Miko Peled has written a fascinating book about his illustrious father—a military hero, a defiantly independent peace activist and politician, and a Ph.D. professor-translator-scholar of Arabic language and literature. But this is in no way a conventional biography of a multi-talented great man. Rather, it is a penetrating, honest analysis of the core beliefs and courageous lives lived by this iconic Jewish leader and his remarkable family. Though the Peled family was always part of the national Zionist political-military establishment, its members have long reached out with empathetic concern for the Palestinians living under Israeli control and have continued to agitate for a just peace, acceptable to both Jews and Arabs. That family commitment to reconciliation has been sorely tested but remained unbroken even after a young granddaughter of the general was killed by a Palestinian suicide bomber... Miko is truly inspiring in the telling of his family's story, and of his own struggles to live up to the moral, ethical, and intellectual legacy from his father.

—LANDRUM BOLLING
Veteran U.S. peace activist,
former President, Earlham College

Out of personal pain and sober reflection on the past comes this powerful narrative of transformation, empowerment, and commitment. It is the personal story that brings home forcefully how one liberates oneself from oppressive ideologies without losing one's identity, family, and humanity. Miko's story is a must-read for anyone who has not lost hope that one day peace and justice will prevail in Israel and Palestine.

—ILAN PAPPÉ
Israeli historian,
Professor of history at the
University of Exeter (U.K.)

ABOUT

JUST WORLD BOOKS
"TIMELY BOOKS FOR CHANGING TIMES"

Just World Books produces excellent books on key international issues—and does so in a very timely fashion. Because of the agility of our process, we cannot give detailed advance notice of fixed, seasonal "lists." To learn about our existing and upcoming titles, to download author podcasts and videos, to learn our terms for bookstores or other bulk purchases, or to buy our books, visit our website:

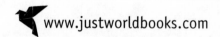 www.justworldbooks.com

Also check our updates on Facebook and Twitter!

Our first title was published in October 2010. By July 2012, we had published twelve titles, including:

- *Wrestling in the Daylight: A Rabbi's Path to Palestinian Solidarity*, by Brant Rosen

- *Watches Without Time: An American Soldier in Afghanistan*, by Matt Zeller

- *The Tragedy of Lebanon: Christian Warlords, Israeli Adventurers, and American Bunglers*, by Jonathan Randal

- *The General's Son: Journey of an Israeli in Palestine*, by Miko Peled

- *Troubled Triangle: The United States, Turkey, and Israel in the New Middle East*, edited by William B. Quandt

- *War Diary: Lebanon 2006*, by Rami Zurayk

JUST WORLD
BOOKS

THE GENERAL'S SON

Peace!

[signature]

9/20/12

This book is dedicated to my mother,

Zika Katznelson-Peled.

THE GENERAL'S SON
JOURNEY OF AN ISRAELI IN PALESTINE

MIKO PELED

WITH A FOREWORD BY

ALICE WALKER

JUST WORLD
BOOKS

CHARLOTTESVILLE, VIRGINIA

The main text of the work, all the photographs in the book interior, and the historic photo of the author and his father used on the front cover: © 2012 Miko Peled.

Foreword, © 2012 Alice Walker.

Portrait of Miko Peled on front cover by David Hebble and © 2012 Miko Peled.

All rights reserved. No part of this book may be reproduced or transmitted in any form or by any means, electronic or mechanical, including photocopy, recording, or any information storage retrieval system, without permission in writing from the publisher, except brief passages for review purposes. Visit our website, www.justworldbooks.com.

Typesetting by Jane T. Sickon for Just World Publishing, LLC.
Cover design by Lewis Rector for Just World Publishing, LLC.
Second printing, 2012.

Publisher's Cataloging-in-Publication
(Provided by Quality Books, Inc.)

Peled, Miko.
    The general's son : journey of an Israeli in Palestine
/ Miko Peled.
    p. cm.
    LCCN 2012931105
    ISBN 978-1-935982-15-9

    1. Peled, Miko. 2. Israelis—Biography.
3. Arab-Israeli conflict. 4. Jewish-Arab relations.
I. Title.

DS126.6.P45A3 2012   956.9405'092
             QBI12-600022

Contents

The Sanity of Friendship
© 2012 by Alice Walker

There are few books on the Israel/Palestine issue that seem as hopeful to me as this one. First of all, we find ourselves in the hands of a formerly Zionist Israeli who honors his people, loves his homeland, respects and cherishes his parents, other family members and friends, and is, to boot, the son of a famous general whose activities during Israel's wars against the Palestinian people helped cause much of their dislocation and suffering. Added to this, long after Miko Peled, the writer, has left the Special Forces of the Israeli army and moved to Southern California to teach karate, a beloved niece, his sister's daughter, Smadar, a young citizen of Jerusalem, is killed by Palestinians in a suicide bombing. Right away we think: Goodness. How is he ever going to get anywhere sane with this history? He does.

I don't remember when I heard Miko Peled talk about the Israeli/Palestinian "conflict" but I was moved by a story he was telling (probably on YouTube) about his mother. I am sensitive to mothers, who never, it seems to me, get enough credit for their impact on society and the world, and so I was eager to hear what this Israeli peace activist, karate master, and writer had to say about his. He was telling the story of the Nakba from his mother's point of view. Nakba is Arabic for the "Catastrophe" that happened to Palestinians when the Israeli army, in lethal force, invaded their communities in 1947-48 and drove them, in their hundreds of thousands, out of their homes; frequently looting and/or blowing up homes, but if the houses were beautiful and/or well situated, taking them for themselves. As the invaders moved in, the coffee, Peled was informed, was sometimes still on the table, still hot, as the inhabitants were forced to flee. His mother, Zika, was offered one of these confiscated houses. She refused it. It was unbearable to her that she might be sitting sipping coffee in the home of another woman who was now, with her frightened or wounded family, sitting, hungry and miserable, in a refugee camp.

Miko Peled's father, General Matti Peled, also rises to full and compassionate dignity in his son's narrative, though somewhat later, and, one feels, with considerably more of a struggle than his wife. He was, after all, a staunch Zionist and a general in the Israeli army, richly praised for his acumen and courage in battle, both in Israel's "War of Independence" in 1947–48 (the Palestinians' "Catastrophe") and in the 1967 war in which Israel pre-emptively attacked its neighbor, Egypt, and proceeded, illegally, to take huge parts of what was until then Palestine.

Although the generals knew that the Egyptian army was too weak at the time to pose a military threat to Israel, Peled and his fellow officers carried out their plan to attack and destroy Egypt as a military power. However, even before this event, Peled had begun experiencing a change of outlook. The aftermath of a massacre of Palestinian civilians by Israeli soldiers made a deep impression on him, and caused him to believe that an army of occupation kept in place indefinitely would ultimately lead to the most hideous violence, and demoralization not only of the Palestinian oppressed but of the Israeli oppressors as well.

After many decades of service to his country, General Peled left the army to become a professor of Arabic Literature at Tel Aviv and Haifa Universities. He learned Arabic and spoke it fluently. He became, as well, a peace activist. He worked with and made friends among Palestinian peace activists and leaders, as his son Miko Peled would do decades later. One such friend was the controversial head of the Palestine Liberation Organization, Yassar Arafat.

What is the prevailing feeling, having read this moving book, given how determined our testosterone-driven world seems to be to make continuous, endless war, and, perhaps, to blow all of us up in one? Possibly soon. I feel immense relief, and gratitude. Someone(s) must take responsibility for being the grown-ups of our human Universe. There must be people, in all walks of life, who decide: *Enough's enough; there are children here.* That even if, in your derangement and pain, or your greed, and covetousness, you do me grievous harm, even to the taking of the life of my child, I still choose to see you and your people as human; though perhaps distorted, warped and tortured almost beyond human recognition. I refuse to turn away from the effort to talk to you, frightened though I might be. Whenever possible, I will not refuse to make friends.

Miko Peled, at first terrified of reaching out to Palestinians because of the false reports he was, since childhood, given of them, realizes the insanity of remaining enemies of a people he has had no opportunity to truly know. What he discovers energizes and encourages him. He begins to understand the danger inherent in living in ignorance of the so-called "other" and begins to realize he would be a far different, a far less open and loving person, had he not, despite his fears, freed himself in this way. His freedom to be at ease with the very people he was taught to hate is, of course, a bonus for his own children and for the next generation of Israelis and Palestinians.

The extreme volatility of the Middle East, with Israel's lengthy list of human rights abuses and contempt for international opinion and law at the center of everybody's fear, is a threat to us all. It is senseless to believe anyone on the planet can afford to ignore or dismiss it.

Miko Peled is a credit to both his parents. As he tries to raise funds for and then to ship 1,280 wheelchairs to those maimed and made invalids in Palestine and Israel, I see his mother's compassion for others who have lost what he still has; in his tireless teaching of Martial Arts to children, especially those in Palestine, I see his father, the General, spreading the faith among the troops that being outnumbered and out-armed is no reason not to win.

A shared homeland, the dream of growing numbers of Israelis and Palestinians, in which each person feels free to be herself or himself, is, or might be, the prize of friendship. In fact, it is only by choosing friendship over enmity that winning makes any sense in a world as on the brink as the one we are living in, where being enemies and attempting to disappear each other has played out, leaving destruction, ugliness, cynicism, and fear. Not to mention a ruined planet, disease, and death.

We will share the earth, and care for it together, as friends of each other and to Her, or we will lose it. I look to the examples of "enemies" becoming friends everywhere in this book to help us continue to carefully choose our way.

The following poem was inspired by watching, on video, home demolitions and house grabbing by Israeli settlers in Palestine. It was a shock to witness the jubilation of the "conquerors" while installing the Israeli flag on the roof a house whose just evicted inhabitants huddled in the street below.

I dedicate it to Smadar, the Israeli, and to the two unknown Palestinian suicide bombers who died with her, perhaps also teenagers, as she was. I wish with all my heart that they might have been friends, playing together rather than dying together, to the grief of all of us who honor the young.

Hope
©2011 by Alice Walker

Hope never
to covet
the neighbors' house
with the fragrant
garden
from which a family
has been
driven by your soldiers;
mother, father,
grandparents,
the toddler and
the dog
now homeless:
huddled, holding on
to each other,
stunned

*and friendless
beneath you
in the street:
sitting on
cobblestones
as if on the sofas
inside
that you have decided
to clean, recover and
keep.*

*Hope never
to say yes
to their misery.*

*Hope never to gaze
down into their faces
from what used to be
their rooftop.*

*Hope never to believe
this robbery
will make you a better
citizen of your new
country
as you unfurl and wave
its recent
flag
that has been given
to assure you
of this impossibility.*

Introduction

On a quiet day in 1997, I sat watching the news from my home in southern California when the broadcast turned live to Jerusalem: Palestinian suicide bombers had struck the heart of the city once again. I caught a glimpse of a young woman's body lying on a stretcher, but before I had time to call my family in Jerusalem and make sure everyone was OK, my phone rang. It was my mother, calling from Israel. "Miko," she said, her voice tense, "there was a bombing on Ben Yehuda Street." Smadar, my 13-year-old niece, was missing.

Smadar's mother, my sister Nurit, is 12 years older than I am; my family always joked that I was her Bat Mitzvah present. As a child, I thought she was the most beautiful woman I had ever seen, with beautiful chestnut hair, a habit of wearing large, shiny earrings, a perpetual tan, and a smile that lit up a room. She is the mother of three boys and a girl. She is honest, brave, forthright, and funny. The thought that she might have lost her only daughter was far too much to process on a peaceful day in southern California.

I had lived in Coronado with my wife and two children for nearly 10 years, (my daughter Tali was not yet born), but still considered Jerusalem, where I was born and raised, home. The two cities could not be more different. Coronado is a picturesque, California beach community—spotless, manicured, and more than a little self-consciously glamorous. It is a place full of optimism and possibilities, a wonderful, safe place to raise children. My family and I lived a peaceful life in our newly purchased condo, within walking distance to beautiful beaches and just two miles from San Diego, across the gleaming Coronado Bay Bridge. I had established a successful karate studio in town, and the work kept me busy and happy in many respects.

But we were a long way from my home in one of the most ancient cities in the world. Coming from Jerusalem—a melting pot of ethnic backgrounds and religions, a city where every newsstand offers papers in five different languages and people passionately discuss politics and daily news—Coronado had always struck me as culturally and politically isolated, and lacking in diversity.

I was born in Jerusalem's Rehavia neighborhood, but spent most of my youth in Motza Ellit, where my parents built a house when I was four. Motza is a quiet, unassuming community hidden in the Judean Hills on the city's western edge. It is surrounded by nature, but not far from the conflict and violence that have come to characterize the city. About five miles away is the walled Old City, sacred to Jews, Christians, and Muslims. It is a city fiercely loved and just as fiercely disputed—it's been captured and destroyed, rebuilt, captured and destroyed again, throughout history. I am a product of that troubled, painfully beautiful place. Its history, both ancient and modern, and the culture of the Jewish people are inseparable from my being.

The fact that I was living in Coronado did not change all of that. I spent hours on the phone with my family each week and stayed abreast of political and cultural developments back home; I even had subscriptions to Israeli newspapers. I faithfully searched TV channels for news about my homeland. And I always made sure to read the latest Hebrew novels and anything new that was published about the politics and history of the region, going as far back as King Herod and Jesus of Nazareth.

Many hours after the phone call from my mother, when it was close to midnight in Jerusalem, the police contacted Smadar's parents. It was as if as if they wanted to allow Nurit and her husband Rami time to reach the inevitable conclusion on their own before escorting them to the morgue. When they returned from the morgue, my other sister, Ossi, called me right away.

"Miko...." I didn't need to hear anything more. Her voice said it all. It was time to fly home. And so it became clear to me that the young woman I saw on the stretcher while watching the news was indeed my niece Smadar. She was dead, killed while shopping for schoolbooks on the streets of the city she called home.

This wrenching tragedy is the starting point of my personal journey, a journey that transformed my heart and ushered me into a life of activism and, some say, risk.

Dignitaries from Israel's entire political spectrum attended the funeral of Matti Peled's granddaughter. Matti Peled, my father, had died two years earlier. A man who had fought fiercely in Israel's War for Independence, oversaw the capture of much of the land Israel now occupied, and then came to question his role as an overlord of the Palestinians, he was a general turned man of peace.

An urgent need to make sense of Smadar's death gripped me. In Israel, war and the casualties of war were a part of life. As a child I had been to countless funerals of young people who were killed in wars or "military operations," and I knew of people who were maimed and crippled as a result of terrorist attacks. But Smadar was my sister's child. For years, I had been frustrated by the Israeli-Palestinian conflict; I was deeply troubled by the lack of progress toward a peaceful solution. Still, the conflict had not become personal until my niece was murdered. Suddenly I needed to understand what brought those two young Palestinians to blow themselves up, taking her life just as it was beginning to blossom. Her death pushed me into a bold examination of my Zionist beliefs, my country's history, and the political situation that fueled the suicide bombers who killed her.

I was born into a well-known Zionist family, which included my father, cabinet secretaries, judges, and even a president of the state of Israel. My maternal grandfather and namesake, Dr. Avraham Katznelson, was a Zionist leader. He signed Israel's declaration of independence and later served as Israel's first ambassador to Scandinavia. My father was 16 when he volunteered to serve in the Palmach, the strike force that fought for Israel's independence. As a young officer, he commanded an infantry company that fought in the 1948 War, and by 1967 he was a general and a member of the Israeli army's top brass. He was later elected to Israel's parliament, the Knesset.

When I was a boy, military legends and dignitaries of all political persuasions passed through our home. But after Smadar's death, I wanted to meet people on "the other side," people who were considered my enemies.

I searched for Jewish-Palestinian dialogue groups in California and made plans to attend. My wife Gila, raised in an Israeli *kibbutz*[1], was apprehensive; neither of us had ever been to the home of a Palestinian, and Gila feared for my life. "What if they do something to you? What if you don't return?" she asked me as I prepared to leave for my first meeting with Palestinians. Although I was 39 and had grown up in the united city of Jerusalem, I never had any Arab friends. Now I faced Palestinians as equals for the first time in my life, and to my relief and amazement, I found common ground. As expatriates we shared both good and bad memories of our homeland.

However, Palestinians told a far different version of our history than I had been taught as a young boy in Jerusalem. The history I knew painted Israel as a defenseless David fighting an Arab Goliath, a story that had compelled me as a young patriot to volunteer for an elite commando unit in the Israel Defense Forces (IDF). Sitting across from Palestinians in California, I learned of mass expulsions, massacres, and grave injustices. We proudly called the 1948 Arab-Israeli War the War of Independence. Palestinians called it *Nakba*, the "Catastrophe." I found that hard to accept.

When other Jews and Israelis stormed out of the dialogue meetings, I chose to stay and listen, even though it pained me beyond words to accept that I was not in

1 An agricultural commune that maintains a strict socialist regimen.

possession of the full truth. Coming from a family of political insiders, I thought I knew more than anyone.

I began traveling to the occupied Palestinian territories. Breaking the acceptable rules of my society, I ventured alone to meet with Palestinian peace activists in areas most Israelis consider dangerous. My sister Ossi was beside herself: "You mustn't go," she said. "It is dangerous and you are a father with responsibilities to your family and your children." My mother, also sick with worry, said: "All it takes is one lunatic."

During a trip to the West Bank, I confronted what emerged in my mind as the greatest obstacle to peace: fear of the "other," a fear I had never realized I possessed. It was December 2005 when I drove from Jerusalem to the West Bank alone for the first time. I drove a rented car with Israeli license plates. As I passed the last Israeli checkpoint, left the wide, paved highway, I encountered the potholed streets and narrow winding roads that characterize the occupied territories. I was now in "enemy territory" and demons ran amok in my head. I imagined myself surrounded by hostile Arabs, waiting in ambush to kill me. As a child, I remembered my father made sure we never traveled through the West Bank without a gun in the car, his AK-47 Kalashnikov. *Hadn't people warned me not to do this exactly?*

When I arrived, I was greeted by activists—freedom fighters who refused to engage in violence and were intent on resolving the conflict peacefully. I experienced no antagonism at all as I spent the entire day there and then returned home to Jerusalem. I felt relieved, hopeful, and discouraged all at the same time. I knew if ever there were to be peace, the fear that ran inside me like a virus had to be conquered. Through centuries of experience and conditioning, fear had become almost inseparable from my culture. It had to be overcome and replaced by trust. This was an enormous task.

Mine is the tale of an Israeli boy, a Zionist, who realized that his side of the story was not the only side and chose to cultivate hope in a situation most call impossible. I feel that my travels and the political insights I gained at my father's side may offer a model for reconciliation not only in the Middle East, but anywhere people look at the "other" and experience fear rather than our common humanity.

PART I

The Early Years

Chapter 1:

Roots

When I was a child, I would sit with my grandmother in her cold apartment on 18 Rashba Street in Jerusalem's Rehavia neighborhood. The apartment was on the first floor of a simple two-story house. Behind the house, there was a small yard with a grapefruit tree in the center. The neighborhood was modest and quiet, but respectable. Most of the residents were professors who worked at the nearby Hebrew University.

Savta Sima[1] would pull out old photos and talk about her life as the wife of an ambassador.

"Avrami," she would say. I was named after my grandfather, but she was the only one to ever call me by that name. "This is your grandfather Avram with King Gustav the Sixth, king of Sweden, and here he is with the Emperor Haile Selassie of Ethiopia."

Dr. Avraham Katznelson or Saba Abba, as he was fondly called, died before I was born, but my mother and grandmother spoke of him and his life all the time. He was a spokesman for the Zionist movement in the early 1920s—traveling to Jewish communities around the world and urging them to return to their historical homeland in Palestine—and then among the signers of Israel's declaration of independence. He was also Israel's first ambassador to Scandinavia.

My grandmother was proud of her husband's diplomatic work: "Your grandfather was both charming and an excellent diplomat, and he knew how to cultivate close ties with people." She was particularly proud of the relationship he had cultivated with the Chinese ambassador. This was quite a feat because, having aligned itself with the West, Israel had no diplomatic ties with China in those days.

One afternoon, as we sat together on her old blue sofa, my grandmother showed me a faded newspaper clipping. Savta Sima's living room was always cold and stuffy because she would seldom turn on the heating or open the windows. The newspaper had turned yellow and must have been more than 20 years old. There was a photo of my grandfather dressed in coat and tails, wearing a top hat and walking alongside a horse-drawn carriage. I could tell from the photo that this was a cold and foggy European city.

---

1 *Savta* means "grandmother" and *Saba* means "grandfather" in Hebrew.

My grandmother told me of my grandfather's presentation as Israel's first ambassador at the court of King Gustaf in Stockholm. "The ceremony took place on a Saturday," she explained, which is the Jewish Sabbath, when Jews are forbidden from driving or riding in vehicles. "He was the representative of the Jewish state—indeed of all the Jewish people—and he felt it would be proper to walk rather than ride in the royal carriage."

"He walked the entire way. He was tall and handsome, his back straight as an arrow, and the royal carriage was rolling beside him." I looked at my grandmother, and I could see how much she missed him.

The glamour of that life reminded her of her years growing up in Batumi, Georgia. Although she lived most of her life in Jerusalem, Sima always missed Batum (what she called the Georgian city of Batumi on the coast of the Black Sea). Every Friday afternoon, she visited us in Motza Ellit, and she would talk to me for hours about the grandeur of her childhood home. They had servants and carriages and were able to truly enjoy the beauty of the city. I imagined Batum to be paradise.

But when I knew her Savta Sima was very thrifty. Her house was always cold in the winter because she only turned the heating on between 6 p.m. and 8 p.m., regardless of the temperature outside, which during the Jerusalem winter frequently drops below zero. I remember one particular winter day, when I visited after school. It was snowing, and I called my mother from my grandmother's apartment, and I whispered into the receiver: "Mom, I am freezing." Savta Sima heard me and quickly came back with, "Freezing, freezing! Well, we are all freezing." Still, the heater remained off. When she watched television in the evening, she had all the lights in her apartment turned off, and she would wear a long dark blue robe and dark sunglasses to protect her eyes from the glare of the television. "I know you think I am stingy. I am not stingy, I am thrifty."

When school was out I would sometimes meet her at the medical clinic where she worked as a dermatologist and walk home with her. She was in her mid-seventies by then and worked only part time, so she was done at noon. I was no more than nine or 10 years old, and she would hold my arm as we walked and say: "Avrami, you are my cavalier." It was no more than a mile or maybe two as the bird flies from the clinic to her home. She would walk 20 paces at a time and then stop to rest. She refused to ride the bus or, God forbid, spend money and take a taxi. "A taxi? What an extravagance," she would say at the mere mention of the idea.

Back then there was not much traffic as we walked by the small shops, cafes, and bakeries. We would pass the compound of Ratisbon Monastery and the Yeshurun Synagogue, two Jerusalem landmarks that stood next to each other, one Christian and one Jewish. Both of them were about as old as my grandmother, and she would captivate me with stories about the people who established and frequented them. "Ratisbon himself was a French Jew who converted and became a Catholic priest," she said with obvious disdain. "When Yitzhak Ben-Tzvi was president he would come to worship right here at Yeshurun Synagogue." From there we would turn into the smaller and quieter streets of Rehavia. These were the 1970s, and to me Jerusalem seemed full of hope and optimism.

I was deeply influenced by the knowledge that my relatives helped shape the history of my country. It made me feel special to know that my namesake signed the declaration of independence, that he moved among kings and prime ministers, representing our country among the nations of the world. Being a proud Israeli patriot was something I did not need to be taught; it was infused in me by the men and women in my family.

Even the way my mother's parents met is a small piece of Israeli history. My grandfather, Avraham, was born in 1888 in Babruysk, a city in Belarus that was about 60 percent Jewish. As a boy, he received an education in a *heder*, or orthodox Jewish preschool, and then in a *yeshiva*, where he studied Jewish religious texts, before he entered a public, secular high school.

My grandmother would boast that he graduated from the gymnasium, as high school was called then, "with exceptional scores. And that is how he was accepted into medical school in St. Petersburg, Russia. He was tall and good-looking and always impeccably dressed." This last part she corroborated with the use of old photos. "He loved the ballet, and when he was a student, he would deprive himself of food for days so that he could afford to buy himself a ticket to the ballet and a bouquet of flowers to present to the prima ballerina after the performance."

I heard stories about my grandfather throughout my entire life, and they were often told to me in no particular order. "He served as a doctor in the Russian army and was awarded a gold medal for bravery by the czar of Russia himself," my mother told me one day as we were sitting in the kitchen. "I even remember playing with it as a child, thinking it was a toy." I was in high school, old enough to appreciate what a medal like that must be worth, and I was stunned. "My grandfather received a medal from the czar of Russia, and they let you play with it?"

"My parents thought very little of it, and the medal was lost."

"Oh my God, I can't believe you lost it!"

"It's a good thing we have a photo of him as a dashing young officer in uniform wearing the medal."

"In medical school your grandfather met Yossef Trumpeldor and the two became good friends," my mother went on with obvious pride. Trumpeldor was a Jewish hero of mythical proportions. When Trumpeldor was young, he too served as a doctor in the Russian army. He was a Zionist like my grandfather, and he founded the British Army's Jewish Brigade, in which many years later my mother served. Trumpeldor served as the brigade's deputy commander. He was killed in

*My grandfather, Dr. Avraham
Katznelson or Saba Abba,
as he was fondly called.*

the battle of Tel Chai in northern Palestine in 1920, and all Israeli children learn in school that Trumpeldor's last words were, "It is good to die for our country."

Trumpeldor asked my grandfather to visit the home of Ze'ev Kaplan, a wealthy Jewish merchant living in Batumi, to see if he would make a financial contribution to the Zionist cause. "Your grandfather did go to Batumi, and he did receive a generous contribution," my mother continued with a smile, "but that was not all he received. Ze'ev Kaplan's daughter, Sima, became his wife and your grandmother to be."

After several years of courtship, Sima and Avraham married, and in 1923 Avraham convinced Sima to immigrate with him to Palestine to participate in building a Jewish state. Avraham rose in the ranks of the Zionist movement and became a member of the executive board of The Zionist National Council, or *Hava'ad HaLeumi*—the *de facto* Jewish government, chosen by an assembly elected by the Jewish community in Palestine, prior to the establishment of the state of Israel. He was the founder of the Jewish Ministry of Health and acted as *de facto* minister of health during the pre-state years. His stature can best be measured by the fact that he was among the select group of Jewish leaders who signed Israel's declaration of independence.

After the state was founded, my grandfather was designated to be Israel's first minister of health. However, he never got the job because in Israel's first major political battle—between Chaim Weizmann and David Ben-Gurion, on who would lead Israel's labor party in the elections for the Jewish state's first prime minister—he bet on the loser. Weizmann, also from Belarus, had a leadership style founded on charm, reason, and diplomacy, and he was pushed aside by Ben-Gurion, whose brand of leadership was militant and uncompromising.

As a child, I heard of my grandfather's disdain of Ben-Gurion many times. My grandmother rather enjoyed describing a particular instance when Ben-Gurion spoke to my grandfather after the elections.

"Ben-Gurion was short and bald, and he came up to Avram, who was tall and handsome, looked up at him, and with clenched fists cried: '*Ata Veitsmanist!*' You are a Weizmannist!"

It was true. He believed in and supported Chaim Weizmann, and he clearly disliked Ben-Gurion's aggressive style. However, since Ben-Gurion won, my grandfather lost his chance to be a member of the first independent Jewish government in more than 2,000 years. My grandfather's good friend and ally, Moshe Sharett, was Israel's first foreign minister, and he asked my grandfather to head Israel's delegation to the United Nations and later to be Israel's ambassador to Scandinavia. My grandfather died of cancer in 1956, at the age of 68, while serving in Stockholm.

After she was widowed, Savta Sima lived alone for more than 20 years. By the time I knew her, she was thin with deep wrinkles, short silver hair, and an air of importance. She had beautiful eyes and was known to have been a beautiful woman in her youth. Or, as my mother put it, "She was so beautiful that when she walked down the streets of Jerusalem everyone turned their head." She was proud of her background as the eldest daughter of the Kaplan family, and of her connection to the Katznelsons, and the sign on her door read: Dr. Sima Kaplan-Katznelson-Nisan.

"We are Katznelsons," she would say.

Being with Sima was not always fun, but it was often interesting. She insisted that I join her for lunch once a week after school, even though she couldn't cook or bake. She lived in Jerusalem for more than 50 years, most of them in the house she and Saba Avram built on Rashba Street, where many years later, I was born. We would sit in her small, almost bare bones, cold kitchen and she would bring out a pair of ivory chopsticks to show me. "These were a gift from the Chinese ambassador," she declared every time she brought them out, and she would show me how to use the strange sticks to pick up the bland rice and chicken she had boiled for lunch.

Regardless of how she may have seemed to me as a child, Sima was an accomplished woman. She completed medical school in Krakow at a time when both

My grandmother, Sima, my mother Zika, and my grandfather Avram.

Jews and women were rarely admitted and only if they had the highest possible academic scores. She became a dermatologist and one of Palestine's first Jewish female MDs. She made major contributions to the development of dermatology in Palestine, then Israel, through her work in the early years of Hadassah Hospital in Jerusalem and Kupat Holim, Israel's vehicle of socialized medicine.

Zalman Shazar, who in 1963 became Israel's third president, was my great uncle by marriage. He was married to Rachel Katznelson, my grandfather Avraham's sister. Rachel was a writer and a Zionist labor leader and established women's unions fighting for women's rights. Shazar himself held several important political posts before being chosen the third president of the state of Israel, a largely ceremonial position. He was also a writer and a poet, and in his youth he would captivate audiences for hours with his long speeches. Sima was very close to them, and every Saturday she would join Zalman and Rachel for a luncheon at the president's residence. She occasionally asked me to join her and we walked together to the presidential residence, a few blocks from her house. In those days, it was a beautiful and respectable home located in a quiet corner of Rehavia, though it was rather humble as presidential mansions go. I was very young at the time, but I remember those visits vividly. They were all very old by then, in their seventies, and the food was never very good. We called the president Dod Zalman, or Uncle Zalman, and his wife Doda Rachel. On Dod Zalman's birthday,

Zalman Shazar, who in 1963 became Israel's third president, was my great uncle by marriage. Here I am shaking his hand, with Savta Sima during Hanukkah celebration at the President's residence in Jerusalem.

which like mine, was during Hanukkah, he would invite the entire family to his house. This meant hundreds of people: judges, cabinet ministers, distinguished doctors, artists, all of whom were members of my extended family. Today Dod Zalman's portrait is on the 200 shekel bill. When my children were young, I showed them the bill with Dod Zalman on it, and they were floored: "We have a great uncle who is on money!"

When Sima turned 80, she received a letter from the general director of Kupat Holim telling her how much they had appreciated her many years of service, and that it was time to make room for younger doctors, mostly new immigrants who had arrived from the Soviet Union, who were in need of her position. She tried to take it well, but it was truly devastating for her. To keep her occupied, my mother took apart old sweaters and gave her the yarn, from which she knitted beautiful bed covers, one of which I still have. Sima died when I was in high school after a protracted struggle against leukemia.

It seems clear to me now that the harsher aspects of Sima's personality were the result of her having lived in an era when women were not supposed to have a career, and emotions were forcibly subdued. This could not have been easy for her. By contrast, Sima's daughter, my mother Zika, is a warm and loving woman, with a small and strong physique and a loud and distinctive laugh. When she was younger, she volunteered to serve in the British Army's Jewish Brigade. She told me that the best part of her service there was that she was able to see Cairo, Beirut, and Damascus, three Middle Eastern cities known for their great beauty. She married my father when she was 19.

When we were kids and my parents had friends over, they would make my mother laugh just to hear that infectious sound. Her children, grandchildren, and great grandchildren could not wish for a better advocate and supporter. She is a wonderful cook, something she says she learned from her mother-in-law. She has impeccable taste in clothes and décor. Her house is always beautiful, and her yard always in bloom.

I learned a great deal about my family from my mother. She taught me to be a Zionist, but not by being dogmatic. She did it by imparting her love for everyone—family members and those outside our family—who played an important role in the revival of the Jewish national home. She also imparted to me her love of the Hebrew language and culture by teaching me to appreciate modern Hebrew poetry and prose. The two most prominent men in her life, her father and her husband, dedicated their entire lives to the cause of Zionism, and she shared their stories with me throughout my life. She was never active politically—she refused to be interviewed or to be in the public eye—but she supported her father and then her husband as they committed themselves to the cause.

I knew my father's mother, Savta Sara, as a short and slightly round woman with eyes that squinted when she laughed. As a child, I clearly preferred her to my mother's mother, Sima. Sara would prepare a great stew with a sauce that I would soak up with fresh white bread and then devour. She baked delicious pies and pastries that smelled wonderful, and she told funny stories. On cold Jerusalem winter days, when I would go to her warm apartment after school, I was always welcomed with a pair of warm slippers, a woolen sweater, and the smell of her delicious, hearty cooking. Her hair was long and thin and always pulled back in a bun, and with her high cheekbones and squinting eyes, her features resembled those of an old Mongolian woman. As a boy, when I was sick and had to stay home from school, the best prize was to have Savta Sara come and tell me stories. "If you want a story you have to take your medicine," she would say, and the sweetness of her presence more than made up for the bitter medicine.

Unlike Sima, Savta Sara completed only three or four years of schooling, but she could speak and read Yiddish, Hebrew, and Russian. She read everything she could get her hands on, including all the Yiddish classics, and would retell us the stories by heart, especially those by the Jewish writer Sholem Aleichem. She read everything published in Hebrew, from newspaper articles to the finest literature.

My father's mother, Savta Sara.

Among her friends and acquaintances were great literary names like poet Haim Nahman Bialik, author Haim Hazaz, and Israel's beloved songwriter Naomi Shemer, whose mother was Sara's lifelong friend.

If Sara had any shortcomings, I was not aware of them as a child. Later in life I realized that in her eyes no one was ever as good or as smart or as right as her brother, her sons, and her grandchildren. And she had an almost insatiable desire to meddle in the affairs of others, mostly her friends and family, and this would often come at the price of broken relationships. But all of my father's comrades in arms who served in and around Jerusalem knew that they could always count on her for a bed and a warm meal should they need it, and that no advance notice was ever necessary. Unlike my grandmother Sima, who was a very independent woman, Sara needed people around her.

She was born in the Ukraine in a *shtetl* (Yiddish for "small town") called Lipowitz in the Pale of Settlement, an area designated by the Russian government where Jews were permitted to reside. She did not know her birth date other than that she was born in 1901, so my mother decided that we would celebrate her birthday on the fifteenth day of the month of Shvat, or *Tu B'Shvat*, as it is called in Hebrew. It is the Jewish holiday dedicated to celebrating trees and nature. The whole family would gather at her house on that day to eat dried fruit, nuts, and her wonderful homemade pastries.

She came from a poor family whose home was made of mostly mud. "If you poked your finger through the wall," she would say, poking a finger at an imaginary wall, "it would make a hole large enough that you could look outside." Then she would laugh her hearty laugh.

My father and his younger brother Dov, who was fondly called Dubik.

In the years immediately after the Bolshevik Revolution, Sara was a teenager and she decided to become a *komsomolka*, a "young communist." She agreed once to go to a gathering of young communists that was held on Yom Kippur, the holiest of the Jewish holidays. But while on the train, she had a change of heart. She knew that if news of her traveling by train on Yom Kippur reached her father it would kill him, so she got off the train and returned home. "She was not meant to be a revolutionary," my mother said. "Her older brother, Eliezer felt that there was no future for young Jews in Russia and that remaining there may be dangerous. So, together, Sara and Eliezer left their home and family and began their journey to *Eretz Yisrael*, the Land of Israel."

They stopped in Turkey for a year in a temporary Zionist camp called *Mesila Hadasha*, where Jews could work while they waited for the British authorities to issue them permits to enter Palestine. From there they traveled by boat to Eretz Yisrael, or *Palestina*, as the Jewish immigrants called Palestine. On the boat from Constantinople to Palestine, Sara and Eliezer met Baruch Ifland, a young Jewish man on his way to start a life in England. Eliezer convinced Baruch to come with them to Palestine and, when they arrived, Baruch married Sara. Together they worked to fulfill the vision of the Zionist labor movement—Jewish people from all walks of life flocking to Eretz Yisrael to work and rebuild the Jewish homeland.

Sara and Baruch had two children, my father Matti and his younger brother Dov, who was fondly called Dubik. Dubik became a farmer. He had six children, and he was everyone's beloved uncle. Sadly, he was 42 when he died of a heart attack.

Eliezer became one of the founders of the Academy of the Hebrew Language in Jerusalem, an institution that turned the Hebrew language, dormant for nearly 2,000 years, into a modern spoken language. He died of cancer when I was three. Baruch passed away in his sleep during Passover, 1962, when I was nearly six months old.

When I was four, my family moved to Motza, and Sara moved into the apartment we had vacated on the upper floor on 18 Rashba Street, just upstairs from Savta Sima.

The relationship between the two grandmothers would make a great script for a BBC sitcom. "She doesn't speak real Russian. She speaks the same Russian our servants spoke," Sima would say with disdain, referring to Sara's colloquial version of the language. Sarah would jab, "She couldn't cook or even boil an egg to save her life," which was also true. They were two accomplished women who, in their own way, contributed to creating a homeland for their people in the Land of Israel. They represent two aspects of the Zionist pioneers: One, an educated Jewish woman with a strong sense of social hierarchy who made it in early twentieth century Europe, and then lent her talents and education to the Zionist enterprise. The other, a working class woman whose world, the world of the Jewish shtetl, had come to an end and who ended up participating in the Zionist project as a laborer and as a mother, which in those days, in the height of socialism, was as noble a position as one could hold. The value and importance of protecting the rights of workers and women and minorities was passed down to me through these two women and their life stories.

As a child, I preferred Savta Sara. As an adult, I learned to appreciate Savta Sima, and I found it puzzling that my mother, who is such a pleasant woman, had a stern mother while my father, who was stern and often severe, had a warm and loving mother.

Chapter 2:

My Father Was Matti Peled

I am my parents' fourth child and by the time I was born in December of 1961, my father was 38 years old. He was 5'11", with broad shoulders, serious eyes, and—ever since I knew him—silver hair combed back from a wide forehead.

As an adult, my father made his mark on Israeli history. First as a young officer, who distinguished himself in battle as a fearless, committed, and levelheaded leader of men during Israel's War of Independence. Then as a career officer who dedicated himself to building a well-organized fighting force for the young state of Israel. But probably most notably as one of the generals of the Six-Day War of 1967, when the Israeli army captured the West Bank, the Gaza Strip, the Golan Heights, and the Sinai Peninsula.

My father later became a professor of Arabic language and literature, a ground-breaking member of Israel's parliament, and a peace activist decades ahead of his time. But whatever hat Matti Peled wore—general, scholar, father—he had a cool and rational way.

I was only 14 or 15 when he caught me smoking. I was outside by the car lighting up, certain that no one would see me, when suddenly I noticed him walking up the hill. He was deep in thought, as always, and his gaze was down. I had no idea how he would react, but I assumed I was going to be in trouble. He was already quite close before he looked up and recognized me. The unmistakable odor of cigarette smoke was all around, and the cigarette was in my hand.

"You smoke?" he asked, with mild surprise. "Isn't it a waste for an athlete like you to ruin your lungs?"

What I said was: "I don't really smoke, and I have no intention of smoking." A stupid reply under the circumstances, but it was true: It was my first or second try, and I didn't like it at all. As he walked away, I added, "Please don't tell mom."

I stood there for a while, waiting for my anxiety to dissipate. I was stunned—not only by the fact that I'd been caught, but also by his direct and dispassionate reaction. Of course my father didn't want me to smoke, but he didn't show any anger. In the end, he left it up to me: It was my body, my life, and my choice.

My father was born Mattityahu Ifland, Matti for short, in the port city of Haifa in what was then northern Palestine. The day was July 20, 1923, and according to the Jewish calendar, it was *Tisha B'Av*, the ninth day of the month of Av—when Jewish people lament the destruction of the Jewish Temple in Jerusalem by Roman legions in 70 AD.

His family lived on a kibbutz, but they didn't stay long. In those days, kibbutz members believed mothers should not raise their own children. The babies lived and slept in the nursery and were raised and cared for by nurses while the parents worked. Parents would see their children for a couple of hours each day in the afternoon. Matti's mother, Sara, could not bear the separation from her son, and when my father was a year old, they moved to Jerusalem, where my grandfather opened a carpentry shop that he operated for many years.

"Your grandfather was a socialist at heart," my grandmother liked to tell me, "and always made sure that his income was the same as his workers."

He grew up to be a Zionist to the core; till the day he died, he firmly believed in creating a Jewish homeland in Palestine, and he acted on this belief. His was the first generation for which Hebrew, a language that had only recently been revived, was the native tongue. From an early age, he made sure his Hebrew was perfect and that he pronounced it correctly. While still in high school, he traveled up and down the country—indeed, he knew it well and loved it dearly. Many years later, when my father came to criticize Israeli policies, it was still in the name of what was best for the future of Israel. Despite his mounting concerns, he continued to believe in securing the future of the Jewish people in their homeland. And when his loyalty to the Zionist cause was put in question, he demanded and was given recognition from the Israeli Supreme Court that he was in fact a patriot and a Zionist.

At the age of 16, he volunteered to serve in the Palmach, the strike force of the Haganah, which was the largest Jewish militia in the years leading to the creation of Israel. He joined without his parents' knowledge or permission, and he would skip school to participate in military training. He served in the Jerusalem platoon with Yitzhak Rabin, with whom he would maintain a lifelong relationship.

It was during that time that my father changed his name. Members of the Palmach were required to Hebraize their names—to make them sound more Hebrew as opposed to the more European-Jewish sounding names that character-ized Jews in exile. It was part of the national Zionist mission to bring about a new Hebrew identity. My father, Matti Ifland, chose the name Peled, because it means "iron" in Hebrew. Later, other officers changed their names to Peled as well.

Fighting the British, who occupied Palestine at the time, and demanding Jewish independence was the premise under which the Palmach had been created. By the mid-1940s, my father had grown disillusioned with the Palmach. He thought they weren't doing enough to fight off the British and if they were not going to fight, he saw no point in staying. So, true to his character, he did something that was con-sidered unthinkable at the time: He quit the Palmach and went to school.

In 1946, he and my mother, Zika Katznelson, were married. In the small Jewish community in Jerusalem, this marriage was no small thing. A daughter of the Katznelson family was marrying a man who came from a family of no consequence or position. "Several friends of my father tried to dissuade me, but I loved your father," my mother told me during one of our conversations in her kitchen. I was an adult by then and in the process of gathering information for a future book.

The family had managed to scrape together enough funds to allow my father to go to law school in London. Because they were still tight, however, he went alone, leaving immediately after they got married. His passport, issued by His Majesty's Government, stated under "country": Palestine. And under "citizenship": Palestinian. Nine months later, my older brother, Yoav, was born, and my father returned. While he was home, in the fall of 1947, hostilities erupted—a war that would later be called Israel's War of Independence had begun. My father stayed to fight and never returned to law school.

He served as a captain in the Givati Brigade's 51st regiment, and commanded the second infantry company, or Company B. The role of Company B became the stuff of legends.

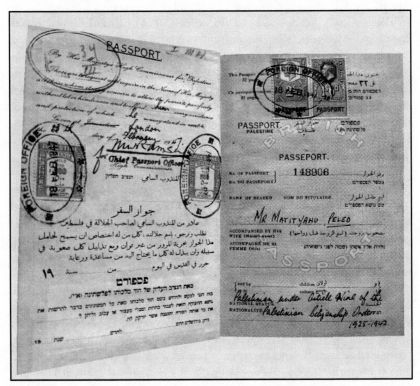

My father's passport issued in February 1947, nationality: Palestinian.

In a journal he kept, my father describes rebuilding the company after it had suffered terrible losses in the war and its commander was removed. He writes about instilling both morale and discipline in his soldiers, who were a mishmash of new, inexperienced immigrants and hardened World War II veterans who volunteered to fight for the Jewish cause. I found what he wrote about soldiers wounded in battle particularly interesting:

> A sergeant and a squad commander were wounded but continued to advance without complaining. I found their behavior responsible and intelligent. Another soldier that was wounded began screaming. I ran to him and yelled at him to shut up….There is nothing worse for morale than wounded soldiers screaming…. Surely a soldier going into battle knows he may be injured, so why scream?

I remember finding this diary while I was going through his desk just a few days after he died. It was fascinating to read, but this particular passage intrigued me more than anything else. Did he really not understand why a wounded young man, scared for his life and in terrible pain, might scream? I suppose he expected everyone to possess the same levelheadedness and dedication that he demanded of himself. He did not see that this was an impossible thing to expect.

His cool and direct reasoning became somewhat of a hallmark for people who knew him. In October 1948, the company took part in a crucial battle as part of Operation Yoav—which coincidentally shared my brother's name—to claim the Negev region, in the southern part of the country. The company suffered many casualties, their communication was lost, and two officers died in battle. My father himself was seriously wounded twice during the battle. Once communication was restored, he was instructed to retreat but insisted they carry on—a third of the company was injured, and there was no one to carry the wounded. He maintained that they could hold on and complete their mission.

Apparently General Yigal Allon, commander of the southern region, intervened at this point. The young company commander convinced Allon that they could hold out through the night. As it turned out the Egyptian forces retreated by morning, and it was an important, albeit costly, victory. My father nearly lost both of his eyes as a result of grenades blowing up near his head, and for the rest of his life he had shrapnel embedded in the back of his head. My mother still has the helmet that saved his life, resting now in his study.

I remember learning about this particular battle in my sixth grade history class. By then my father was a professor teaching Arabic literature at Tel Aviv University. I sat and listened with a mixture of awe and discomfort as we learned that he commanded the legendary Company B which, as the poet Abba Kovner wrote, "distinguished itself beyond any other… turned weakness into courage," pushed the Egyptian army back, and opened a crucial intersection that connected between the central and southern parts of what was to become the state of Israel.

My father as a young officer.

The awe I felt was partly a result of having never heard the story placed in a larger context. I had heard bits and pieces about this battle from my father when we would drive south and pass by the region where the battle took place. On Independence Day, we used to take trips with friends, many of whom participated in the War of Independence, and during lunch everyone sat together and the dads would tell stories of the war. People always asked that my father tell the story of that particular battle, and he always agreed. But I was already at that age: though my father was a hero, he was still my father, and I couldn't help feeling a little embarrassed when he told stories in the company of my peers.

During the war my mother and older brother Yoav lived in Jerusalem with my mother's parents. Being the wife of an officer, my mother was offered a house in Katamon, a Palestinian neighborhood whose inhabitants were forced to flee as a result of the war. The homes of the Palestinians, spacious and beautiful, were all seized by the Israeli army and given to Israeli families. My mother recalls how the contents of these homes, which belonged to well-to-do families, were taken by looters.

"I knew the Palestinian families as a child growing up in Jerusalem," she said. "On Saturdays I would walk through the neighborhood and see the families sitting on their balconies. There was usually a lemon tree in the front and a garden with fruit trees in the back."

She refused to take another family's home. "That I should take the home of a family that may be living in a refugee camp? The home of another mother? Can you imagine how much they must miss their home?" She told me this story many times as a child, insisting that I hear her message. "I refused, and we all stayed living with Savta Sima, which was not easy for any of us. And to see the Israelis driving away with loot, beautiful rugs and furniture. I was ashamed for them; I don't know how they could do it."

By refusing the house in Katamon, she gave up an opportunity to have a beautiful, spacious home for her family in a choice neighborhood in Jerusalem, and at no expense. It wasn't until many years later that my father's military paycheck could afford them a comfortable house, and even then it came at some sacrifice and with help from my grandmother Sima. I wish I could recall the first time my mother told me this story, but I can't. I only know that I've known it for as long as I can remember myself.

After the war ended, my father was asked to remain in the army as an officer. He was sent back to England, this time to the Royal Military Academy at Sandhurst. By then, Nurit had been born, and the four of them spent one year in England. When my father came back from England, he was assigned to a team of officers,

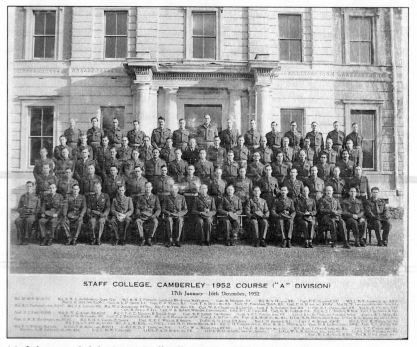

My father attended the Senior Staff College at Camberly in 1951.

My father at Camberly (seated on the right at the end of the first row).

My father participated in the first military delegation to visit the United States. Here with Haim Hertzog, Yitzhak Rabin and Moshe Dayan.

all graduates of the Royal Military Academy, who established the Israeli army's Senior Staff College. In 1954, he was part of the first Israeli military delegation to visit the United States.

Political rivalries and upheaval in Israel during the mid-1950s determined, to a large degree, the relationship between the elected civilian government and the army—and also impacted my father's career. One could roughly categorize two main approaches to Israeli-Arab relations within the ruling labor movement. There was a moderate, diplomatic approach led by Moshe Sharett, Israel's first foreign secretary and then its second prime minister. Sharett believed Israel should avoid war and seek a negotiated peace settlement with its Arab neighbors. There was also an aggressive approach that wanted to establish Israel as the supreme military force in the region, so that it would never need to negotiate a peace settlement. David Ben-Gurion, who was Israel's first prime minister, led this approach and was supported by the army's senior command. In 1953, Ben-Gurion decided to resign as prime minister, leave politics, and live in a remote desert outpost in the southern part of the country, allowing Moshe Sharett to take his place.

Then in 1955, as a result of a failed covert military intelligence operation in Egypt and the resignation of Defense Minister Pinhas Lavon, Ben-Gurion returned to politics as defense minister. As soon as he returned, he and army Chief of Staff General Moshe Dayan tried to advance a plan for an Israeli attack on Egypt. Prime Minister Sharett was opposed to the plan and led an effective coalition and succeeded in derailing it. This infuriated Ben-Gurion. When general elections were held in July of that year, Ben-Gurion ran a tough campaign and won back the prime minister's seat. In a political "musical chairs" that is quite common in Israeli politics, Sharett was now once again foreign minister. But Sharett posed a problem for Ben-Gurion. He stood firm in his opposition to Ben-Gurion's plan to attack Egypt, a plan Sharett believed would lead to an unnecessary all-out war, and he foiled several of Ben-Gurion's attempts to engage in military operations. Finally, Ben-Gurion fired Sharett. Moderates and liberal-leaning people within Israeli society who viewed Sharett as "the last bastion of moderation" were furious, but Ben-Gurion's decision was irreversible.

In 1956, with Sharett out of the way, Ben-Gurion signed a secret pact with France and Britain to attack Egypt. Israel conquered the Gaza Strip and the Sinai Peninsula in what was called the Sinai Campaign, or *Mivtza Kadesh*. The war lasted from October 29 to November 5. Israel suffered 171 casualties, and the Egyptians lost between two and three thousand men. Israel captured 6,000 POWs and the Egyptians captured four Israelis. Just as Ben-Gurion and Dayan had anticipated, it was a devastating blow to the Egyptian army.

This was the first time Israel had occupied the Gaza Strip—an artificially delineated region on the southeastern coast of the Mediterranean Sea surrounding the ancient city of Gaza—where Palestinians refugees exiled in 1948 were herded. After the Sinai Campaign, my father, by then a full colonel, was appointed military governor of the Gaza Strip. This was a defining role for him, and it influenced his entire life.

My father did not usually have conversations with me or with my siblings. If he had something to say, he would lecture us and then get up and leave when he was done. For several years while I was in high school, his classes ran late into the evening, and he did not return home until close to midnight. Before going to sleep my mother would prepare a nice hot soup for him to have when he got home. I would often wait up for him, and we would both have a bowl of soup and talk.

It was during one of those late nights that he revealed to me his thoughts on his time in the Gaza Strip. "When I was given the orders that described my role as military governor, I was aghast. They were identical to those of the British high commissioner, or governor of Palestine. I was not only representing the foreign occupier, I was the governor. I could not help recall how I, as a young man, was determined to fight the British who ruled Palestine and whom I considered foreign occupiers. You really never know how things will turn out in this world."

When I first went to the army archives in Tel Aviv to look for information about my father's career, an employee who assisted me immediately recommended that I look up the Gaza Report. "It is one of the defining documents written by your father," he said. In this document, he expresses how appalled he was when he entered Gaza to take up his command. I have come to recognize the document's language and tone as my father's voice: he comes across as clear, unemotional, and analytical, yet unyieldingly critical of his superiors and the military establishment in general.

It was several days after Gaza was captured that he was sent in. Chaos reigned: "Israeli soldiers and border police were there with no clear orders and no clear command center, which led to rampant disorder and looting." My father quickly set up his command, arrested the looters, collected arms from the locals, and restored order. He set up guidelines to restoring basic services like healthcare and education. He conducted a census that accounted for each family, whether they were refugees and if so from what town or village they had been exiled. The report had accounts of education levels, property, livestock, and a whole host of information about the place and its people.

As military governor of hundreds of thousands of Palestinians, my father realized that he knew virtually nothing of their language, culture, or their way of life. He did not like the fact that he needed translators in order to communicate with the people he governed so he made a personal decision to study Arabic, receiving a bachelor's degree in Arabic from the Hebrew University in Jerusalem. "In conversations with the locals, I was amazed to learn that they were not seeking vengeance for the hardship we caused them, nor did they wish to get rid of us. They were realistic and pragmatic and wanted to be free."

Under immense pressure from the Eisenhower administration, Israel was forced to give up the conquered territories in March of 1957. Although in

My father inspecting groups with Israel's second president, Yitzhak Ben-Zvi.

those days Israel was receiving no money from the U.S. government, when the American president gave the word, my father had two weeks to get out. He was out in two days, but he was deeply troubled. My mother and my sister Nurit told me many times that this issue tormented him for months. "He could not sleep at night, and he would talk of nothing else," Nurit said. My mother told me similar stories.

I was not yet born, but I can imagine his frustration when he learned he would have to go back on his word. I heard him talk about this many years later, saying: "I was assured by my superiors that I could tell the people of Gaza that if they cooperated with us they would not be returned to Egypt. The local leadership believed me and cooperated and then when we left Gaza they paid a heavy price for this."

In an article he wrote after he retired, he brought this up again:

> As the one whose destiny it was to inform the leaders of the towns and villages in Gaza on that cold day in April 1957 that the Israeli government decided to forsake them, I can testify to the looks on the faces of people who at first did not want to believe what they were hearing and then realized what they had brought upon themselves by believing the Israeli government.[1]

My father's next major assignment was commander of the Jerusalem Brigade, which secured and protected West Jerusalem's precarious border with Jordanian-

---

1 Matti Peled, "The Palestinian Problem," *Ma'ariv*, June 27, 1969.

Commander of Jerusalem Brigade with Israel's Prime Minister David Ben Gurion.

controlled East Jerusalem. Jerusalem was not just another region. Jews, Christians, and Muslims had a deep regard for the city, which meant that my father had dealings with diplomats and religious leaders from all around the world. It was a highly sensitive diplomatic post as well as a difficult military one.

In the early 1960s, he served as special advisor on armaments to the deputy minister of defense, who at the time was Shimon Peres. This was the period when, under Peres's supervision, Israel began developing its nuclear weapons program. It was one role about which my father never spoke, and about which I could find no information, presumably because of its highly classified nature.

In 1964, when I was three years old, my father was promoted to major general (*aluf* in Hebrew) as chief of logistics of the Israeli army. This is the highest rank in the Israeli army with the exception of one person, the army chief of staff. His responsibilities included armaments, technology, logistics, the medical corps, weapons and other purchases, and overseeing an enormous budget. The job he wanted was head of army intelligence, and since he was the only general who spoke Arabic at the time, it would have been a logical choice. But chief of logistics was an important position that carried a great deal of responsibility, and the state of logistics in the army was in dire need of reform. So army Chief of Staff Yitzhak Rabin nominated him to that position, and he remained in it for four years.

He felt that war was imminent and that the logistical operation needed modernization, and so in the first one hundred days of his command he planned a complete overhaul of the system. A book on the IDF logistics command that was published years later by the IDF, described his reform:

"In a fashion that is uncharacteristic of the army the discussions he led were short and efficient and within six months of him taking command the reforms were approved by Chief of Staff Rabin. Within three months after that the reforms were implemented."

The description ends by stating that,

Only an officer with a broad vision, an understanding of the needs of the military and an extraordinary determination in implementation (as general Matti Peled possessed) is capable of executing an overhaul of such dimensions.[2]

My father served as chief of logistics of the Israeli army. His rank was Major General, the highest rank in the Israeli army with the exception of one person, the army chief of staff.

On Fridays, my father would come home from work early, and after dinner he would sit in the living room and turn on our beautiful, large wooden radio. I was no more than four or five years old, but I remember it like it was yesterday. He would sit there, still in uniform, and listen to speeches in Arabic given by President Gamal Abdel Nasser of Egypt and other Arab leaders of the time. My father spoke Arabic fluently by then. I remember hearing the massive applause the speakers received and thinking that they sounded like a lot of chess pieces being tossed around in a box. Even though I could not understand a word, I would sit in complete silence as he listened for hours to these speeches. He was absorbed in what he was doing and did not acknowledge me or anyone else that may have been there. Still, I felt as though I was witnessing something very important.

Soon war was on the horizon again. In the late spring of 1967, Egypt's President Nasser expelled the United Nations peacekeeping forces that had been monitor-

---

2 Israel Defense Forces, *The History of the IDF Logistics Command*, (Ma'arachot, publishing arm for the Israel Defense Forces).

ing the ceasefire between the two countries from the Sinai Peninsula. He sent Egyptian troops across the Suez Canal and into the demilitarized Sinai Peninsula, and he threatened to blockade the straits of Tiran and not permit Israeli ships to proceed toward the Israeli port city of Eilat. These were acts that blatantly violated the terms of the ceasefire that was signed between Egypt and Israel. The army was calling it a plausible *casus belli*, or justification for war.

According to documents I found in the IDF archives and other sources, the Soviet government fed misinformation to the Egyptians, claiming that Israel was planning a surprise attack against Syria. The Soviets claimed that Israel had amassed troops on the border with Syria. Syria and Egypt had a mutual security pact, and President Nasser had to act in defense of his Syrian allies. As the Israeli cabinet was considering its options, on May 26, 1967, the Russian prime minister sent the Israeli prime minister, Levi Eshkol, a letter through the Soviet ambassador in Tel Aviv, calling for a peaceful resolution to the conflict. When the Russian ambassador presented Prime Minister Eshkol with the letter, Eshkol invited the ambassador to see with his own eyes that the claim had no merit and that Israeli troops were not amassed at the Syrian border.

The army was recommending that Israel initiate a preemptive strike against Egypt. The cabinet was hesitant and wanted time to explore other options before committing to a full-scale war. Things came to a head in a stormy meeting of the IDF General Staff and the Israeli cabinet that took place on June 2,

Israeli generals preparing for battle. Generals Rabin, Bar-Lev, Peled.

1967.[3] After opening remarks, my father told the cabinet in no uncertain terms that the Egyptians needed a year and a half to two years in order to be ready for a full-scale war. The other generals agreed that the Israeli army was prepared and that this was the time to strike another devastating blow.

During this meeting, my father said to the prime minister: "Nasser is advancing an ill-prepared army because he is counting on the cabinet being hesitant. He is convinced that we will not strike. Your hesitation is working in his advantage." In his reply to my father, the prime minister said: "The cabinet must also think of the mothers who are likely to become bereaved."

The generals were getting more and more frustrated and tensions ran high. Rabin, who was a heavy smoker, was said to have suffered nicotine poisoning and a nervous breakdown. They all knew what my father knew, which was that victory was imminent. In his role as chief of logistics, my father also warned that a prolonged mobilization of reservists, who had already been called up by then and comprised a significant percentage of Israel's workforce, would cripple the country's economy, perhaps even cause it to collapse, unless the cabinet acted decisively. "The army morale is high, and we will be victorious whether we strike today or in three weeks. But the Israeli economy cannot hold for very long. We are not prepared nor are we meant to hold through an extended period of waiting," my father said. General Ezer Weizmann, a lifelong friend of his, threatened to resign his post as deputy chief of staff. General Ariel Sharon, who many years later would be prime minister, said that Israel must engage in a preemptive strike against the Egyptian army "and destroy it entirely without delay."

According to all accounts I had heard over the years by people who were present at this meeting, my father's words to the prime minister were particularly scathing. He demanded an explanation: "Why must this army which had never lost in battle endure such an insult by the cabinet?" This exchange between the two power centers was later known as the "General's Coup."

Many years later, when the issue came up in public debate, I asked my father: "What do you say to the claim that this was a coup?"

"Nonsense!" he retorted in his typically dismissive way. He did not like to have his commitment to the state of Israel questioned, and when it was, he made his displeasure known. But he believed firmly in the superiority of the civilian government and in the rule of law. He defended his actions in speeches and articles many times. His exact words were, "The army leadership had an obligation to advise the cabinet and to make their point clear. Just as the other arms of government had obligations to advise in matters of state or economics, so were we obliged as military experts to give our expert opinion." In an article he published in *Ma'ariv*

---

3 Minutes of the meeting between IDF General Staff and the Israeli cabinet at IDF headquarters on June 2, 1967, The Israel Defense Forces and Defense Establishment Archives (IDFA), Tel-Hashomer military base.

on June 15, 1973, he mentioned this again: "I can testify that there was not a single senior officer in the army who questioned the government's undeniable authority to decide or the army's duty to obey."

Still, as one reads the transcript of that meeting it is obvious my father spoke to the prime minister in a harsher tone than would otherwise be acceptable in a civilian democracy.

I heard the story of this meeting more than once related by Ezer Weizman (who we fondly called Eyzer) himself when he visited us: "You should have seen your father," he recalled with great enthusiasm. "He knew how to pound on the table and get the job done." The whole thing visibly pleased Eyzer to no end.

Well, the generals made no progress and the members of the cabinet chose to wait. They preferred to see the impasses resolved through diplomatic means, and a tug-of-war of unimaginable proportions ensued. This was more than a difference of opinion on how to resolve the crisis. A generational difference factored in as well. The Israeli army generals were in their early to mid-forties, and most of them volunteered in their youth to serve in the Palmach. All but five were Israeli-born, and they were zealous in their belief that Israel must always be decisive and forceful. The members of the cabinet, on the other hand, were mostly in their sixties. Most were from my grandfather's generation, had immigrated to Israel from Eastern Europe, and had fresh recollections of Jews being persecuted and killed. After all, this was taking place only thirty years after the Holocaust.

The army decided to announce that: "The delay in attack is due to diplomatic considerations, but the existential threat remains imminent." Israeli citizens were led to believe that the Arab armies were coming to rape and murder them, as the Nazis had done less than three decades earlier.

The government was pressured by public demands on the one hand and by the generals on the other to act decisively. Eshkol, who acted as defense secretary in addition to his capacity as prime minister, something that is quite common in Israeli administrations, was pressured to give up his role as defense secretary. This was a personal insult for him as well as a major political setback. He called the highly admired former army chief of staff and Ben-Gurion protégé, General Moshe Dayan, into the cabinet as minister of defense. Eshkol then called the opposition parties into a national unity government, which authorized a preemptive strike against Egypt. Once again, the militant approach gained the upper hand.

I was five years old at the time, but I remember the ensuing flurry and the preparations for the war: the adults unable to conceal their worry, the news broadcasts playing more often than usual, and the newspaper headlines striking even my five year-old eyes as more intense. My father was spending his nights and days at army headquarters. My older brother Yoav, by then a lieutenant and a platoon commander in the Armored Corps, was in active duty, and we neither saw nor heard from him.

I was particularly anxious because we were notified that Motza Ellit, where we lived, was in grave danger. Less than a mile from our house is an ancient crusader castle called, plainly, *The Kastel.* In 1948, in a bloody battle that took place there between the Haganna forces and Palestinian fighters, Palestinian commander and national hero, Abdel Kader el-Husseini was killed and his death was a severe blow to the Arab forces. It was said that the Arabs planned to take *The Kastel* and avenge the death of el-Husseini. What did that mean? Would they come and kill us all? I kept my worries to myself, relieved to see that the army positioned an artillery battery in the valley nearby.

Our house had no bomb shelter and may well have been the only one in the entire country without one. "Bomb shelters are useless and unnecessary," my father insisted, and no amount of convincing would sway him to build one. When he made up his mind about something, he seldom offered an explanation. He had no patience for people who questioned his knowledge or authority as an expert.

So even though our house had only recently been built, there was no place for us to sit when the sirens went off. We did have one spot in the house that was somewhat guarded. The small downstairs bathroom, situated on the ground floor and directly under the upstairs bathroom, was the safest place in the house. So my mother and sisters and I, who were alone at home during the war, would rush to sit there whenever we heard the sirens. To give the place some dignity, my mother put a vase with flowers in it, and she hung an autographed photo of David Ben-Gurion on the wall. The bathroom is barely large enough to fit two people at a time.

Our house was an imperfect shelter in other ways. Because my father wanted us all to be able to enjoy the view of the Judean Hills surrounding our home from the kitchen and living room, there were massive glass doors on the main floor. This meant danger of glass being shattered. So I helped Ossi and Nurit to plaster the windows with strips of cloth.

During the day, it all seemed like some sort of festive occasion, because there was no school and my sisters and I were home together. But at night I was frightened. From my bedroom window I saw the endless stream of helicopters bringing wounded soldiers to the Hadassah hospital that sits on a hill directly across from our house. I would get up and go down the corridor to my mother's bedroom, only to find that my sisters were there too. We all tried to calm our fears by cramming into my mother's bed.

I was a child; I had no inkling what war meant, I just knew that we Israelis were heroes, and we would surely win. Like other Israeli children, I was taught that we were descendants of the Maccabees, who beat the entire Greek Empire, and King David, who was but a child when he killed Goliath the Philistine. I knew that even though we were few and they were many, we won every war since Israel was established. I heard stories from my mother about the brave fighters of the Haganah, who fought the British and the Arabs with their superior weapons. We outsmarted and beat them every time.

As it turned out, the whole thing did not last long. The surprise attack led to the total destruction of Egypt's air force, the decimation of the Egyptian army, and the re-conquest of the Gaza Strip and the Sinai Peninsula in a matter of days. Israeli army intelligence confirmed that the Syrian and the Jordanian armies were no match to the IDF. After the campaign against Egypt went smoothly, the field commanders, in collusion with Moshe Dayan, decided to take the West Bank and the Golan Heights, two regions Israel had coveted for many years. Both had strategic water resources and hills overlooking Israeli territory. The West Bank contained the heartland of Biblical Israel, including the "crown jewel," the Old City of Jerusalem.

The fact that the West Bank and the Old City of Jerusalem remained in Arab hands in 1948 was a sore spot for many of the senior officers. So when the opportunity arose again they acted swiftly and decisively. They referred to it as "finishing the job."

In 1953, when my father was still a young lieutenant colonel, Moshe Sharett had invited him to speak in front of a delegation of American Jews. Both Sharett and Ben-Gurion were present and both expressed their delight at the eloquence and the content of the lecture. In his memoirs, Sharett writes that my father said in no uncertain terms that the army is preparing for war "in order to complete the conquest of the Land of Israel and to push Israel's eastern border to its natural location on the banks of the Jordan River."

When the opportunity arose, the army did this without waiting for orders from the civilian authorities.

In six days, it was all over. Arab casualties were estimated at more than 15,000. Israeli casualties were 700, and the territory controlled by Israel had nearly tripled in size. Israel had in its possession not only land and resources it had wanted for a long time, but also the largest stockpiles of Russian-made arms outside the Soviet Union. Israel had once again asserted itself as a major regional power.

I remember the jubilation. The radio played victory songs, and *Yerushalaim Shel Zahav,* Jerusalem of Gold, written by Naomi Shemer, became an international hit. My father finally came home, and there was news that my brother Yoav was OK. In a sheer coincidence, he and my father met in the field after the Sinai Desert was taken. My mother has a photo taken by a friend showing a very young and tired Yoav, full of dust from the desert, and my father facing one another and talking. Then there were the ceremonies. I recall we went to Army Headquarters in Tel-Aviv as the victorious generals were all awarded their victory pins. In a photo I have and treasure, Israel's president, Zalman Shazar, *Dod Zalman,* is surrounded by the entire Israeli army General Staff with an autograph of each of the generals at the bottom. I was so proud at that time, I felt that I could fly.

Israel's president, Zalman Shazar, surrounded by the victorious Israeli army General Staff after the 1967 war.

I had no idea that my father was concerned about any unintended negative consequences this victory posed to the Jewish state.

The late Ze'ev Schiff, who was Israel's most prominent military analyst, would later say that in his role as chief of logistics, my father's contribution to the war's success was unprecedented and cannot be overstated. He and his comrades who, as young officers made the victory of 1948 possible, were now the generals who led the victory of 1967 and the complete return of the historic Eretz Yisrael after 2,000 years to Jewish hands. And on top of that, this was taking place less than 30 years after Nazi-controlled Europe was systematically murdering Jews.

But this massive conquest of lands troubled my father. When he was pushing for the war, he had imagined it would be a limited war with Egypt to punish the Egyptians for their breach of the ceasefire and to assert Israeli legitimacy and military might. Taking the West Bank, Gaza Strip, and Golan Heights was never part of any official plan. In an article in the daily *Ma'ariv*, journalist Haim Hanegbi vividly describes the first weekly meeting of the General Staff after the Six-Day War. [4] He

4 Haim Hanegbi, "Peled, His Mouth and His Heart," *Maariv*, April 7, 1995.

states that Chief of Staff Yitzhak Rabin and the other generals were beaming with the glory of victory, but when the meeting was nearing its end, my father spoke.

Never one to rest on his laurels, he cleared his throat and in his unmistakably dry, analytical manner, he spoke of the unique chance the victory offered Israel to solve the Palestinian problem once and for all. "For the first time in Israel's history, we are face to face with the Palestinians, without other Arab countries dividing us. Now we have a chance to offer the Palestinians a state of their own." He later also claimed with certainty that holding onto the West Bank and the people who lived in it was contrary to Israel's long-term strategy of building a secure Jewish democracy with a stable Jewish majority. If we kept these lands, popular resistance to the occupation was sure to arise, and Israel's army would be used to quell that resistance, with disastrous and demoralizing results. He concluded that this would turn the Jewish state into an increasingly brutal occupying power and eventually into a bi-national state.

My father said all this as the gun barrels were still smoking and before Israel began its settlement project in the West Bank and Gaza. The other generals listened, but they did not want to discuss the issue. They claimed the Palestinians would never settle for the West Bank and Gaza and would demand more land. So he proceeded to bring intelligence reports that showed clearly that an overwhelming majority of Palestinians thought as he did. Finally, Yitzhak Rabin took him aside privately and told him it wasn't the right political climate to discuss this.

Even though I was only six years old when my father retired from the IDF, my entire life has been affected by his military career. In Israeli terms—where the army is regarded above all else, and the generation of 1948, or the "Palmach Generation," have all but been made into gods—it was no ordinary career.

It was during these early years that I was infused with patriotism and a belief in the Zionist cause. Having been born an Israeli Jew at this time in history, I had a desire to fulfill my destiny and to serve when my turn came. At the time, I wanted very much to be a hero and a great general like my father.

Chapter 3:

Against the Current— Academia and Activism

My father planned to retire immediately after the 1967 war, but was asked by the new army chief of staff, Haim Bar-Lev, to stay another year. There was a need for major armament and logistics organization after the war, so he agreed to stay and get the job done. But my father had no interest in governing an occupied nation, and he was eager to move on with his life. So in 1968, he opted to retire from the army and embark on a much-anticipated academic career. He donated his huge military library to the IDF and filled his study with books on Arabic literature.

The transition from the intensity of military life to civilian life is not easy, and naturally it took my father some time to adjust. The first few years after he retired from the military, he would not answer the phone—he was used to having a secretary; that was understandable. If I answered the phone, I would need to find out who was on the other end, and once I told my father he would sharply ask, "Well, what does he want?" To which, of course, I had no answer. At one point, he decided to answer the phone by himself, but always in a tone that suggested the he was being pulled away from something important.

And indeed he was. Matti Peled was always doing something important. His greatest joy was work, and he took himself and his work extremely seriously. Interruptions were never welcome.

Upon his retirement, my father had lucrative career options. As IDF chief of logistics, he headed an immense logistic, administrative, and financial organization, and he did this with unprecedented success. When he retired, he was only 45 years old, and already considered an enormous hero. He could have done pretty much anything he wanted to at that time. He fielded offers to head some of Israel's largest and most successful corporations. He also had several attractive options in government and politics, but he found none of those appealing.

He did not believe that one should choose work because of money or position. "One's work," he used to say, "should to be determined by principles, by the ability to contribute, or by one's own interests in life."

For him, building an army for the Jewish state was based on principle. Becoming a scholar of Arabic literature fulfilled his interests. Being involved in politics and being an advocate for Palestinian rights was his contribution to the moral fiber of the state that he fought to establish for the Jewish people. When I was old enough to appreciate the benefits of having money, I asked him why he turned down those lucrative offers. "What do you mean why? Do you think I should spend my life manufacturing zippers?" "Zippers" was his way of referring to anything that he thought was of little consequence to the world.

So, immediately after my father retired from the army, our family moved to Los Angeles for three years in order for him to pursue his second career, as a professor of modern Arabic literature. During this time, he managed to complete his PhD at the University of California, Los Angeles (UCLA).

I was six years old, and I was ecstatic to go to America. I would show off my vast knowledge about America to my friends: "In America, they have cars with automatic transmission and phones where you can see the person on the other end of the line through the phone!" I actually imagined the stick shift moving on its own, and I was seriously disappointed when I learned that it was not like that at all. "Plus we fly in an airplane to get there."

Although I loved America, these turned out to be three very difficult years for the rest of the family. My father was given a scholarship, but it was not a very generous one, and so we lived in an apartment in what was called the UCLA Married Student Housing. There were several poor married students, some with kids. There were also a few respectable international refugees who, more often than not, had fled their own countries as a result of a coup. And there was one Israeli couple who had two cats and with whom I would spend a great deal of time. My best friends were Vita from Tanzania, Berno from Ecuador, and Piyush from India. Vita's family lived on one side of our apartment; on the other was the Babikian family, Armenians from Lebanon. I remember the mother, Margot, and my mother became good friends. They also had a son who was younger than I, Ariel, with whom I would often play.

The army retirement plan was not generous at the time, and so money was very tight. Although I was never in want of anything, I realize now how hard and stressful it must have been on both my parents. I was always a cheerful young boy and my mother, my sister Nurit, and friends of the family all made sure that I was having a good time—and I did. We would go to the pool on campus a lot and participate in summer camps there.

My brother, Yoav, left after a year and returned to Israel. Nurit left shortly thereafter to study at the Sorbonne in Paris. Ossi, the sister closest to me in age, and I remained the entire three years. Realizing the amount of stress under which my father had placed himself and how his mood affected the rest of the family, my mother did her best to remain cheerful and make our life livable.

When we first arrived in Los Angeles, we stayed in a very nice apartment building not far from UCLA. The apartment was spacious and the corridors leading to it were carpeted like a plush hotel. There was a swimming pool, and since most of the residents were older, my sisters and I had it all to ourselves. But it turned out that my father's stipend could not afford us this arrangement and we ended up moving into a smaller apartment on Sawtelle Boulevard, among families who were younger and far less affluent. I knew no English when we arrived but, being six and having a TV set, I picked it up quickly. I went to second, third, and fourth grade at the Clover Avenue School in Los Angeles.

I loved living in the U.S., and the experience gave me an edge that cannot be overstated. I became completely fluent in English, which made me bilingual at a very young age. I was exposed to American culture and, more than that, to the diverse nature of Los Angeles and particularly the UCLA campus during the late 1960s and early 1970s. I remember going with my father to the drive-in theatre to see the famous fight between Joe Frasier and Mohammad Ali, where Frasier knocked out Ali. When we returned, I saw that the entire neighborhood was in uproar, particularly the African Americans who lived there. More than a boxing match, this was a huge social and political match even though both Frasier and Ali were African American. Ali represented the antiwar, anti-establishment African-American rebellion of the time. His defeat was viewed as unfair, and as a loss for the African-American struggle.

We were also there during the presidential elections when Richard Nixon beat Hubert Humphrey. It's almost hard to believe today, but my father supported Nixon over Humphrey. As he supported the U.S. bombing of Cambodia and Vietnam—because he was completely and thoroughly anticommunist and pro-American. Watergate began to surface during our final days in the U.S.

Even after we returned to Israel, I kept up with American politics and culture, much more so than most Israeli kids my age. And I held on to certain pop culture associations from the time: Peanuts, the young Michael Jackson, and all the television series and shows that marked that period and remained iconic in American culture. So that when I moved back to Southern California as an adult, I was in some ways returning home.

My father had an office at UCLA on the tenth floor of one of the tall buildings on campus, and he spent most of his time there. In the evening, after dinner, he would watch the news and then I would join him on the couch for an episode of Bonanza or The Wild Wild West, or a police drama, before going to bed.

While I enjoyed America, I was glad to eventually return to Jerusalem. But in Israel things did not go so smoothly for me. I had first-grade Hebrew skills and was sent to fifth grade, but received no help in order to catch up. Plus, what was cool in the U.S. was not necessarily cool in Israel. Here no one cared about UCLA beating USC at basketball; I knew nothing about local sports; and the American mannerisms I'd picked up made me an outsider from the get-go.

The first day of school my mother dropped me off at the house on 18 Rashba Street—our old building where my grandmothers now lived—and said, "Just follow all the other children, they are all going to the same school." I didn't know my way around so I was terrified, but I did what she said. Then once I got to school, I had no idea where to go. There were hundreds of children who seemed like they knew what to do and where to go, and I was embarrassed to admit I was clueless. Eventually, I found my class, and the teacher gave me name cards to hand out to all the students, not realizing I could not read Hebrew well enough to read the names.

The first couple of years back in Israel, my greatest fear was that I would be asked to read out loud and people would find out that I couldn't read very well. I fell behind in all subjects and that, along with my father's unpopular views, made for some tough times for a ten-year old. Because my father, the retired general, called for compromise and criticized the state, he was called an "Arab lover," and so was I—although I still hadn't formed any particular political views. It's safe to assume that the other kids repeated at school what they heard at home, and it made little difference if I held the same views as my father or not. It took me three years to catch up, both socially and academically. By eighth grade, I felt pretty good and I had a few friends. As far as school was concerned, other than English, with which I felt at ease, my confidence was always low and my performance poor. So while three years in the U.S. was a great opportunity, because no one thought to work with me through the transition, the return home was very difficult.

Meanwhile, my father helped to found the Arabic Literature Department at Tel Aviv University. He gained a reputation as a serious and innovative scholar and later became the first Israeli professor of Arabic literature to introduce studies of Palestinian prose and poetry into the academic curriculum. He taught at Tel Aviv and Haifa Universities until he retired for a second time in 1990.

While we were still in the U.S., my father started writing a weekly opinion column in *Ma'ariv*, a mass-circulation daily newspaper published in Israel. Because of his résumé, everyone expected him to align himself with the Israeli government's narrative, which claimed that Israel had been viciously attacked by three Arab armies in 1967 and defended itself heroically because it had the wits and, more importantly, the moral high ground. This narrative also claimed that Israel's rights to the land of Israel were absolute, if not for religious or historical reasons then for military and security reasons.

But he saw things differently. He came out and stated publicly that the 1967 War was not an existential war but a war of choice:

I was surprised that Nasser decided to place his troops so close to our border. He must have known the grave danger into which he placed his forces. Having the Egyptian army so close allowed us to strike and destroy at any time we wished to do so, and there was not a single knowledgeable person who did not see that. From a military standpoint, it was not the IDF that was in danger when the Egyptian army amassed troops on the Israeli border, but the Egyptian army.[1]

He fiercely criticized the army's building of an expensive defensive line in the Sinai Desert along the shores of the Suez Canal. He thought the army should be mobile and agile and that throughout history defensive lines had proven themselves to be costly and ineffective. This line was later named *Kav Bar-Lev*, or The Bar-Lev Line, after Chief of Staff Haim Bar-Lev. During the 1973 Arab-Israeli War[2], the Egyptian army stormed through the Bar-Lev Line and it proved to be a disaster, providing no defense at all. After the war everyone liked to joke:

Question: "What remained of the Bar-Lev Line after the war?"

Answer: "The villas of the contractors who built it."

In response to a comment made by Israel Galili, who was a cabinet member and a major policymaker under Golda Meir's premiership, my father wrote yet another article, calling to allow the Palestinians in the West Bank and Gaza to conduct democratic elections[3]. Galili's claim, often heard since, was that had there been democratically elected Palestinian representatives, Israel might have considered negotiations, but in the absence of such representatives Israel had no choice but to maintain the status quo. My father thought Galili's claim disingenuous—after all, it was Galili's Israeli government that was preventing the Palestinians from conducting elections in the West Bank and Gaza.

In another article my father wrote in his column on the third anniversary of the Six-Day War, my father compared the government's inaction and lack of courage to act to achieve peace, a peace that he said was made possible thanks to the tremendous victory that the army delivered, to the lack of courage and inaction that characterized the same government in the weeks leading up to the war. He wrote of the great sacrifice he along with everyone else felt in having to return portions of the Land of Israel in return for peace. "I would be less than

---

1 Matti Peled, "The beauty has not faded," *Ma'ariv*, June 15, 1973.

2 The 1973 Mideast War, also called The Yom Kippur War, began on the Jewish Holiday of Yom Kippur, October 6, 1973. Egyptian and Syrian forces attacked Israel and caught the IDF by surprise, which resulted in panic and many casualties. A special inquiry, the Agranat Commission was set up to investigate the IDF failings. It found IDF top brass responsible and several generals, including the IDF chief of staff, had to resign. Prime Minister Golda Meir, who remained unscathed by the commission, had to resign as well as a result of popular protests.

3 Matti Peled, "The Palestinian Problem," *Ma'ariv*, June 27, 1969.

honest had I denied that I too have deep regard for these lands that for the sake of peace must be left outside the boundaries of our State." And he continued to speak with great emotion of the experiences of his youth: "It was not out of obligation, but rather love for this country that in my youth I traversed its length and breadth."[4]

In 1973, Prime Minister Golda Meir gave a speech in the southern Israeli city of Eilat, in front of an audience of high school students. It was during this speech that she claimed that, before 1967, she had never heard of the Palestinian people and that they were somehow invented and had no real national identity—and therefore could have no national claims to the land of Palestine. In his column, my father immediately wrote a scathing reply to Golda's speech where he asked:

"How do people in the world refer to the population that resides in the West Bank? What were the refugees of 1948 called prior to their exile? Has she really not heard of the Palestinian people prior to 1967? In discussions she must have had over the years in her capacity as ambassador and then as foreign minister, how did she refer to these people? Yet she says she had not heard of the Palestinian people prior to 1967? Truly amazing!"[5]

Still, it came as a shock when in the mid-1970s my father called on the Israeli government to negotiate with the Palestinian Liberation Organization, the PLO. He agreed that the PLO was the legitimate representative of the Palestinian people and as such must be Israel's partner to the negotiating table. He claimed that Israel needed to talk with whoever represented the Palestinian people, the people with whom we shared this land. He constantly wanted to remind everyone that only peace with the Palestinians could ensure our continued existence as a state that was both Jewish and democratic.

In those years, I occasionally traveled with my father when he gave lectures around the country. He was often invited as an expert to speak about the major political and military issues of the day. It was a great way to see places I had never seen and to spend time with him. I recall once we visited the Kibbutz Bar'am in the northern region of Galilee. Bar'am sits on the lands of the former Palestinian village Bir'am. The lecture was at the Kibbutz in the evening, and the next day we went to see the ruins of the village. At the time, I was not fully aware of the state's role in the displacement of Palestinians.

Sometimes my mother would come on these trips as well. The lectures were typically on Friday night, so we would drive Friday afternoon, and then eat dinner and spend the night at the Kibbutz. Then on Saturday we'd see whatever the area had to offer.

The lectures were quite often very tough and people were not at all polite when they heard my father's opinions. I will never forget the anger and venom directed

---

4 Matti Peled, "Thoughts at Beginning of the Fourth Year," Ma'ariv, June 5, 1970.
5 Matti Peled, "Who Heard of the Palestinians?" Ma'ariv, March 23, 1973.

at him when he spoke of *Ashaf*, the actual Hebrew acronym for the PLO. "How can you talk to terrorists who want our destruction?" some would ask. "They want Yaffa and Haifa and Ramle, and they want to slaughter all of us."

"Terrorism," he would reply, "is a terrible thing. But the fact remains that when a small nation is ruled by a larger power, terror is the only means at their disposal. This has always been true, and I fear this will always be the case. If we want to end terrorism, we must end the occupation and make peace." He insisted that the Palestinians could become our natural allies, our bridge to the entire Middle East, where we Israelis had decided to build our home.

A military general was suggesting that we negotiate instead of fight; this was hard for Israelis to swallow. I think it angered people that he did not go along with the established thinking, which always placed Israel on the right side and the Arabs on the wrong side. Moreover, he was suggesting we turn away from what had become basic Zionist principles: to never give up land and to never accept the claims of the Arabs regarding Israel and the Palestinians.

He was suggesting that we talk with the people we had been taught to hate and fear the most. Unlike Egyptians, Jordanians, Syrians, or Lebanese, who had their own states, "these so-called Palestinians," people would say to him, and to me when I opened my big mouth, "wanted *our* homes and *our* land." I, like most Israelis, learned the terms *fedayeen*[6], *infiltrators*, and *terrorists* long before I knew they were actually called Palestinians. People would voice their fears in ways that were aggressive and even belligerent: "You want to make peace with these terrorists who blatantly claim they want to take back the cities of Jaffa and Ramle and Lod and to push us into the sea." People thought General Peled had lost his mind, or at the very least, lost his direction.

I am often asked how it was that he had developed such clear and far-sighted opinions on this issue, and the only answer I can think of is that he was a principled man through and through. He did not accept the double standard that we, the Jewish people, deserve to live on the same land as the Palestinians and yet deprive them of their rights. He also had grave concerns for the nature of the Jewish democracy, and he knew that the occupation of another people would destroy the moral fiber of society and of the IDF. He did not want to see the IDF turn into a brutal force charged with oppressing a nation that would surely rise to resist the occupation. There were other Zionists, like the revered professor Yesha'yahu Leibovitch and journalist Uri Avnery to name but two, who thought and spoke as he did. But when he said these things, it was particularly troubling to people because he was a military general of the Palmach generation.

It wasn't long before friends stopped inviting him and my mother to social events. He became a political and social pariah. For my father this meant more

---

6 Fedayeen are people who volunteer to fight for a cause. They were Palestinian freedom fighters, but to us the name meant terrorists.

time to work, so he didn't mind. But I remember many occasions during that period when my mother would tell me, sadly, about old friends who were gathering without her: "They invited everyone but us." My mother agreed with his political views, but she would always insist that the harsh and impatient manner with which he expressed them was counter-productive because it isolated him, and her. "People don't hear the message when you are so harsh. It is only hurting you," she'd say.

Somehow I, my sister Nurit, and my brother Yoav, all reached the same political conclusions as our father did. His rationale was always clear and convincing. There was a time for war, and now it is time for peace. His generation fought so that ours could live in a democracy, and the occupation and oppression of Palestinians was getting in the way. Ossi has never been, and still is not, as engaged politically as the three of us. And while we all criticized and disagreed with my father plenty, albeit not in front of him, on this issue we were all aligned—even though it sometimes came at a heavy price.

Being the youngest son of a public figure with such unpopular opinions was difficult. I was as patriotic as one could be, and I knew my father was a patriot. So I could not understand how people doubted him. While I felt myself being pushed out of the mainstream, at first I was not sure why.

Over the years, his views became more and more at odds with mainstream Israel, even though in theory everyone claimed to espouse the principles he preached: democracy, free speech, and above all, peace. With time I too established firm views that were aligned with his, and so I too found myself at odds with my environment. But to my surprise, no one wanted to hear the rationale behind our views. On occasion, I would voice my opinions in school and get in over my head, arguing with teachers and other students. These arguments did hone my debate skills, but I was mostly yelled at for being an Arab-lover. I remember once in fifth grade, a parent of a classmate who was a well-known journalist came to speak to us. The first thing he said was: "I understand that one of you is Matti Peled's son. Which one of you is it?" I felt my face burning as all eyes turned to me, and I raised my hand and identified myself. I had to constantly negotiate my patriotism and my love and admiration for my country and its army with the fact that I, along with my father, was going against popular opinion.

In the early 1970s Israel still held military parades during Independence Day. My father believed whole-heartedly that they ought to be part of the Independence Day festivities—that without the IDF there wouldn't have been an independence day at all. It was a huge affair and I loved it: there were tanks and missile launchers and infantry brigades displaying their colors. They would enter the stadium at the Hebrew University in Jerusalem, where a stage was set up for the VIPs. The stadium was packed with people who looked up at the IDF air force flyovers by U.S.-made F-5 Fantoms and French-made Mirage fighter jets. We got to sit in the VIP section, and I thought it was the best thing in the world. In those days, it was quite common to see the retired generals show up in their uniform for the Independence Day parade, but my father refused to follow the tradition.

"Come on dad, why not?" I was dying to see him wear his uniform again.

"This is not a masquerade and the uniform is not some costume," he said sharply. I would look at the one clean and pressed uniform he had sitting in the closet with admiration, and wonder when if ever he might wear it again. He never did. I would play with his older ones, wearing the hat and the medals and pretending to be a general myself, but he never encouraged this. He saw no particular pride in the military; he thought of it as a tool, not an identity.

In the aftermath of the 1973 Arab-Israeli war, which we named the Yom Kippur War because it began on that holiest of Jewish holidays, my father shifted even further from the mainstream and aligned himself with Israel's Zionist socialist left. His association with Uri Avnery for example, a veteran journalist who was a leftist, anti-establishment political activist his whole life, was a major shift. It was a relationship that lasted many years.

Then, along with Avnery, Yaakov Arnon, and several other dissident members of the Zionist establishment, he founded the Israeli Council for Israeli-Palestinian Peace.

The council sought to promote private and unofficial dialogue between Israelis and Palestinians, which they hoped would lead to official negotiations between Israel and the PLO. Its charter called for Israel to withdraw from the territories occupied in 1967 and for an independent Palestinian state to be established in the West Bank and Gaza, with Arab East Jerusalem as its capital. At the time, the idea was unthinkably radical.

I remember that I and everyone else were surprised at the amount of attention the council received, particularly from the foreign press. Soon word came through back channels and intermediaries that key members of the PLO, Yasser Arafat's people, wanted to meet. It was a big step for both sides. Until that point, the PLO had a policy of talking only to non-Zionist Israelis who were open to the idea of a "secular democracy" in all of Israel/Palestine, where Jews and Arabs would live in one state. This notion was totally unacceptable to my father: He was a Zionist—he believed in a state for the Jewish people in the Land of Israel. For him, any other solution would lead to endless bloodshed. Still, I wonder if his devotion to Zionism would have waned at all had he been alive today.

Great precautions were taken and a great deal of mistrust had to be overcome before the first meeting took place. It was in Paris where my father was first

A close friend of my father's, Issam Sartawi was a close confidant of Yasser Arafat and the PLO's representative to Paris.

introduced[7] to Dr. Issam Sartawi, a close confidant of Yasser Arafat and the PLO's representative to Paris. To borrow from the classic movie *Casablanca*, this was "the beginning of a beautiful friendship," as Dr. Issam and my father became peace partners.

In an article he published in 1977, my father described in great detail both that first meeting with Sartawi and his own thoughts immediately before, and during, the meeting.[8] (When the article was published, Sartawi's identity had not yet been made public, so he never mentioned him by name.) "How does one feel when one is about to meet his enemy?" my father asked.

He continued,

> As I recall I was sitting in a comfortable armchair trying without success to read an article in *Le Monde* when the doorbell rang and two men entered. These were the two men for whom I had made the trip to Paris.
>
> My role was relatively easy. The story of my people since the return to our homeland began is etched in my memory...

As my father saw it, the main question was this: "Will we be allowed to live our lives in peace and security... and be masters of our own destiny? Anyone who allows us to do this is a friend. Is the man with whom I am speaking willing to be our friend?" He also asked, "Can reality be transformed?" His answer there: "Anyone who does not believe it can is depriving himself of the great powers that nature has bestowed on mankind."

---

7 Henri Curiel, an Egyptian-Jewish communist, living in exile in Paris, played a key role in facilitating the opening of these contacts. He was assassinated in 1978. It remains a mystery who killed him.

8 Matti Peled, "My meetings with PLO representatives," *Ma'ariv,* July 1, 1977.

Over the years, my father met with Sartawi in various locations all over Europe and North Africa—they spent time in Palma De Majorca off the coast of Spain, in Morocco, and in Tunis. The late Austrian Chancellor Bruno Kreisky, who was Jewish, facilitated many of these meetings, as did Landrum Bolling, a Quaker and former President of Earlham College in Indiana, who also became a good friend of my father's. Landrum, a lifelong devoted peace activist, told me once about the time he and Chancellor Kreisky were with my father and Issam in Majorca. He and Kreisky stayed behind and let the other two walk along a secluded beach resort, deep in conversation. "If it was left up to these two men," Landrum said to the Austrian Chancellor, "this conflict would be resolved immediately." Kreisky agreed.

Before leaving for these meetings my father would say, "I will be away for a few days, I can't talk about it but don't be alarmed." My mother worried sick until he was safely home. As we sat together late one night my father told me about a meeting at a remote resort in North Africa. "It was luxurious beyond imagination," he said, "and miles from anywhere. Issam wanted to reassure me that we were safe, and he said there was no way anyone could possibly know that we were here." He paused before getting to the main point of his story. "I looked around and pointed out the beautiful young receptionist. 'Do you know for a fact that she does not work for the Mossad?' I asked him." My father took nothing for granted, and he knew just how far the arm of the Israeli intelligence could reach.

The contacts between members of the council and the PLO were largely kept secret, as few Israelis could comprehend the idea of talking with the *Ashaf,* and many Palestinians were fiercely opposed to a dialogue with Zionist Israelis. Over the years, Issam and his wife, Dr. Widad Sartawi, developed a personal friendship with my father and mother. Many years later, when my eldest son Eitan was 10, he and I—along with my mother and my sister Nurit and other family members— spent a memorable time with Widad and her family at her home in Paris.

In 1977, Israeli Television set up a roundtable discussion with the entire general staff of 1967—on the occasion of the tenth anniversary of the war. The roundtable was held on a news program called "Moked," and was later featured in the excellent documentary by Ilan Ziv that came out in 2007 called *Six Days in June.*

At one point, my father remarked that he did not recall ever hearing or seeing a directive from the cabinet to take the West Bank. It was the first time that I heard him criticize the IDF commander's decision to take the West Bank without first seeking cabinet approval. "It had always been considered an important strategic directive to avoid conquering areas that were heavily populated, he said, "Taking the West Bank with its Arab population was a clear reversal of this principle, and I don't recall ever hearing or seeing such a directive come down from the Israeli government."

As he was saying this, the camera began pulling back to show the faces of the others around the table. Their unease at his words was obvious. Not only was my father reminding everyone that the West Bank and the Golan Heights were taken without cabinet approval, an act that in the past he had defended, but he was now

Israeli generals 10 years after the war.

pointing out that the generals themselves reversed an important strategic directive without proper authority.

For his leftist politics, my father received occasional death threats and was sometime accused of treason by extremist Jewish groups, most of whom had not served a single day in uniform. He would report these to the police and although he did not seem troubled, he always slept with a loaded pistol by his bed. At one point word got out that there had been a death threat made, and reporters called to interview him on Israeli radio. "Are you afraid for your life, sir?" the reporter asked.

His response was as cool and rational as ever: "The incident was reported to the police, and I have every confidence that they will deal with it appropriately."

"I understand sir, but, General Peled, my question is, are you afraid for your life?"

"The police took a report, and I am sure they will know what to do."

"Yes sir, I understand you have faith in our police force, but are you afraid?"

"I have nothing more to add."

He refused to say any more than that, and he ended the interview. In a way it was not unlike his attitude toward building a bomb shelter for our home. If something made sense to him, he would not allow emotions like fear get in the way of good reason, and that was the end of the conversation.

In hindsight, I think he was right to answer the way he did in so far as he did not want to give in to the extensive myth that there was some horrible, pervasive threat and that we all had to live in fear. No, there was a rational, reasonable way to resolve these issues, and my father had faith in people's ability and in the state of Israel. He certainly could have done a better job expressing himself at times, and at giving some validation to the fact that the rest of us were afraid and may have needed reassurance as opposed to orders and edicts. But then again, he was a general.

Whenever Dr. Sartawi called our home from Paris, his code name was The Friend. "Hello, is Matti home? This is the friend speaking." When I heard that, I would be filled with a sense of excitement and importance, and I would rush to get my father. Then I would leave the room immediately.

One discussion they had was about creating a Palestinian state in the West Bank and the Gaza Strip, what was later named, "The Two-State Solution." For Yasser Arafat to give up all of Palestine with the exception of the West Bank and Gaza—two pockets of land that amount to 22 percent of Palestine—was an enormous concession to make before official negotiations began. The official line of Fatah—a main Palestinian liberation party and a major faction of the PLO—was to support one secular democratic state that would include Arabs and Jews and allow the return of the Palestinian refugees. Arafat had serious people around him who saw the two-state solution as an option that was both pragmatic and practical. Others within Fatah vehemently disagreed, claiming they could not abandon the millions of refugees who wanted to return to their homes and land in what was now Israel. Arafat had to tread carefully between these two camps. He wouldn't officially endorse a two-state solution until 1988, but the idea was born in these early years when he let his advisors speak with prominent Zionists.

Upon his return from these trips, my father would meet with Yitzhak Rabin, then in his first term as prime minister. He wanted to brief Rabin on his talks with the Palestinians and to convince him that the time was right for the Israeli government to engage in official talks with the PLO. Everyone thought highly of Rabin as a person and of his abilities as an officer and a leader. When I would hear my father start a sentence with "Yitzhak said," I knew it was important. But it was never blind admiration; there were many times where my father forcefully criticized Rabin.

I remember one occasion when Rabin came to our house to be briefed. He had visited our house before for social gatherings, weddings, and other family celebrations, and our families knew each other well as a result of the many years the two men worked together while in uniform. Even in the early days it was always a big deal when Rabin came to visit because he was the subject of great admiration. "Will Yitzhak be there? Will he be coming?" people would ask my mother. "Yes, Yitzhak will be coming."

Now when the prime minister visits your house, it is a big deal. A team of secret service agents positioned themselves at each of the many entryways to our house. Military jeeps positioned themselves at the main intersections leading to our home and a helicopter hovered overhead. And then the prime minister's motorcade appeared, and we went out to greet him.

The two men sat in our spacious living room, and my father asked that they have the room to themselves. I was 12 or 13 at the time, so I went outside and talked with the secret service guys.

✆

I grew up believing that peace, even if difficult, was sure to come. That belief was bolstered in November 1977, when it was announced that Egyptian President Anwar Sadat would visit Jerusalem. And he would do it with no guarantee that his gesture would bring any tangible results.

It was unthinkable, unbelievable—an unprecedented and truly courageous act of good faith. An entire nation sat glued to their televisions as the Egyptian presidential plane landed in Tel Aviv. Many people simply did not believe it would happen until they saw the impressive figure of President Sadat step out of the plane.

The Israeli honor guard played a marching tune as he strode down the stairs and ceremoniously inspected the troops. Highway 1, the main highway that leads from Tel Aviv to Jerusalem was closed for the occasion. We lived only minutes from the highway, so I ran with dozens of friends to see the motorcade and wave signs in Arabic that said, *Ahlan wa Sahlan Rais El Sadat!* Welcome President Sadat!

Sadat was welcomed at the entrance to Jerusalem with traditional bread and salt by the chief rabbis. He went to pray at the Al Aqsa Mosque in the Old City of Jerusalem, and then he spoke at the Knesset in Arabic in front of a full house and a packed visitors' gallery. It was a day of profound, almost delirious jubilation. Peace with an Arab nation was at hand.

I was in high school at the time and my father was on sabbatical at Harvard. He had good relations with the Egyptian ambassador to the United States, and this, along with the goodwill that came about as a result of Sadat's visit, resulted in an invitation for him and my mother to visit Egypt. Theirs must have been the very first Israeli passports stamped with Egyptian visas.

They toured Egypt and met the famed Egyptian writer Naguib Mahfouz, who later received the Nobel Prize for literature, at his home in Cairo. My father had written his dissertation about Mahfouz, but being an Israeli and a retired general, he had not been able to meet him until then. Over the years, my father returned to visit Mahfouz several times. He loved the normalcy of taking a bus from Tel Aviv to Cairo, going to the café that Mahfouz was known to frequent, and sitting there with the great writer for hours. He loved the Arab world—the neighborhood in which Israel was founded, not just the piece of land on which it had set up its state.

Riding the success of the 1979 peace pact with Egypt, in the 1982 national elections Menachem Begin won a second term in office as prime minister. However, this term was marked by the invasion of Lebanon, a devastating war that would later be known as Israel's Vietnam. Testing the limits as he always did, in early

*My father in Cairo with
Egyptian author and Nobel
Laureate for Literature,
Naguib Mahfouz.*

1983, shortly after Arafat was driven out of Lebanon by the Israeli invasion, my father embarked on a secret mission to Tunisia to meet with the PLO chairman himself. He was joined by Uri Avnery and Dr. Yaakov Arnon, an economist, former general director of the Israeli department of treasury and a close friend of my father. And on the Palestinian side, along with Chairman Arafat, were Mahmoud Abbas and Dr. Issam Sartawi. The meeting was later publicized, and the photo of them together made the press worldwide.

It wasn't long after this historic meeting that Dr. Sartawi was murdered. It happened April 10, 1983, during a meeting of the Socialist International Conference in Portugal. The presumed culprit was the Abu Nidal terrorist gang operating out of Iraq, whose loyalties are shrouded in mystery to this day.

Sartawi's death was a dark day for my family. I happened to be watching TV when it took place. Dr. Issam lay on the ground in a pool of his own blood in broad daylight in a hotel lobby. It took me a few seconds before I could utter the words: "Dad come quick, Issam Sartawi was shot!" Surrounded by parliamentarians and heads of state, including Shimon Peres, who was there as the Labor Party leader, Issam Sartawi was gunned down.

Israeli Council for Israel-Palestine Peace meeting with Yasser Arafat in Tunis.

My father was in his study when I called him. When he realized what had happened, he was stricken and motionless. Though he did not say a word, I could see that after the death of his beloved brother Dubik, this was the saddest day of his life. Later on, he gave a statement in which he said, "Sartawi was killed because he was reaching out to Zionists. He had literally given his life for peace." My father reminded people of this each time doubt was cast upon the sincerity of the Palestinians' desire for peace.

The next year, my father was among the founding members of a joint Jewish-Arab political party, the Progressive List for Peace (PLP). Their Palestinian-Israeli[9] partners were headed by Mohammed Mi'yari, a veteran activist and human rights lawyer, and Bishop Riah Abu-el-Assal, vicar of the Anglican Church in Nazareth, who was later the Anglican bishop of Jerusalem. My father had lent his name and reputation to several political parties over the years, but he had no real interest in becoming a politician. For the PLP however, he agreed to be the number two on the list in the 1984 national elections.

Right-wing nationalist parties made several attempts to outlaw the PLP and prevent it from running in elections. They compared it to the racist Kach Party, led by US-born Rabbi Meir Kahane, and said that the elimination of both would be a fair trade. Kach was an overtly racist Jewish party that ran on a platform calling for forcibly transferring all Palestinians out of the country. One party called for peace and reconciliation and one for ethnic cleansing, yet the claim was that they were equally extreme. The Israeli Supreme Court, which

9 Palestinian-Israelis are Palestinians who live within Israel and have Israeli citizenship. Israelis usually refer to them as "Arab-Israelis." Around 1.5 million Palestinians live in Israel as Israeli citizens.

considered it utterly ridiculous that a party cofounded by Matti Peled should be considered "a danger to state security," ruled that both parties should be allowed to run. The Progressive List for Peace won two seats in the Knesset in the next elections, and my father served one four-year term.

He enjoyed his years as a parliamentarian, and as with everything he did, he poured all of his heart, soul, and intellect into it. His term coincided with the tense atmosphere of the outbreak of the first Palestinian Uprising, or *Intifada*, but he did not confine himself to speaking about the conflict. He took great interest in an array of subjects, in some cases finding common ground with staunch right-wingers.

He quickly gained a reputation as one of the most diligent and industrious members in the history of the Knesset. He would read for up to a week to prepare a ten-minute speech, and his speeches were said to resemble academic lectures. It was not uncommon for radical right-wing adversaries, many of whom had never served in the armed forces, to try to shout him down as a traitor. He felt disgusted by the chase for media attention that was common among Knesset members and refused to insert provocative lines into his speeches that would be sure to grab headlines. He didn't miss a single meeting in four years, which was highly unusual in a Knesset whose chamber is usually mostly empty.

He still preferred Arab literature to politics, and when his four-year term in parliament was over in 1988, he was pleased to return to academic life. Immediately he and my mother left for another year-long academic sabbatical to Harvard, where they had a terrific time together.

Gila and I were already married at this point. At the end of 1987, before my father's term was up, we left Japan—where we had been living for close to two years—and spent a few weeks in Israel. We actually got to see my father at the Knesset. He took us on a tour, and we met his colleagues, and we sat in on a session in the chamber. Then, in the fall of that year Gila and I moved to the U.S., intending to spend no more than two years before returning to Jerusalem. When my parents arrived at Harvard, my mother came to visit us in California, after which Gila and I went to Massachusetts and spent a very pleasant week with them at their apartment in Cambridge.

By then, the Palestinian uprising had begun. Images were beamed around the world of Israeli soldiers beating and shooting Palestinian children wielding nothing but stones in their hands. This was a bona fide grassroots revolution, and it caught everyone by surprise. As Israel was looking for ways to crush this popular revolt, the widely circulated, unofficial order from the defense minister was to "break the Palestinians' bones and deliver casualties" and indeed, many civilians were shot. Israel's defenders claimed that Israel was using rubber bullets, in order not to kill or harm but merely scare them away.

My father kept a rubber bullet in his coat pocket, and he would take it out when he gave talks about the conflict back home. He'd scratch the rubber off the bullet to demonstrate that the bullets were made of steel and only thinly covered with rubber.

Speaking in America was nothing new for my father. He had first visited as an Israeli VIP, a general who spoke for the government. Gradually, as his opinions began to shift, his speeches did, too. He was invited by various peace groups and would sometimes spend weeks traveling and speaking. Having been a member of the Knesset and a military expert in the area of logistics and armaments, he was ready to argue from both a political and a military standpoint that Israel was much better off making peace than arming itself and maintaining the occupation of the land it had conquered in 1967.

One point he came back to often was that the best thing America could do for Israel was to stop selling it weapons and giving it free money. "Until 1974," he told the audience of Temple Emanuel in San Francisco on one occasion, "Israel had not received foreign aid money and we did fine." He then looked at the people seated in the audience and continued: "Receiving free money, money you have not earned and for which you do not have to work, is plain and simply corrupting." He argued that the weapons the U.S. sold to Israel were corrupting the country and were being used to maintain the occupation and oppression of the Palestinians.

"It is bad for Israel, it is morally wrong, and it is illegal," he always said.

At the end of 1992, Yitzhak Rabin was elected as prime minister once again, vowing to make peace. By the end of 1993, he seemed to come to the same conclusion as my father, and he signed the Oslo peace agreement known as the Oslo Accords and shook hands with Yasser Arafat. This was done on the White House lawn as the entire world looked on, and I believed at that time this was the beginning of the end of the conflict, built upon the hard work of my father, Dr. Sartawi, and others like them. The two-state solution, which before had been unthinkably radical, had gone mainstream. I felt certain that peace was now inevitable.

The process was a long one, but the pace of reconciliation seemed very fast. The Israeli army was pulling out of major Palestinian cities, and Palestinian expatriates began returning to build what they thought was their soon-to-be independent state. Israelis were visiting Palestinian cities as tourists and guests rather than as soldiers. Things were moving rapidly, and euphoria was in the air.

My father strongly supported the Oslo Accords at first, and he wrote that Rabin had "crossed the Rubicon." (He was referring to Julius Caesar and his army crossing the Rubicon River upon Caesar's return to Italy. In other words, it was an irreversible act of great significance.) They were signed the same year my father, Uri Avnery, and others formed Gush Shalom, the grassroots Israeli peace bloc.

But as time wore on, my father lost patience. "Settlement expansion in the West Bank continued, and good faith deadlines passed due to Israeli inaction," he claimed. He knew that a slow pace of peace coupled with ongoing settlement expansion would give ample opportunity to extremists on both sides to renew the violence. He criticized and described what he saw: "Rabin is stalling and disregarding aspects of the agreement that would solidify Palestinian statehood, like ending the total Palestinian economic dependency on Israel." Also that "Arafat, who had put everything on the line for peace, was being treated with contempt." In contrast with Sadat, who visited Jerusalem with great fanfare and was allowed to pray at the Al Aqsa Mosque, Arafat was never permitted to enter the city.

My father, true to his nature, read the fine print and found that the Oslo Accords were seriously flawed. On the occasion of his 70th birthday, he gave an interview with *Ma'ariv* that became the weekend cover story. The headline read, "Rabin Does Not Want Peace."[10]

This statement permanently severed the relationship between Rabin and my father, two introverted men of steel who for thirty years had fought side by side and worked together to build the Israeli army, and in 1967 led it to the final conquest of the "Promised Land."

In another interview he gave to the daily *Yedioth Ahronoth* in late 1994, my father said, "The Palestinians believed the Oslo Accords would lead to a Palestinian state, but Rabin had no intention of letting that happen." Again in his dry, analytical style, he claimed "the Palestinians might be allowed to collect their own garbage and print their own passports, but this mini-state would ultimately be controlled by Israel." Meanwhile, the rest of us chose to follow our hearts and believe that the leadership would produce the peace we all hoped for. Ultimately, my father was right about the Oslo Accords.

In late 1994, a few months after my first son Eitan was born in San Diego, a sharp pain in my father's lower back presaged the diagnosis of incurable pancreatic cancer. We had known about the pain for some time, and we hoped it was an orthopedic issue that could be fixed. But then we got the call that it was cancer.

Despite pain and rapid deterioration of his health, my father remained active until his last days, dedicating himself to his research of Arabic literature, to advancing a dialogue of mutual respect between Israelis and Palestinians, to mitigating the plight of soldiers jailed for refusing to serve in the occupied territories, and to his political writings.

His final academic work was the translation, from Arabic to Hebrew, of a book called *The Sages of Darkness* by the Syrian-Kurdish writer Salim Barakat. It was a big project, and he had many exchanges with the writer, which he greatly enjoyed. He used a modem to communicate with Barakat over the Internet. For this last work of his, he was awarded the Israeli Translators' Association Award. He gave me an inscribed copy, which of course I cherish.

My father's last political article was titled "A Requiem to Oslo" and appeared in a magazine published by The Israel Council for Israeli-Palestinian Peace.[11] There

---

10 Sima Kadmon, "Rabin Does Not Want Peace," *Ma'ariv*, August 16, 1993.
11 Matti Peled, "A Requiem to Oslo," *The Other Israel* 65 (February-March 1995).

When my my father was making a point, he was often compared to one of the prophets who chastised the people of Israel.

he predicted the disastrous end to the peace process. He argued that the process had already reached an impasse from which it may not recover. "The failure was due, quite clearly," he wrote, "to Rabin's refusal to redeploy forces on the West Bank and allow general elections to be held in the Occupied Territories." He continued:

> The real cause for Israel's position is that the results of general elections confirming Arafat as the unchallenged leader of the Palestinian people, would place the Palestinian side closest that they ever came to statehood status.

This he said during the years that Rabin was receiving the Nobel Peace Prize and the world saw him as *the* man of peace. So, once again, he was saying the unthinkable.

When we learned of my father's illness, Gila and I decided not to wait to take Eitan to see his grandfather. We ended making two trips to see my father, going once in October of 1994 and then again in December.

It was very moving to see Father so frail yet still sharp and smiling. We took several pictures of him as he held Eitan. We also had a wonderful family gathering with all four siblings, Yoav, Nurit, Ossi, and I with our spouses and children. My father told stories, and we all listened intently, suspecting that this might be our last gathering where he was still well enough to speak. Now I wish I had recorded the moment, because try as I may I can't recall what stories he told us that evening. Over the days and weeks that I was with him, I kept asking my father to write about himself and about his life, but he refused. "I find it boring to write about myself," he insisted, and he wouldn't consent for me to record him either. He was very optimistic about his recovery and his mood for the most part was quite relaxed.

Smadari was there too. Naomi Shemer, Israel's most beloved songwriter and an old friend of the family, wrote a poem in his honor. The poem begins with the words, "The body's betrayal, the loyalty of spirit," alluding to Father's sharpness of mind even as his body was being eaten by the cancer.

I continued to visit every few months on my own. As his condition got worse there was no point in Gila and Eitan coming along. The third time I visited, my father had just begun receiving chemotherapy, and I went straight from the airport to the hospital. "How are you?" I asked. He looked terrible.

"Miserable," he replied, and then added, "You should go home and rest, you must be exhausted from the long flight." He was never an easy man, but he was a little more relaxed as a grandfather than he was as a father. The disease accentuated his moods so when he felt good he was actually quite jovial, but when the pain hit him or the chemo was in him, he was miserable.

I stayed about 10 days. My mother decided to care for him at home as opposed to a hospice. On my fourth visit I stayed till the end. He held on to life as long as he could, believing until the very end that medicine would cure him. Finally, in the early morning hours of March 10, 1995, he succumbed to the disease. My mother and siblings had been taking shifts staying by his bedside. I was with him at 4 a.m. when he took his final breath. He died in his bed in the home he loved so dearly.

We decided against burying Father at the military cemetery on Mount Herzl in Jerusalem. His legacy was so much more than his military service, and if he'd been buried in the military cemetery, his tomb would have said simply that he was a general and when he was born and when he died. However, more than half his life was about other things—Arabic literature, activism, and peace. So my mother purchased a plot on a hillside cemetery in Kibbutz Nachshon, just outside Jerusalem. We felt it more appropriate to lay him to rest in a beautiful forest near his home in Jerusalem, where we could put what we wanted on his tombstone.

The funeral was a full military ceremony. When the Jeep showed up at our house with the coffin—on its way to the cemetery—we stepped out to see it and say goodbye. Six generals would carry my father's coffin, and they sat around the coffin chatting. As we walked up to the Jeep, they hurriedly hushed one another to look dignified. My mother rested her head on the coffin and cried.

My father's generation, the bright, young officers who won the war of 1948 for us and then went on to become the generals of the 1967 war, were

Eyzer Weizman, former commander of the Israeli Air Force and Deputy Chief of Staff. He was one of my father's few life long friends. Here he is in his last formal post, President of the state of Israel.

iconic, and my father's role in the buildup to the Six-Day War reached almost mythical proportions. That alone would have made the funeral a major event. It also brought together an unprecedented combination of Israeli generals, heads of state, and radical peace activists as well as Palestinian leaders. Messages of condolence were read from both the government of Israel and Yasser Arafat. Dr. Ahmed Tibi came to represent Arafat (as Arafat himself was not permitted to enter Jerusalem) and lay a wreath on the grave on his behalf. It was placed next to the wreath from the President of Israel. As I recall this, I still find it hard to believe: The first Palestinian president presenting a wreath and a message of condolence on the grave of an Israeli general. The press noticed this, and the photo of the two wreaths side by side made its way into many newspapers.

From Uri Avnery on the left to Ariel Sharon on the right, everyone came to pay respects. The army chief rabbi who ran the ceremony asked me to say the *kaddish*, or "prayer of the bereaved," and he added, "It's for father." I did say the mourners' *kaddish*, but I couldn't help thinking that if he knew anything about my father, he would know not to say such nonsense. Father had no tolerance for religion or religious ceremonies.

My father's death prompted countless news stories in Israel and around the world, many of which attempted to analyze his career and his personality. I found two pieces, one by a Palestinian and indeed world-renowned professor Walid Khalidi[12] and the other by Israeli veteran journalist and lifelong peace activist Uri Avnery[13], particularly effective. My father's close ties with these two men and the kind words they wrote upon his passing demonstrate the quantum leap he had taken over the years since his military service ended. Dr. Khalidi wrote among other things, "Matti was no diplomat. Well ahead of his time and against daunting opposition, he had cut through the century-old Arab-Zionist conflict and had developed deep convictions with regard to its resolution."

Avnery summed up his written eulogy with the words, from Shakespeare's Hamlet, "He was a man, take him for all in all—I shall not look upon his like again."

It's true that Matti Peled could be difficult, but he was greatly respected and admired. He distinguished himself with his commitment first as a military expert and then as a peace activist and advocate. True, he did not allow for much discussion, but his lectures at the dinner table were always illuminating, and I received much of the confidence I have in my identity as a Jewish Israeli from him.

Yitzhak Rabin, then prime minister, also attended my father's funeral, as protocol called for it. But he never called to say farewell to my dying father as all his other comrades in arms did, nor did he visit our home during the *Shiv'a*, the traditional seven days of mourning, to express his condolences. Tragically, eight months later, Rabin too was dead—murdered by a Jewish boy who was raised on the toxic mix of Orthodox Judaism and radical Zionism. It was the end of an era and the beginning of great uncertainty.

---

12 Walid Khalidi, "Converging tracks," *The Other Israel*, April 1995, Cambridge, MA. http://israelipalestinianpeace.org/issues/66toi.htm#Converging
13 Uri Avnery, "I shall not see his like again," *Ma'ariv*, March 3, 1995. Archived at http://www.israelipalestinianpeace.org/issues/66toi.htm#I

PART II

A Long Way from Home

Chapter 4:

The Red Beret

It was 1974, and as I moved from elementary school to high school, it became clear that I was not only still behind academically, but that I had another issue as well, one that had not surfaced until then and may well have been genetic: a big mouth. There were subjects about which I could not and would not keep silent, regardless of who I was facing. Later on, I realized that there was one exception, one person in front of whom I did keep silent—my father.

During the first talk my class had with the vice principal on the issue of discipline on school grounds, I argued with him that his idea of discipline was archaic and unfair. My homeroom teacher, who taught math and physics, topics with which I had trouble anyway, was a recent immigrant from Eastern Europe. He was stern, uncompromising, and insecure. He never smiled, and he did not believe in second chances. I was terrified the entire time I was in his class and couldn't function.

By the end of my first year in high school, I had even alienated the physical education teacher, although I was a good athlete and actually liked both the teacher and the class. He was an old-fashioned instructor, and he would make the lives of kids who were not athletic miserable. One day, the teacher insulted a student who was overweight and invited the entire class to make fun of him as he stumbled through gym. I waited for the end of class, when all the students had left, to approach the teacher: "Aren't you ashamed of yourself? Was it really necessary to insult him like that and have the class join in?"

Needless to say, he was not accustomed to being reprimanded by a freshman, and I found myself in the principal's office and in serious trouble. "You dare to think that you know better than I?"

When the year finally ended it was clear that this particular high school was not going to work for me. In tenth grade, I transferred to a school closer to our home in Motza and actually had a great year. I had a charismatic homeroom teacher who taught history and civics and who welcomed my big mouth and was in awe of the fact that my father was Matti Peled. We got along great, I did well in all my subjects, and I was quite happy.

That year, at the suggestion of a few friends, I began practicing karate, and I fell in love with it. Karate eventually became a lifelong pursuit. Still, after eleventh grade

I realized that the traditional school environment was too restrictive for me and not one in which I could succeed. So for my senior year, I decided to go to what is called an "external" school, a high school that merely prepares students for the matriculation exams. You go to school for three or four hours each morning, and then you are free. There was a bit of a stigma attached to these external schools—they were not exactly the kind of school that "good kids" attended, but I really didn't care. I knew I would not do well if I stayed at a traditional school, and that I would never make it through the matriculation exams. My father was on sabbatical at Harvard at the time and had no particular opinion on this, and so it was up to my mother to agree. It was tough for her, and she was not crazy about the idea, but after she met the principal, who was a terrific man and a great educator, she agreed.

My mother's fears proved unfounded. I met great kids at the school, and it turned out to be a fine year for me. Highly motivated, I did quite well on my matriculations, which in Israel is extremely important.

As my school years were coming to a close and I was approaching draft age, I began to have mixed feelings about joining the military. My father had convinced me that Israel's occupation of the West Bank and Gaza was wrong. But as a staunch Zionist, I was also convinced that Israel had to have an army—and not just any army but the best military force possible. I believed that if more people like me joined the IDF, it would be a good, moral army. So I was conflicted; I wanted to serve and to set an example, but I also wanted to protest the injustice.

I had been practicing karate for two years by then, and that too influenced my thinking and my motivation. Karate teaches discipline and non-violence. And yet I found karate training more demanding, both mentally and physically, than anything I had previously experienced. What's more, I enjoyed the rigor, and I was eager to continue to challenge myself in those ways—the army could offer that.

As a young Israeli who was healthy enough to be a combat soldier, I had two choices: I could volunteer to serve in a particular unit and hope to be accepted or I could let the army decide where to send me. My father thought very little of the Special Forces units—in his opinion they were over-glorified—and he was concerned by the fact that new ones were being established all the time. "The armored tank brigades are the most important force in the battlefield," he said, in an effort to persuade my decision. "A tank is a sophisticated machine and understanding how to operate a tank, with all of its computerized components will be useful to you once you return to civilian life." But there is no glory in tanks, only grinding, dirty, oily work.

In the end, I did what so many good Israeli boys do. When I was drafted in February 1980, I volunteered to join one of the many Special Forces commando units. I was attracted by the physical and mental challenges of the training, which I knew would be tough, though going in I had no idea just how tough it would be, and I was completely sold on the image of the Israeli hero. I wanted the status symbols that included the red beret, the special semiautomatic weapons, the brown shoes, and the pins that are the mark of Israel's finest. How much of this was vanity and how much patriotism is hard to say; both played a role in my decision.

I was sent to basic training at the famous paratroopers training camp in Sanur, in the West Bank near the Palestinian city of Jenin. At the entrance to the base a sign read, "If we don't rely on one another, we will find ourselves hanging next to each other." It makes sense in Hebrew because the word for "rely" and the word for "hang" is the same: *taluy*. The point was that we are a team, and we have to be able to count on one another; if we can't, we will all end up dead. Another poster read: "Paratroopers—the long arm of the IDF."

Sanur was located in a green and pastoral area of the northern West Bank. The base sat by a tall, menacing hill on top of which sat a tomb of a Muslim sheikh. We marched up and down that hill more times than I care to remember.

I did not think much of the fact that this was Palestinian land until our first nightlong march. We had to carry heavy equipment and move quickly and in complete silence. Despite my exhaustion, I couldn't help but notice that we were marching on cultivated land and trampling somebody's crops. I walked as fast as I could to catch up to our sergeant and tried to tell him the crops were being destroyed. I had no idea how naïve my comment was. He ordered me to remain silent and keep marching.

The training was so tough both physically and mentally that pretty soon we were drained and all that mattered was making it through the week. The hardest thing for me was not being allowed to sleep through the night. Our sergeant would wake us up at all hours for surprise inspections, marches, and drills. He also kept a small notebook in which he recorded everything we did wrong throughout the day. At night he would get us out of bed and give us all sorts of exhausting punishment-drills.

But there were privileges to being part of an elite unit. Even as a new recruit you had better food than the rest of the army, and you got to go home almost every weekend. Going home meant uninterrupted sleep, good home-cooked food, and seeing your girlfriend—the only things a new recruit cared about.

When it was time to go home, an army bus took us out of the West Bank to a major bus depot in Israel, and from there we each took a public bus. I will never forget those long rides to Jerusalem on Fridays. The buses were crowded with exhausted soldiers like me, as well as a few civilians. The soldiers would often sleep, even while standing. If you were lucky enough to get a seat, you fell asleep with your head resting on the stranger in the seat next to you, your semiautomatic poking him in the ribs.

As our training advanced, we began participating in simple security missions that included patrolling the streets of Palestinian towns like Ramallah, the Old City of Jerusalem and remote villages in the West Bank. Not once did I have a clue why we were there or what we were securing. All I ever saw were civilians going about their business. When we were in more remote areas, we saw nothing but the typical pastoral landscape of the West Bank, terraces with grape vines and olive groves.

I remember once getting prepped before a patrol in Ramallah. We were given batons and handcuffs. In those days there was no uprising, no protest to speak of, no Intifada. We were a small, highly skilled infantry unit, specializing mostly in anti-tank warfare, and I remember thinking, *Why are we in a city full of civilians, and what are we supposed to do with these batons and handcuffs?*

Our lieutenant briefed us before we were sent to Ramallah. He said we were to walk up and down the streets and that if anyone so much as looked at us we were to beat them, or as he put it, "Break every bone in their body." This seemed pretty extreme: *to break people's bones just because they looked at us?* How could anyone avoid looking at us? We were a platoon of fully armed infantry soldiers in the middle of a city full of civilians. I seriously did not get it. But soldiers do not ask questions; they follow orders. When you are in basic training, your lieutenant is your God, even if your father is a general. I was too intimidated to ask questions and far too tired to think it through.

Many years later, when I learned that people under military occupation have the legal right to engage in armed resistance, I also realized it was a stroke of luck that I was never attacked because there were times when our commanding officers carelessly put us in serious danger. When I realized this, the first thing that came to my mind was a particular instance when we were sent to secure a remote spot in the West Bank. It was Friday morning, and we hadn't slept since the early hours of Thursday morning. The routine was that we trained all day Thursday and after dinner we went on a grueling nightlong march. After the march, we had to prepare for Friday morning inspection, which meant there was no time to sleep. This particular Friday we expected to go on leave, but instead of going to the bus depot we were all piled into a large army truck and taken to some remote spot in the West Bank. We were sent to secure different places in the area, and I and one other soldier were sent to secure a secluded hill. We had our guns, water, and a communication device, and our only instructions were, *"Dir Balak, mi sheyashen!"* You better not fall asleep! *"Ken Hamefaked!"* we replied. Yes sir!

There was no power on earth that could have prevented us from sleeping. We were exhausted from a week of physically and mentally draining days, capped by a long, hard, sleepless night and a grueling expedition to this remote spot. To top it off, it was a hot day, and the sun was in our eyes. Our commanders did not permit us to wear sunglasses or chew gum, two things that may have helped us stay awake. "Anyone caught with gum will spend the weekend on base!" That was enough to keep us from ever looking at, never mind chewing gum. In short, the moment our superiors left us, my partner and I slept like bears in winter.

We were grateful not to get caught sleeping because the penalty for that would have been severe. Our ignorance was such that this was our only concern. It did not occur to us that anyone might harm us and that our lives were in danger. We should have been thankful that the Palestinian resistance did not find us. The carelessness our commanders displayed by placing young, inexperienced, and exhausted soldiers in such a predicament only occurred to me many years later, when I met Palestinians we imprisoned for attacking and even killing soldiers in similar situations. They wait in ambush for days for such an opportunity. We were lucky, but there were many who were not.

The symbol of the elite special forces in Israel is the red beret. Every kid wants one. To earn the red beret, each unit has its own "Beret March." It is longer and harder than any one march a soldier has to go through. Ours was a fifty-mile trek with open stretchers. That meant that every six or eight guys were responsible for carrying a stretcher with a soldier lying on it. Four guys at a time carry the stretcher on their shoulders and switch off at set intervals. Typically no one wanted to be on the stretcher, so this role would fall to someone who was not fit to march due to an injury.

It really was a backbreaking march. The night was hot and extremely humid. We wore a full uniform of long-sleeved shirts and long pants. We had army boots on our feet, and besides the stretchers every soldier had to carry his semiautomatic rifle and all sorts of other heavy equipment. We sweated so profusely that our uniform was wet the entire march, and that meant terrible rashes and constant, almost unbearable and unquenchable, thirst. Water was rationed, and we only drank when we were told. When we did drink, there was a discipline to it. We carried our water in canteens, and because not even the slightest noise was permitted the canteens had to be either completely empty or filled to the brim and covered with a small sheet of Saran Wrap before it was sealed shut with the cap. If it was done right, the water did not make a sound when we walked. Once opened, a canteen had to be emptied completely.

Our team had a new commanding officer, a young ensign fresh out of the Officers Academy who had completed a highly classified course in Special Warfare. Before he came, there was a lot of talk and excitement because he was a veteran of our unit now returning as an officer. He took command just prior to the Beret March. We marched through the night, and by daylight it was clear that he had navigated incorrectly and got us lost along the way. So not only did the march end up much longer than planned, but we also failed meet with the unit command at the appointed time and place.

Because these marches are so difficult, they are taken seriously by the army and the highest level of command is involved with every detail. In the morning we could see our unit commander, an army major, and the brigade commander—a full colonel—fuming at the young officer for his navigation blunder: "Is this what we are to expect from you?" Several months later he was dismissed from the unit.

Instead of finishing the march in the early morning hours, it was midday when we finally arrived at our destination, Kfar Yehoshua, a beautiful agricultural community in northern Israel.

We were greeted like heroes, with a feast fit for kings laid out for us by a pool. But we were far too tired and in too much pain to enjoy the food and festivities. Our legs and shoulders hurt so badly we could not stand, but we could not sit or lie down either. It took several days before we all recovered fully. We were extremely proud when we received those bright red berets to wear home that afternoon. I remember heading to the bus depot and making sure the beret was in full sight the entire time.

I remained in this unit for close to a year, but before the training was finished, I injured my knee. I was at the base clinic for a few days, and when it became clear that I wasn't getting better, they sent me to the hospital in Be'er Sheva, where it was determined that I needed knee surgery. Fortunately, the best orthopedic surgeon and the best facilities in Israel were at the Hadassah hospital on Mount Scopus in Jerusalem, a brand new modern hospital just a few short miles from home.

After the surgery, I was sent home for a few weeks to recover, and that was truly a gift. Then my unit commanders decided that for the remainder of my recovery I would train to become the team's medic at the army Medical College near Tel Aviv. The medic's course was three-and-a-half months, and by the time I graduated I would be ready to return to full active duty with my team.

I was excited about this turn of events, and I was determined to do well and rejoin my team. However, during those months of medic training, something happened. I liked the intensity of the training it took to be a combat solider and the camaraderie it engendered, but before I had committed myself to being a combat soldier and pursuing the red beret, I'd had another point of view, one that was more humanistic. Being a student of karate, I was opposed to violence and killing. Plus, I was raised to oppose Israel's treatment of the Palestinian people. We, the Jewish people, deserved our own state in our historical homeland and the state needed an army to protect its people. These were our rights—I had no doubts about that—but the brutality of the occupation was seriously bothering me.

At the medical college, away from all the intensity, I had time to catch my breath and to think things through. I felt that I was among my own people again. There was more intelligent discussion and more diversity—in other words, it was more like a college than an army base. The medical corps wasn't as mindlessly enthusiastic or conformist as the rest of the army, certainly not as much as the combat units. This gave me time to reevaluate who I was and what I wanted to do.

Over time, I realized that I could not continue to be a combat soldier. I became less and less comfortable with my hard-earned red beret, and I couldn't ignore the fact that what I had seen was simply wrong. I did, however, like the idea of teaching people how to save lives. At the end of each course, the class instructors would recommend to the course commander the names of students they thought were fit to remain as instructors. I later learned that this required several criteria. You had to be liked by the teaching staff and have a good command of the material. The toughest requirement was the ability to lead and maintain order while teaching thirty young soldiers—who were constantly hungry, horny, and wanted to go home—to become responsible medics.

I was thrilled that at the end of my medic's course, my instructors recommended my name to the course commanding officer, who in turn requested that I remain at the IDF Medical College to become an instructor. That meant leaving my unit—my team of fighters who were on the cutting edge of Israel's fighting force—to serve on a base a few miles from Tel Aviv.

It was a long shot. My unit was not likely to let me go after so many months of training and when they were in need of a medic. However, since I was left with some disability as a result of the surgery, they did let me go and I was able to begin the course to become a medic's instructor.

I began my new military life with a decision that I would leave my hard-earned red beret at home. I found an old black beret and some used black army boots that were lying around the house, and that was how I showed up for the first day of instructor's training. My instructors and friends were stunned. They had never seen anyone give up the right to wear the red beret. It sounds silly now, but these symbols are immensely important in that environment. The men who supplied me periodically with new boots, beret, and a uniform thought I was nuts. Most guys would literally kill to go home in brown boots and a red beret. I told them they could have mine.

The instructor's course lasted two-and-a-half months, during which I learned a great deal and felt good about what I was doing. Then, when I began teaching students and watching them become fully prepared, qualified medics, I finally felt I was really serving my country.

In 1979, after several years of negotiations, Israel signed a peace agreement with Egypt, and one aspect of the agreement called for Israel to return the Sinai Peninsula to Egypt and to dismantle the Israeli settlements that were built there. Sinai is an enchanted desert with endless sand dunes, magnificent mountains, and spectacular coral reefs along the Red Sea coast. It also has a few oil wells and the all-important access to the Suez Canal. However, returning all of this did not seem to be as serious a problem for Israel as dismantling the settlements and relocating the Israelis that lived there.

It was common knowledge that these settlements were built on occupied land, and that whoever chose to make a life there knew they were taking the risk of being evacuated one day. Still, a serious problem arose when it was time to evacuate the Israeli settlements that were built in the northern part of the Sinai, near the Israeli border.[1] When the time came for the evacuation, extremist Israeli militants took over the settlement of Yamit and refused to leave peacefully. Most of the women and children had already been relocated by then, and the army was sent in to get the extremists.

I was there as part of the army's medical outfit. It was actually a good feeling—for the first time in my life I felt that people who believed in peace were winning. After all those years of being mocked as an Arab-loving peacenik, I finally felt vindicated. My country was on my side—the army was there to get the Israeli militant extremists out and to allow peace in. I beamed with pride to be part of this history. I remember standing and watching the busloads of militant Israelis being sent back to Israel. Some of them were so hysterical they tried to jump out of the moving buses. I stood with a friend, who was also pleased by what was happening, when a woman who had just jumped out of a moving bus yelled at us, "How can you just stand there? This is a dark, terrible day for Israel and all you do is stand there and smile!"

"On the contrary," I said. "This is a good day for Israel. Peace is becoming a reality."

Israeli politics had taken a turn. There was a new cabinet in power and Prime Minister Menachem Begin brought in General Ariel Sharon as the new defense minister. While in uniform, Sharon was revered as a brilliant military man. He had charisma and was often compared to General George Patton in his ability to accomplish things with his soldiers. My father often spoke and wrote of his unique ability as a military man. When Sharon entered politics it became clear that he was a man with a mission. He believed that the fight against the Palestinians had to continue to the bitter end, their bitter end. The peace agreement with Egypt called for talks to continue and include the Palestinians, but a comprehensive peace was the furthest thing from Ariel Sharon's mind.

From an Israeli perspective, Egypt was the only Arab country that could possibly deter Israel militarily. Now that it was neutralized due to the peace agreement, Sharon saw an opportunity to decimate the Palestinian leadership, which at the time was in exile in Beirut, Lebanon, and place a pro-Israeli, Christian-dominated government in power in that country.

I was home on weekend leave on that fateful June in 1982 when, not six months after the peace agreement with Egypt had been concluded, Israel began its heavy-

---

1 In contravention of international law, Israel had been building settlements on the lands occupied in 1967—the Sinai, the Golan Heights, the West Bank, and Gaza—and populating them with civilians. The reasons for this are numerous—from Messianic to security-related to the fact that it was a profitable enterprise for many businesses.

handed invasion of Lebanon. I got the call that I had to return to the base due to an emergency situation. It is a call every Israeli soldier expects to receive one day. I immediately got my uniform on and ran to the main road to hitch a ride back to the base.

The base where I was serving was Sarafend, or *Tsrifin*, an old British army base not far from Tel Aviv. When I got back to the base, a few of us began talking about the impending war. It was said to be a nearly 25-mile incursion into southern Lebanon, something Israel had done many times in order to get rid of terrorist cells along the Israeli-Lebanese border. As the war progressed, reports came back from soldiers who were already on the outskirts of Beirut. They too were listening to Israeli radio talk about a "limited" 25-mile incursion into southern Lebanon.

Beirut is much farther into Lebanon than 25 miles, and advancing an army toward the capital city of a sovereign country was no small matter. The first inkling Israelis got of how bad the situation really was came after a fierce battle for control of the Beaufort crusader fort in southern Lebanon. Prime Minister Menachem Begin was flown in to see the place and talk to the soldiers. His visit was broadcast live. A young officer with a quiet sullen expression met him as he got off the helicopter, and you had the feeling from the officer's expression that things were not good.

The TV cameras were on Begin as he asked the young officer, "So, how was the battle? Did they fight hard? Did they have automatic weapons?" The officer, still quiet and sullen, replied in a barely audible voice, "Yes, they fought hard." It was obvious the prime minister didn't have a clue about the strength and firepower of the enemy. Was he expecting them to fight with bows and arrows?

After the visit, Prime Minister Begin said that the fort was captured with no Israeli casualties. It was later made known that the Palestinian fighters fought hard, and it was a fierce battle. At least six Israeli soldiers were killed, and many were wounded. Among the dead was Major Guni Hernik, the commander of one of Israel's finest elite units. His mother later became the leader of a movement to end the war and bring the boys home. Begin's ignorance about the war was embarrassing, and it was obvious that Ariel Sharon was running the show.

Discontent with the war was spreading, and at the first antiwar rally, which took place in Tel Aviv, my father spoke: "Friends, this is the first time in Israeli history that people protest a war even as the fighting is carried out." He later supported soldiers who refused to go into Lebanon and participate in the war. He said over and over that Israel's bombing and siege of Beirut was a war crime in which no Israeli soldier should consent to participate. When Eli Geva, a renowned army colonel with a promising career, resigned his commission in protest of the bombing of civilian targets in Beirut, my father supported his decision and said, "It was the only morally right thing to do." However nothing changed, and no one in the cabinet or the army could stand up to Sharon, until he finally crossed the line.

A great deal has been written about the massacres that took place in the Palestinian refugee camps of Sabra and Shatila west of Beirut. It was September 1982, Sharon had a plan to "clean up" the Palestinian presence in Beirut and allow the pro-Israeli Lebanese Christian militia, the Phalangists, to take control. The Israeli army sealed the two camps and allowed the Phalangists to enter, illuminating the dark night with flares that lit up the sky. They killed indiscriminately for hours in full view and with the logistical support of the IDF top command. Later on it became clear that young Israeli soldiers and officers who realized what was going on and tried to alert the chain of command were reassured that everything was under control. Arabs were killing Arabs, and it was not our problem.

Sharon's involvement in the massacres at Sabra and Shatila was his downfall. Massive protests in Israel and around the world resulted in a formal inquiry that found Sharon to bear personal responsibility for the carnage. He was forced to resign and was barred from ever heading the defense ministry. For the next 18 years, he was a political pariah.

Back on our base, the militant macho types were chomping at the bit to be sent to Lebanon. Armed with the brown shoes they got from the supply guys (some of which were probably once mine), they were full of combat spirit. The ones that were sent there returned with all sorts of memorabilia, mostly loot. As for me, my willingness to serve was being stretched to the limit, and under no circumstances would I agree to cross the border into Lebanon as a soldier, or the West Bank for that matter. Luckily I didn't need to.

This was the final year of my service, and it was becoming increasingly intolerable. The war, politics, and my convictions were constantly at odds, and many of my friends, who were supposed to be discharged before me, had their service extended because of the war. I was terrified mine would be extended as well. I became tense and angry as the months went by, and it reflected on my work and my relationships with my superiors.

"Miko is an antithesis to a soldier," one of them said. I and my left-leaning friends on base were all branded "gay lefties, *homoim smolanim.*" Those of us who were critical of Israel did not hide it and since in the army being gay and being an "Arab-loving lefty" are equally unacceptable, we were all lumped together. Once, during a trip with the entire unit, I got into a seemingly friendly exchange with my commanding officer while on the bus. He was a lieutenant colonel who adored the army and hated people like me and my friends, people who were critical of Israel and the IDF's actions in the West Bank and Gaza. At one point, I decided to lay a trap for him. "Moshe," I said (we were all on first name basis), "it's really too bad you don't live on a settlement in the West Bank."

"Really, why?" *It was too good to be true.* He fell for it.

"Because when they finally return the West Bank to the Palestinians, they'll return you as well." The entire bus burst out laughing. Moshe was silent for the remainder of the ride, but friends told me that he swore to make me pay as soon as we returned to base. His frustration with me grew to the point where he once actually picked up a chair and threw it at me.

The one good thing I took with me when my army service ended was Gila. The army base where I served was coed and so there were plenty of opportunities to meet girls. During my final year, Gila became a student in the Women's Medic's course. Her instructors liked her and she had all the makings of a good instructor so she was recommended to stay as one. One of my best friends on the base, someone I am still in touch with, was Shlomo Amir. He retired many years later as deputy surgeon general with the rank of full colonel. At the time, he was a major. He did not care for the army's pomp and circumstance, so we got along great. Amir was charged with interviewing instructor candidates and determining who would ultimately be accepted to the instructor's course. I remember hanging around by his office when Gila's turn came to be interviewed. I didn't know her well, but I thought she was charming. She had black curls down to her shoulders and warm dark eyes that always seemed to smile at you.

Gila began her instructor's training, but it wasn't until it ended and she began teaching that we started seeing each other. By that time I was in my last months of service and she still had another year to go. I approached her for the first time as she taught a class. She was more than a little embarrassed when I came by and the girls she taught, all 25 of them, giggled as she came out to speak to me. We decided to go to the movies. After she agreed to go out with me, I ran to Amir's office to tell him. I think he was even more excited than I.

Being with Gila was a godsend during those last few months of my service. We had a lot of fun together on and off base. She'd been born and raised on a beautiful little kibbutz on the coast, and we spent lots of time on the beach and at the pool there.

Thankfully, my service was not extended and it came to an end in December 1983—after two years, 10 months, and 14 days. For the first time in my life I was free. I was done with school, and I was done with the army, two very conservative institutions with which I was not comfortable. At last I could do what I wanted. It was one of the happiest days of my life.

Ironically, before I was discharged, I received the pin that was awarded to all who served in the military during the Lebanon campaign. The war was named "Operation Peace in the Galilee." As we were presented with the pins, several friends and I let them fall to the ground and we buried them in the dirt with our boots.

Chapter 5:

Karate

Gila was one of very few people on base who knew about and appreciated my love for karate. I had loved karate since the day I began practicing it in 1977, while I was still in high school.

The karate school, or *dojo*, was at a large school gym in the neighborhood of Ma'alot Dafna in Jerusalem. The intensity of the classes was in many ways similar to what I had later experienced in the army. I became fascinated by the severe demands of both karate and military combat training. But as I found out, contrary to the military, karate possesses a strong, uncompromising moral foundation.

On cold and rainy Jerusalem nights, our instructor, Sensei Dan, would take us on long runs, barefoot. Along the way we would stop to do pushups in the deep puddles of cold water and by the time we returned to the dojo we were soaking wet—but warm under our skin and energized. I would often stay for two classes, which meant that I was at the dojo from four in the afternoon till nine in the evening. I remember sitting on the late night bus on the way home and thinking about the dinner my mother had waiting for me.

Unlike military training, where the aim is to break you down and then turn you into a killer, Sensei Dan wanted to build us up and develop us as confident and compassionate people. Okinawan and Japanese martial arts traditions are established on firm moral principles. The martial arts student is taught to never misuse or abuse his power. Okinawan Goju-Ryu Karate-Do[1], the art that I practice, is no different. While popular culture often confuses karate with violence, the truth is that karate, like all traditional martial arts, espouses a philosophy of compassion and non-violence.

My instructor, Dan Russell, whom we called Sensei Dan, was a Brit who decided to live several years in Jerusalem. He was a student of Tibetan Buddhist meditation before it was fashionable. His meditation teacher was Chögyam Trungpa, the renowned master of Tibetan Buddhism, who pioneered the study of Tibetan Buddhism in the West. Dan knew Trungpa well and spoke a great deal about

---

1 Okinawan Goju-Ryu, is one of the original forms of karate, and is unique in that it has maintained its initial form and traditional training methods along with its principled moral foundation.

him and his unique approach to meditation and life. Sensei Dan, originally from Newcastle, had a master's degree from Cambridge University. A fellow meditation student introduced him to karate and, as he put it, he was "struck by the tremendous mental and spiritual potential that exists within karate practice."

As soon as I began my karate training, I was captivated by this art's combination of grace, beauty, and intensity. I could endlessly watch the students who were higher belts execute their forms. This was the time when Chinese martial arts movies began to debut in the West, and I would go to see them all. Dan was a harsh teacher, and even though the classes were physically demanding they were always packed with students eager to train and learn. He had a few assistant instructors, some of whom were not much older than I, who knew how to emulate his intensity. It was clearly sink or swim for me in the beginning, and I was not going to sink.

I understand now that I found karate at a time in my life when it was a perfect fit. I had participated in school sports—mostly track and field—for several years, but I had grown unsatisfied and bored, and I saw little point in working so hard only to beat someone else at a competition. I was looking for something that offered meaning as well as a physical challenge. Karate has a deep philosophy that touches on all the issues that interested me then, and still do to this day. These include ideas like understanding violence and the difficulty in defining non-violence, overcoming an opponent that is seemingly impossible to defeat, spirituality, mind and body connection, longevity, and health.

Traditional martial arts recognize that we change both physically and emotionally as we mature, which allows us to practice and improve our skills even as we get older. I was particularly attracted by the fact that in karate practice the challenge was never to overcome the other but to overcome my own preconceived notions of what I could or couldn't accomplish. This was something that came to my aid later, during the very difficult parts of my training in the army. In basic training, it often seemed as though we were asked to do the impossible, but the notion that there is no such thing as impossible was ingrained in me by then, and it helped me to persevere.

At the dojo, I quickly went from practicing two days a week to six, and soon I knew that for me it was not merely a hobby. Sensei Dan would often travel back to Britain, and in his absence the assistants would teach the classes. It wasn't long before I was one of those instructors, and I discovered that I loved to teach karate.

"I have a surprise for you," Sensei Dan told me one day before class began, and he introduced me to his friend and karate instructor, Sensei George Andrews. Sensei George is a proud Englishman who'd lived his entire life in the rough neighborhoods of London's East End. His accent was textbook Cockney, and he liked his English cup of tea as much as he liked his beer. He had to learn karate as a way to survive the rough streets of his childhood, or as he put it, "Oy hyte runnin' so oy ad t'learn 'ow to foyt, dit'n oy?" Karate eventually became a spiritual path for George, and he became a remarkable teacher.

When Sensei George met Dan Russell, Dan encouraged him to leave his environment, where drinking and fighting were a way of life, to teach karate in Israel for a few months. George fell in love with Israel, and it became his vacation spot as well as a place to teach bright-eyed young disciples like me. I met him for the first time in 1979. We were told that we were going to the Sea of Galilee for a weeklong retreat— *gasshuku*, in Japanese. One of the students owned property right on the lake, and we all spent the week there as his guests. We trained, ate, slept, and then trained some more, outside on the banks of the *Kinneret*.[2] We learned a tremendous amount, and George became a hero and a great role model for me. When I was drafted into the military, I decided that upon my discharge I would go to London and train at his dojo, and whenever things got tough, this thought kept me going.

When my military service was done, I found a few friends from the old dojo and we would train together at someone's house or outdoors at one of Jerusalem's parks. At the time I was also feeling motivated to get involved in peace activism. This was in the aftermath of the Lebanon War, the Sabra and Shatila massacre, and the conclusions of the Kahan Committee[3] inquiry, which investigated the massacre and found Defense Minster Ariel Sharon personally responsible. Sharon's negligence in protecting the civilian population of Beirut, which had come under Israeli control, amounted to a non-fulfillment of a duty, and it was recommended that Sharon be dismissed as defense minister. Prime Minister Menachem Begin refused to fire him and Sharon refused to resign. On February 10, 1983, a nongovernmental Israeli organization called Peace Now had organized a march in Jerusalem to demand that the cabinet, led by Begin, accept the recommendations of the Kahan Committee and fire Sharon. The mood was tense and there was a lot of opposition to the march from Israel's extreme right wing.

I had karate practice that evening, and I had to make a decision whether I should go to practice or participate in the march. This was much more than a schedule conflict—it was a very difficult choice for me, a choice between two different career paths, and I was torn for several days. After giving it a great deal of thought, I decided that I could contribute more to this world as a karate teacher than as a political activist. So I went to practice. That night, while the protesters were gathered in front of the prime minister's office in Jerusalem, a member of one of Israel's Jewish right-wing terrorist organizations threw a grenade into the crowd. Emil Grunzweig, a peace activist, was killed and nine other Israeli peace

---

2 Kinneret is Hebrew for the "Sea of Galilee."

3 Commission of Inquiry into the Events at the Refugee Camps in Beirut, was established by the Israeli government on September 28, 1982, to investigate the Sabra and Shatila massacre. The Kahan Commission was chaired by the president of the Supreme Court, Justice Yitzhak Kahan.

activists were injured. Who knows where I would have stood and what might have happened had I been there.

For me this was a watershed moment. I felt I had made the right decision in attending karate practice that night. It was not until many years later that I found my way back to activism.

In the summer of that year, I finally traveled to England to train with Sensei George. Gila's grandparents lived in London, and they graciously allowed me to stay with them. Their home was in the upper-middle-class neighborhood of Mill Hill in North London. I trained with Sensei George for about a month, and then I traveled to see Sensei Dan, who by that time had returned to the United Kingdom and was living on the Scottish-English border. I had intended to stay longer, but I missed Gila terribly and so I cut the trip short.

"Don't fly back, it's boring," Dan's said. "Hitchhike, you will be surprised how many nice people you will meet." His instructions were to avoid France and go through Germany instead. So rather than flying straight to Israel, I took the ferry from Dover to Holland, hitchhiked across Europe to Italy, and from there I flew back to Israel.

By the end of the year Gila had completed her military service, and in February 1984, we decided to travel to England together. I wanted to continue training with Sensei George, and she was excited to get out and see the world. It was a dream come true for me to live and train in London. I admired Sensei George, and I wanted to live in a place where I could participate in a full-time dojo.

Gila and I took a bus from Tel Aviv to Cairo and spent a couple weeks in Egypt. Then we flew to Greece, traveled by ferry to Italy, and from there by train to London. Even though going to London was an adventure with no clear ending, my intention was always to return to Jerusalem to teach karate.

We stayed in London for two years, during which we both worked and I trained as much as I could. London was cold and wet and unwelcoming, and we had no money. For the first few months we lived in a tiny flat that was used as storage space under the dojo. But then, once we both got steady work, we moved to an apartment in Brixton Hill and our life settled into a routine.

Sensei George's dojo was in a rough part of town and that meant that the crowd was rough too. The dojo was housed in an old historic building on Camberwell Road called The Marble Factory, about a mile from the well known Elephant and Castle tube station. There was no glass on the windows and no heating or cooling system so the winters were freezing cold and the summers were unbearably hot.

George had a great sense of humor and no regard for laziness. He didn't care who you were—if you didn't sweat happily, he made sure you perspired through suffering. By then I had the training at the Jerusalem dojo and the military train-ing behind me, so I was prepared for Sensei George and his physically demanding classes. Still I could see without doubt that his intentions were aligned with the principles of karate, and he sought to build up his students and help them become better people.

By the end of two years in London, two important things had happened to me: First, Gila and I got married in a modest ceremony in the London borough of Southwark. Gila's grandmother Rose and Aunt Nunnie came, as did our friends Charlie Ramble and his wife Frances. My sister Ossi and her husband Haim came to London to visit us for the occasion and after that the four of us traveled by car to Wales. The second thing that happened was that I fulfilled my dream and received my black belt in Okinawa Goju-Ryu karate from Sensei George.

Having received my black belt, I realized I wanted to learn more. I knew that Goju-Ryu karate, the Okinawan discipline that I had been practicing, offered a great deal of depth, and I did not want to miss any of it. I spoke with Sensei George, and he suggested that I travel to Japan to train with *the* master of Goju-Ryu karate, Morio Higaonna.

"I can do that?" I asked, astonished. "I'm just a first-degree black belt. Will he take me?" George said he would speak to Sensei Higaonna himself. Since Gila and I had wanted to travel to Asia anyway, we decided to go to Japan.

I was completely taken by karate at this point, and all I wanted to do was train and learn more so this was one of the easiest decisions I ever made. I was in no hurry to return to Israel—I assumed that once I was done with my training, I would go back to Jerusalem to teach. I had by then decided that my goal was to reach third-degree black belt, which is considered the appropriate rank to become an instructor.

I was extremely excited by the possibility of going to Japan, and I can safely say that all my preconceived ideas and expectations were shattered when I landed in Tokyo in October 1985. I am not sure why, but I was expecting an ultra-modern society where everyone spoke English and everything moved quickly and effi-ciently. What I found was that English was spoken by precious few. People I met went out of their way to be friendly and polite, yet I always felt that Japanese people kept a safe distance from me because I was a *gaijin*, or "foreigner." The metro-politan centers in Tokyo were fast and bustling, but as I went into neighborhoods where people lived, I saw that life moved at a different pace, one that conformed to age-old Japanese traditions.

I expected hundreds of students to be lined up for classes with Master Higaonna, a master with an international reputation who'd reportedly taught in Tokyo for twenty years and had upwards of one thousand students. However, he had just moved back to Tokyo after spending a few years in his native Okinawa, and his previously huge following had lost momentum. He didn't even have a per-manent dojo of his own and would teach at various dojos around Tokyo.

None of that mattered. I enjoyed most aspects of life in Japan, and the karate training was rigorous and at times painful, which was what I wanted. I trained two and sometimes three times a day, five days a week, and spent as much time as I could with Sensei Higaonna. At the time, there were mostly British, Australians, New Zealanders, and Europeans training. Most of them had come for a few weeks or months to experience karate in Japan. I was able to see and meet some of the greatest Japanese masters within the traditional martial arts world, and I came to realize the immense respect that martial arts masters of all disciplines had for my new teacher.

Gila and I soon met a community of Israelis there, and we all lived together in a "gaijin house," where we rented a room. It was the first time we were in close contact with Israelis since leaving Israel, and we both loved it—although Gila felt more at home in the group than I did. Even though we did not talk much about politics, it didn't take long for the other Israelis to figure out that I was the son of Matti Peled and where I stood on the important issues.

I was also set apart by the fact that I was following a strict and very demanding training regimen. Six days a week, I was out of the house by 8:30 in the morning and did not return till midnight. Our housemates kept a more leisurely schedule, waking up at noon and relaxing together before heading out to work or to explore. I would return home exhausted and go straight to bed, and the others would stay up socializing until two or three in the morning. This led to some friction between Gila and me—she wanted me to go along with everyone else's routine a little more.

Still I enjoyed being there with the other Israelis, and I felt that everyone respected what I was doing. For money, I worked as a waiter in a fancy Italian restaurant called La Scala, in Tokyo's upscale Kojimachi district. It had a piano bar upstairs and the pianist, an Italian named Ciro, would sometimes grow bored or want a drink. If so, he would play the Israeli tune *Hava Nagila*, and I'd go up and chat with him.

The training took place each morning from 10 a.m. till noon. I would then go with Sensei Higaonna and one or two other students to have lunch. Training would resume at 1 p.m. and last until 3 p.m. During those lunches, Sensei would tell stories and talk about interesting things. He spoke of his own Sensei, An'ichi Miyagi, who was a behind-the-scenes type of person and not widely known. "If people don't see, I don't tell them," Sensei Higaonna said, referring to his own teaching methods. He believed knowledge had to be gained the hard way. At the time, he was also in the middle of an intense research project on the roots and history of Goju-Ryu karate, and he shared a great deal of what he was finding with me. I was glad I was there, and I even had the chance to train with Sensei Miyagi many times over the years.

One day on the way to lunch, Sensei Higaonna said to me, "October, you *Nidan*[4] grading." Which meant that I could take my exam for second-degree black

---

4 Black belts ranks are called "dan" in Japanese, which simply means level. Nidan is second-dan or second-degree black belt.

belt that October. I was floored. It had only been about a year since I received my first-degree black belt, and getting my second degree so soon after was a huge distinction and reward. Later, Mrs. Higaonna, an American and karate student herself, said to me, "Miko, you have been training hard and this is a well deserved reward for the many hours of training you put in since you got to Japan." It was another shock to hear praise for my hard work after a year with the reticent Sensei. This was one of a handful of times where he gave me praise, albeit in an indirect way.

I guess that Sensei Higaonna was in many ways similar to my father. Higaonna did not readily express affection or concern, and except for rare occasions I did not feel that my hard work was of much interest to him. Not unlike my father, he spoke little and when he did he lectured, wanting little conversation or feedback from others. Meanwhile, I was in awe of his mastery of karate and his authority just as I was in awe of my father's intellect, military achievements, and ultimately authoritarian personality. It was many years later, after I became a father and a teacher myself, that I realized the shortcomings of this type of silent authoritarianism. Ultimately, it must come from a severe sense of insecurity. Certainly the never-ending demand for perfection and endless hours of practice that Sensei Higaonna imposed upon himself reminded me of the way my father was with his own work.

Around the time I received my new rank, Gila and I had enough money saved to go on our dream trip to Asia. Charlie Ramble, an Oxford PhD and an old friend from the London dojo, who had also attended our wedding, lived in Kathmandu at the time, and he invited us to stay with him. We knew he could point us in the right direction in terms of travel, so we decided to start there. We spent two-and-a-half months living, traveling, and trekking in Nepal. The country was underdeveloped and sanitary conditions were appalling, and yet at the same time it was an enchanting place. I got so sick with amoebas that I lost 20 pounds. At one point Charlie suggested that we go to see a young Indian astrologer who lived in Kathmandu. His name was Indu, and he came from a long line of Indian astrologers. The only problem was that I had to find out the exact time of my birth, and the only way to do that was to call home. As I waited for someone at home to pick up the phone, I found myself thinking, "Please let it be my mother who answers, because I don't want to have to explain this to my father." Sure enough I heard my father's short and impatient "hello" on the other end. We had a brief chat and then, trying to sound as casual as possible, I asked him, "By the way do you know what time of day I was born?"

"Why, are you going to see an astrologer?" He was too sharp, and there was no chance of concealing my intentions, which I assumed would seem silly to him. I had no choice but to confess that that was indeed why I wanted my time of birth. He did not disapprove, but he was a rational person and his only reaction was, "Oh well, just don't take what he says too seriously."

Charlie advised us to travel overland from Nepal into India. For me, India was love at first sight. Yes, poverty was widespread, but that could not hide the immense beauty of the country and its people. We took a bus from the border and as soon as I saw the Indian landscape I sensed the richness of the country: enormous rivers and endless forests, huge tracts of cultivated land, and a vast countryside.

It was a very long ride and because in India schedules ran differently than in the West or Japan—in other words, keeping with a schedule was not a priority—we did not know when we would arrive at our destination. The bus stopped several times along the way for people to buy tea and food. A tea *wallah*, or "seller," would set up a huge pot with strong spicy Indian tea cooked in milk. He would serve the tea in a cup set on a saucer. I remember the first time I saw an Indian pour his tea into the saucer and then drink from the saucer itself—I remember wondering, "Why in the world would anyone do that?" It occurred to me later that it was a way to cool the boiling tea so it was drinkable.

We arrived at our destination, Patna, the capital city of Bihar state, after midnight—instead of the originally projected 9 p.m. The city was completely quiet, and there was not a soul in sight. We walked around for a bit, not knowing where to go or what to do, when a rickshaw driver came up and offered to take us to a hotel. We had a good night of sleep and the next day we were off to Bodhgaya, following in the footsteps of Gautama Buddha.

I had never been in a country with so much beauty and generosity until then. I felt that the country and its people were offering so much and asking for so little in return. When I toured the monumental statues of Mount Abu or the breathtaking architecture in Fatehpur Sikri near Agra, I thought of the great works of art and architecture one sees in Italy. In India, there was no mention of the artist or architect as though it was all offered selflessly, as opposed to the West where every work of art and every building seems tied to its creator's ego. It's not that the art in India was any more or less beautiful than the art in Europe, but in India I felt that the creators demonstrated a sense of selfless generosity.

In February of 1987, after two-and-a-half months in India, we went back to Japan to continue working and training. A few months later, Sensei Higaonna dropped a bombshell: "We moving to America, if you want come, welcome." He and his California-born wife decided to take their son and move to southern California, where they planned to open a dojo. I still wanted my third-degree black belt and the thought of going back to Southern California after all these years appealed to me. So it was a no-brainer for me to follow him, and Gila agreed.

We decided we would visit Israel first before going to the U.S. It was our first visit since we left in 1984. We spent six weeks with our families and both of us felt that we did not want to leave. We realized how much we loved and missed our homes and our families. Our siblings had young children at that point, and we wanted to be part of it all. In some ways it would have been a lot easier to stay, rather than starting over once again in a new country. But something stronger than all that was pulling me away. I felt I had to continue to train and study, that what I had accomplished so far was not enough. We decided we would go to California for two years, enough time for me to reach third- degree black belt and for Gila to study something, although she was not yet sure what that would be. As the time for us to leave came nearer, we were torn and heartbroken.

We landed in Los Angeles on Halloween day, 1987, with $3,000 in our pockets. My first feeling was that I knew Los Angeles and remembered it fondly. A friend drove us to San Diego, where Sensei Higaonna had already opened his dojo. We arrived at night, and I got into my uniform and went to class immediately. The following day was the grand opening of the dojo, or opening ceremony as it is called, and I was scheduled to take part in the black-belt demonstrations.

At first we felt a little adrift in the U.S., but we quickly became focused. I spent endless hours training with Sensei Higaonna, teaching at his dojo, and doing odd jobs, and Gila worked as a nanny and eventually enrolled in acupuncture school. It was not easy though. I did not want to be a waiter any more. I remember working at a particular restaurant, pretending I was local but not really knowing what anything on the menu was. A customer asked for a salad with no croutons, and I had no idea what those were so of course I gave him a salad with lots of croutons. I was waiting for the day when I could earn my living another way.

In 1989, I received my third-degree black belt, and I was ready to open my own dojo when an opportunity arose to do just that. A Japanese acquaintance told Sensei Higaonna he was opening a karate school and wanted him to recommend an instructor to run it and teach. It was the beginning of a fascinating, fulfilling, and fun career. In fact, it was another dream-come-true and the thought of ever returning to teach in Jerusalem had completely left my mind. From that point on one thing led to another, and there was no stopping it.

I opened the karate school on May 27, 1989, in a residential area of San Diego. A few friends helped me take down the walls and convert a regular house into a karate studio. We decorated two pillars and the front porch with the Japanese words for Goju-Ryu Karate-Do. It didn't occur to me that I needed a sign in English as well. When I finally thought to place one along with a phone number in one of the windows, people began calling. A year later, I had 10 or 15 students and needed to move to a different location. I found a basement in a newly built apartment building around the corner.

The next year, 1991, San Diego experienced more rainfall than it was able to absorb. The result was flooding everywhere, including the basement of the building that housed my dojo. Even when the walls began turning green from moss, parents still brought their kids to my classes.

After a few months in the basement, an advertising representative from a local family magazine found me. This was amazing enough because while I could not even afford a proper sign, he actually sold me an ad. The ad cost $400, which I didn't have, so I decided to call my brother Yoav, a political science professor at Tel Aviv University, who happened to be on sabbatical in Florida at the time. He was kind enough to lend me the money.

It made an unbelievable difference. I quickly went from ten to fifty students, many of them from what I perceived to be the glitzy suburb/city of Coronado. By the time my second anniversary came around, I needed to move again. I found a spacious studio that had formerly housed another martial arts school. It was perfect—long and wide with an office and meeting room. The number of students grew steadily, soon nearing 100. I eventually began teaching classes in Coronado a few times per week and finally opened a full-time dojo there. After trying to juggle the two schools for some time, I realized that 80 percent of my students came from Coronado. Following another year of heavy rains and another flood that ruined parts of my building, I closed that chapter and dedicated myself full-time to the dojo in Coronado.

Once again things were moving fast. I went from 100 to 200 students practically overnight. On January 26, 1994, our first son, Eitan was born. Six months later, we moved to Coronado. Two years after that, on August 19, 1996, our second son was born. Because he was born on my mother's seventieth birthday, we decided to name him Doron, which in Hebrew means "gift." Another six years later, we had our third child, a daughter who we named Avital Zika, or Tali for short.

In 1998, Israeli television produced a series called *Tkuma*, which means revival in Hebrew. It had 22 chapters covering the first 50 years of the state of Israel. My brother-in-law Rami bought the entire set for me and sent it to me in the U.S. He added a handwritten, heartfelt letter in which he wrote,

> This is a special gift from me to you as a token for the love and admiration that I have for you...from time to time I am reminded of a young, passionate boy arguing with me as if going to battle. Armed with little but great enthusiasm, half formed ideas and ambivalent historical facts, only to be met by my unforgivable cold, cruel cynicism and my inability to listen and be persuaded.

As I read this letter I was reminded of heated political arguments Rami and I had, when I just a young teenager, sharpening my mind and debate skills. They were always about the smallest, minute details because when it came to the bigger issues we agreed with one another and with my father, whom we both adored.

Rami's letter continued,

But we have since matured and calmed down and we understand the hard, painful facts of life…this series will not be easy to watch. At times it will bring you to tears, or cause you to raise your fist in anger, but it will remind you and your children from where you came and to where you will one day, hopefully, return. With Love, Rami.

I watched every chapter of that series. When the show turned to events that I knew from family stories, like the immigration of the Arab Jews to the new home- land and the awful discrimination they experienced in Israel, or to events I had actually lived, like the visit of President Sadat or the Lebanon War, my debates with Rami would come back to me. And the words in his letter echoed in my head. I knew this country would always be a part of me, but would I ever return?

Things were moving along smoothly for me in California. We had purchased our first home in Coronado and for the first time in my adult life I was establish- ing roots and I was doing it away from my family and far from the country I loved so much. I was back in southern California, as though drawn by fate, building a home and a family here.

Chapter 6:

Black September

Then, in the fall of 1997, an unthinkable disaster befell our family. Two young Palestinians blew themselves up on Ben Yehuda Street in Jerusalem and killed my niece. Smadar was with friends, shopping for books for school. My mother had just returned to Israel from visiting us in California, and had my niece chosen to meet her at the airport instead, she would not have died that day.

All this was unfolding while I sat, helpless and dumbstruck, in my peaceful home in southern California. Smadar was the first granddaughter in our family, and she would have turned 14 two weeks later. She was the kind of kid you couldn't get enough of, with eyes that seemed at once innocent and wise. She'd visited us in Coronado two years earlier, just before her Bat Mitzvah, the twelfth birthday ceremony when a Jewish girl becomes a woman. Her hair was long and straight and honey-colored then, and she was sweet and a little shy. She refused to let us take her picture, but we managed to do it anyway. After a few days with us, we noticed that she began every sentence with "Anyway..." emulating the way Gila talks.

Gila and I and the two boys had visited Israel just a few weeks before the terrible day. By that time, Smadar had become tall and more confident, her body already that of a young woman. She had dyed her long hair black. "She has such beautiful hair, why does she have to dye it?" my mother complained. But Smadar was now a teenager and in need of asserting herself. She could go from serious and independent to childlike and joyful in a matter of moments. She played with my sons—Eitan, who was three, and Doron, who was one—and she was even comfortable changing Doron's diapers. We have a picture of her playing with Doron as a baby.

When my mother first called from Israel to say that my niece was missing, I quickly rationalized: Smadar must be at a friend's house, oblivious to the bombing. When I grew up in Jerusalem, even when I heard about a bombing while I was out with friends, I wouldn't always take the trouble to call home. "*Kulam beseder*?" I would ask, when I eventually walked through the front door. "Is everyone all right?" It was a kind of dissociation, the thick skin a young person cultivated to create some semblance of normality in a place where catastrophes were a part of life.

Still, I had a terrible feeling that something was wrong—that the worst had in fact happened. I kept telling myself my emotions were misplaced, that she was too smart, too alive. Nothing could happen to a girl like that.

A few cars passed by on our quiet cul-de-sac, and an ocean breeze blew. I was alone in our children's playroom watching the news on CNN. "The previous suicide attack had taken place six weeks earlier at the open-air market in Jerusalem," someone on TV commented. *Yes, I remember.* It had been a Friday; the market was bustling with shoppers buying food in preparation for the Sabbath, and it was a massive bloodbath. As soon as I'd heard the reports, I called home to Israel as I always did after a bombing to make sure everyone was safe. It was a relief to hear the voices of my mother and sisters reassuring me everyone was safe, and I went about my day pretending all was well. But even when my own family had not been harmed, things were not well. Every act of violence was always followed by retaliation, and the cycle did not stop. Deep down I feared that it was only a matter of time before something like this might happen, that someone close to me would be killed.

CNN went live to a scene in Jerusalem. My eyes were fixed on the images streaming from the television, my ears hearing the sirens wailing thousands of miles away. I saw medics carrying the dead and injured and noticed the body of a young woman on a stretcher lying with her back to the camera.

No. I had a terrible feeling as I wondered who this young lady might be. *Impossible.* This young woman's hair was cropped short. I had seen Smadar a few weeks earlier and her hair was long and dyed black.

Calls continued back and forth from Jerusalem to California as the day wore on. Every call would raise my hopes and then dash them. Smadar wasn't with this friend. She wasn't with that friend. She hadn't been seen in any of the hospital emergency rooms in town. I was not certain if this was good news or bad.

Soon it was time for me to drive up the coast to teach a class. I had recently opened a second karate school in Poway, about 30 miles north of Coronado. I was trying to keep to my schedule and retain a sense of business as usual. I was determined to be focused and present, telling myself that the call reassuring me that Smadar was fine would come at any minute. In the car, I found myself phoning my travel agent, an Israeli who I knew would understand: "I might need a ticket to fly home right away." As I hung up, I realized that I was holding back a choking feeling.

The police waited until late at night to call, as if allowing Nurit and her husband Rami to reach the inevitable conclusion on their own. After Smadar's parents returned from the morgue, where they identified their little girl, Ossi called me.

As I was packing, I realized with horror that my passport had expired. I couldn't fly with an expired passport, and the renewal process would take days. I did not have days. I did not have even one day. Jewish people must bury their dead within 24 hours. I had to get to Jerusalem now.

I discovered that grief intensifies some memories and blurs others. To this day, I cannot remember how the arrangements were made or how I got to the Israeli consulate in Los Angeles. I have no idea if I flew to LA or drove. I remember being greeted at the consulate in hushed tones. They knew my niece had been killed in the recent suicide attack and that she was the granddaughter of the late General Matti Peled. They knew that the state funeral was being held up until I, her uncle living in America, went home to Israel. They quickly ushered me into the office of the consul general herself.

I was treated with great kindness and the reverence given to anyone in my position. In Israeli society, those who have lost loved ones in war become members of a holy order. They become untouchable—they are The Bereaved.

The officials waived every formality. Still in a daze, I was out the door with my new passport in 20 minutes and on my way to the airport.

On the plane, I was overwhelmed by grief and engulfed by terrible thoughts. I found myself hoping that those responsible would be caught and killed, which was absurd because they had already killed themselves. Anyway, how could there possibly be vengeance for a death such as this? As the Hebrew poet Haim Nahman Bialik wrote and Nurit would repeat over and over again, "Satan has not yet invented vengeance suitable for the blood of a young child."

I landed in Israel at dawn. My brother Yoav picked me up at the airport and took me to Nurit and Rami's apartment in Jerusalem. We drove in silence, Yoav deep in thought. He finally said, "Of all of us why did it have to be her... I mean so many of us had fought in wars and survived, and yet it had to be this innocent little girl walking down the street. It makes no sense, no sense at all."

He was so right. When we arrived, the street was empty and I sat in the car for a while. Then I got out and glanced at the morning paper in the yard—I saw the headline: "Granddaughter of Peace Activist General Matti Peled Killed by Palestinian Suicide Bombers..."

I walked up the stairs to Nurit and Rami's apartment. They lived in the house where I was born, 18 Rashba Street in Jerusalem. It was the longest flight of stairs I ever had to climb. When Nurit opened the door, we fell into each other's arms sobbing with the abandon of small children. I still don't know what to say or think as September 4 approaches each year. I feel the same way I did then, crying in my sister's arms, over and over again, even all these years later.

Smadar was laid to rest near my father, her grandfather, in the small hilltop cemetery just outside of Jerusalem. As police motorcycles cleared traffic for the funeral procession, I felt a sense of déjà vu. Two years earlier we had driven the exact same route escorted by police motorcycles. Only that time we'd been following my father's coffin to his final resting place. That too had been an emotionally charged state funeral attended by Israeli and Palestinian dignitaries, representatives from Israel's entire political spectrum, and the press. The difference was that he

*My niece, Smadar, who was killed
in a suicide bombing in Jerusalem.*

was nearly 72 years old and an accomplished man. Smadar was 13, just beginning to bloom.

I never imagined we would be taking the same route again so soon, and under such unthinkable circumstances. Nor did I know how dramatically my life would change, and what an unexpected quest awaited me as a result of this searing grief.

As we got out of the van, someone approached me and said, "Would you help us carry the coffin?" My heart felt heavier than the small coffin on my shoulder.

Israelis and Palestinians, family members and friends from across the political spectrum, famous leaders and ordinary people, came to give eulogies or express their sorrow at this unspeakable loss. To this day Nurit cannot forgive herself for leaving her baby girl alone in the cold, damp ground.

For the next seven days, Nurit and Rami's apartment was packed from 6 a.m. to midnight. Dignitaries, reporters, mourners, friends, and family members walked through their door. The door through which past statesmen, generals, and diplomats had once entered, and which today has a sticker on it reading: FREE Palestine.

Among those who came to pay respects were Ehud Olmert, then the mayor of Jerusalem and future prime minister, and Ehud Barak, who holds the distinction of being Israel's most decorated soldier. Barak later rose to be Israel's prime minister and defense minister, but at the time he was the head of the opposition party and doing everything he could to be elected prime minister. Barak was largely seen as Yitzhak Rabin's designated successor. The expectation was that if elected he would take on the role of peacemaker, a role which Rabin had paid for with his life. Here he was, sitting among us, trying to convince people that in order to really make peace he had to run without making it look like he wanted peace so he wouldn't lose votes for being a peacemaker. I sat quietly wondering if anyone really believed such nonsense. Finally, I couldn't take it anymore and said, "Why not tell the truth?" The room became silent. "Why not tell people that this and other similar tragedies are taking place because we are occupying another nation and that in order to save lives the right thing to do is to end the occupation and negotiate a just peace with our Palestinian partners?" All of us in the family felt this was true, in fact we had known this for years. At this moment I could no longer keep it in. Here was a major decision maker and future key policymaker in the room, and he wanted our support.

I received a withering look from Barak, and when he prepared to leave and made the rounds of handshakes, all I got was a cold shoulder. I also received a lecture from one of his cronies about not understanding politics and being naïve.

One person who played a significant role in this tragedy was actually Benjamin Netanyahu, or Bibi[1]. He was prime minister at the time of Smadar's death. Nurit had gone to school with Bibi, and his first wife is one of Nurit's lifelong friends. I remember him from my childhood neighborhood in Jerusalem. He'd been the picture perfect young Israeli, a paratrooper and a member of Israel's elite commando unit, *Sayeret Matkal*. Known simply as "The Unit," it's the cutting edge of Israel's Special Forces. To my five-year-old mind, he was a subject of immense admiration with his uniform, good looks, and of course the red beret. Bibi also served as a reservist in The Unit and had participated in several heroic missions. We would visit him when he returned home to hear his stories. He was slightly injured in an operation to rescue a Sabena Belgian airliner that was hijacked in May 1972 and landed in Tel Aviv. The Unit commandos dressed as repair technicians and managed to get into the plane, rescue the passengers, and kill the hijackers. Bibi was shot and suffered a flesh wound in the arm. After the operation, I went with Nurit to visit him. The bandaged arm seemed to me like a medal of honor.

Bibi's older brother, Yonatan (Yoni) Netanyahu, was also a legend. He served as commander of The Unit and was killed in July 1976, during the famous Operation

---

1 In Israel, we address people by the most common and diminutive name possible. Ehud is Udi. Avraham is Avi, Rami, or in my case Miko. Benjamin is Beni or Bibi, even if he is the prime minister.

Entebbe.[2] After Yoni was killed, Nurit and I visited the family again. I will never forget the look on their father's face, the unmistakable look of a bereaved father.

My naïve admiration for Bibi went on for many years. However, when he entered politics, my admiration quickly faded. He seemed insincere and opportunistic, and his views were uncompromisingly hawkish. It was obvious to me that no government under him was going to advance the cause of peace.

Netanyahu was elected prime minister in 1996, sweeping into office after Yitzhak Rabin's murder—capitalizing on the country's total disillusionment with the Oslo peace process and a rash of suicide bombings, which Netanyahu promised to put a stop to. He had campaigned under the slogan, "Making a Safe Peace." Things didn't seem very safe or peaceful at the moment.

After it was confirmed that Smadar was killed, Bibi had called Nurit to offer condolences, adding, "I don't suppose Rami would want me to come." He was smart enough to know Rami and the rest of us abhorred his politics and held him responsible for Smadar's death. Nurit's response was unambiguous: "No, he would not."

Nurit and he were like brother and sister, yet Bibi did not go to Smadar's funeral, and he did not visit, even once, during the week of mourning, the *shiva*.

Ten years later, in the summer of 2007, Nurit and I and my boys ran into Bibi at the coffee shop by the pool at the Hebrew University in Jerusalem. Bibi was there with his oldest daughter. He was not in office at the time, and he was as cordial and personable as ever. We all talked, and he mentioned that he still remembered me as a child. Nurit, too, was friendly and relaxed. After he took his leave, Eitan, who by then was almost 13, noticed that this person seemed important. "Who is this guy?" he asked.

"He used to be the prime minister, which is kind of like the president."

Doron, who was almost 11 and missed nothing, asked, "Why does he have bodyguards?"

Nurit quietly sipped her Earl Grey tea. "He must have done something really terrible and now he is afraid for his life," my sister said, comparing the hawkish politician to mafia bosses who have blood on their hands. As she saw it, every Israeli

---

2 On June 27, 1976, two Palestinians from the Popular Front for the Liberation of Palestine (PFLP) and two Germans hijacked an Air France flight en route from Tel Aviv to Paris and diverted it to Entebbe, Uganda. They demanded the release of 40 Palestinians held in Israel and 13 other detainees imprisoned in Kenya, France, Switzerland, and West Germany. They threatened that if these demands were not met, they would begin to kill hostages. The hostages were held for a week in the transit hall of Entebbe Airport. Four Israeli planes flew secretly to Entebbe Airport under cover of night, infiltrated the terminal, killed the hijackers (three hostages were also killed in the crossfire), and evacuated the hostages under fire from the Ugandan military, killing about 45 Ugandan troops. Yonatan (Yoni) Netanyahu was the only Israeli soldier killed.

politician who did not end the Israeli occupation and oppression of Palestinians was responsible for the deaths of Israelis and Palestinians. She reasoned, and still does, that this is not a question of policy or inability to reach an agreement but callousness, greed for land, a desire to rule, and a lack of will to end the conflict.

After Smadar's death, I stayed in Jerusalem for the week of shiva and then had to return home and resume my routine. *How do people do this?* I kept thinking. *How do people keep on living as though nothing happened?* So many songs have been sung, poems and stories written, about this feeling—the feeling one has when the unthinkable happens, yet the world doesn't end. Bialik described it in his epic poem "*Ir Hahariga*" ("In the City of Slaughter") when he wrote: "The sun rose, the trees bloomed and the butcher slew."

It seemed impossible to carry on. My mother Zika always said that life was stronger than death, and she was right. Doron was a year old, Eitan was barely four, and both Gila and I had businesses to run.

I had always taken the political situation in Israel to heart, but after Smadar's death, it became deeply personal, even more so than before. Up to that point, I was fine with the decision I had made many years earlier not to be active politically, but after Smadar was killed I was no longer content to sit still.

Unfortunately, no one around me cared much about the Middle East. Our lives in southern California did not include any Israeli or even American-Jewish friends, and in our immediate surroundings people knew little and cared little about my homeland and its problems. Besides, bringing up the issue of Israel-Palestine with the friends we did have seemed burdensome, outside the realm of topics people cared about. On top of that, talking about Smadar was always awkward. It took me a long time before I could even mention what happened to her without choking up. And when I did, people didn't know what to say or think. I couldn't really talk to anyone unless I called my mother or sisters in Jerusalem.

As time wore on, the urge to get involved, to be active, became stronger and stronger, but I couldn't find an outlet for it. Rami became involved with the Bereaved Families Forum, an organization that brings together Israeli and Palestinian families dedicated to promoting reconciliation. In 1998, my brother-in-law met, as he describes it, "a large and impressive man with a knitted *kippah* on his head." Rami assumed this meant the man was a member of Gush Emunim, the right-wing Israeli settler organization. (The *kippah*, or yarmulke, was a sign of a casual Jewish Orthodoxy that had been co-opted by the settlers.) He was mistaken. Itzhak Frankenthal told Rami that his son was kidnapped and murdered by Hamas militants in 1994, and that after that he had founded an organization for people who lost their loved ones to the conflict but still believed in peace.

Suddenly Rami recognized the man's face. He had been one of the thousands of people who had visited their apartment during the shiva. Rami was furious. "How dare you walk into the home of someone who just lost a child and talk about peace and reconciliation? Where do you get the nerve to do that?"

Frankenthal was undeterred; the pain of the bereaved was not new to him. According to Rami, "He was not offended by my words. He calmly and patiently invited me to come and see with my own eyes what the meetings were like."

So Rami went to a meeting. "I stood watching as people arrived by bus. Old Palestinian women who had lost their children, Palestinian fathers alongside Israelis from all walks of life who had lost loved ones. For the first time in my life I was deeply and truly feeling hopeful." From that moment on Rami gave his heart and soul to the Bereaved Families Forum and the cause of reconciliation. The forum's message was simple: If bereaved parents could sit and talk with one another, so could everyone else. There was a partner for peace, and peace was possible.

"From that day on, I had a reason to get out of bed each morning," Rami said. He dedicated his life to this one thing, going from place to place, from person to person, and telling anyone who would listen that ours was not a fate that could not be changed. "It was not written anywhere that we had to live like this and sacrifice our children."

Meanwhile, Nurit had been speaking and writing extensively about the need to stop the bloodbath, pointing an accusing finger at anyone who sent children to kill or die. The *New York Times* quoted her saying that the Israeli government led by Netanyahu "sacrificed our children for their megalomania – for their need to control, oppress, dominate."[3] Two days later, she was quoted in the *Los Angeles Times*: "This is the fruit of their (Israel's) misdoings...they want to kill the peace process and blame the Arabs."[4] Her words drew an enormous amount of attention both in Israel and abroad. In December 2001, she received the Sakharov Prize for Freedom of Thought from the European Parliament. She received it jointly with Izzat Ghazzawi, a Palestinian writer and peace activist whose son was shot by Israeli soldiers.

I took Eitan to the ceremony; Doron was still young so Gila stayed home with him. The two of us met the rest of the family in Paris, where we spent a few days, and then we all took the train to Strasbourg, France, where the European Parliament sits in session. It was a moving event and Nurit invited Dr. Widad Sartawi, the widow of our father's partner Issam, to join us. Nurit delivered her speech in French at a session of the parliament.

"I dedicate this award to the memory of my father Matti Peled and Dr. Issam Sartawi," she told the audience. "And I thank my mother and Madame Sartawi for joining us here today." I couldn't hold back my tears, and it seemed neither could anyone else, for there was not a single dry eye.

Rami and Nurit's devotion to reconciliation had increased my already considerable admiration for them. When I visited Jerusalem, I would often accompany

---

3 Serge Schmemann, "Netanyahu's Hard Line Faces Rising Israeli Dissent," *The New York Times*, September 9, 1997.
4 Rebecca Trounson, "Mother Blames Israelis Policies for Child's Death," *The Los Angeles Times*, September 11, 1997.

them to meetings or go with them when they gave talks in schools or visited groups who wanted to learn about the conflict. I had never encountered such deeply devoted and principled people in my life. The connection between those who lost loved ones and chose to reach out instead of lash out is a deep and intense one. Through my sister and brother-in-law I met many fascinating people, and I found myself wishing I could do something similar back in San Diego. Only I had no idea where to start.

PART III

The Road to Palestine

was becoming more chauvinistic and constantly shifting to the right. When my best friend's son was about to be drafted, I asked the boy where he was going to serve and he told me he wanted to join the Special Forces.

I looked at my friend in surprise.

"You know that what they do is wrong—didn't you tell him?" I asked my friend later.

"You don't understand," my friend said. "You don't care about my son, all you care about are your Palestinian friends."

"Yes, I care about my Palestinian friends and what the Special Forces do to them, but this will backfire, and this will hurt your son, too. How could you not tell him?" That was the last time we spoke.

When I met Jewish Americans, my position on the Arab-Israeli conflict made them uncomfortable. American Jews for the most part wanted to believe that Israel was good and that Arabs were bad. I remember visiting a foot doctor who was Jewish. Once he realized I was Jewish and from Israel he allowed himself to unleash a few venomous anti-Arab remarks, thinking I must feel the same way about "these fucking Arabs." At first I was so shocked I was speechless. Then I dropped off a brochure published by the Bereaved Families Forum, to give him some food for thought. I never went to see him after that.

He was not the only one to do that around me. More and more I could sense an anti-Arab and anti-Muslim sentiment taking over what I had always thought was "moderate" America. If I had any regular contact with local Jewish people I could not talk about politics in the Middle East because it would get in the way of our friendship. Needless to say few of these friendships lasted very long. I remember thinking once that if I were to set the issue aside, stop talking and thinking about it, and move on with my life, then maybe I would just "get over it."

But after Smadar died, I cared so much that it hurt and I realized that getting over it was not an option. The political reality in my homeland would continue to follow me, not to say haunt me, for as long as I lived, regardless of where I chose to make my home. I searched and searched for an outlet, for something I could do in southern California, and the final push to make me become more active came almost three years after Smadar was killed.

As always, the process was tied to internal Israeli politics. In 1999, Israel had elected Ehud Barak, who promised he would negotiate with the Palestinians and end the conflict once and for all. My mother was visiting us in Coronado right after the elections and we had dinner with Marshall Saunders, a good friend and mentor of mine. He asked my mother, "So Zika, what do you make of Mr. Barak, your new prime minister?"

Chapter 7:

A Journey Begins

My journey into Palestine began in San Diego in 2000. I was 39 years old.

I used to think of Jerusalem as a "mixed" city because both Israelis and Palestinians live there. The sad reality is that Israeli and Palestinian communities in Jerusalem are completely segregated. As I look back on my childhood in Jerusalem, I realize that I never had an Arab friend, or even a close acquaintance. There was "us" and there was "the Arabs," and we might as well have been living on different planets.

I assumed that we lived separate lives because we were so different: Arabs spoke a different language, they went to different schools, and it seemed to me that they even wore different clothes; their schools usually required uniforms and they generally dressed in a more formal and conservative manner than we did. Their food was different, and whereas the society I knew was very relaxed about mixing men and women, in Arab circles that was not common. All of this I somehow knew without ever meeting or speaking to Arabs. When, on a trip somewhere with family or friends, we would stop at an Arab town, it seemed dusty and backward, which reinforced my preconceived notion that Arabs were poor and less developed than us.

I was 10 or 11 when I began asking questions. I remember once during a trip we visited a very poor village somewhere in the Negev. The children did not look like us, and I asked my father why they were so dirty. He did not reply. I remember asking him once why it was that Arab men beat their wives, as though this was a fact that everyone knew. It was another stereotype I had picked up somewhere. He became very angry and once again he did not respond, which of course I did not understand. My mother tried to get him to engage and talk to me about this, but he was not willing to even acknowledge such questions. By then he was teaching Arabic literature, and I think he was angered by these characterizations, and by the fact that his own son was bringing them home. Not knowing how to deal with this other than through anger, he chose to say nothing.

As an adult, my more liberal views on the Israeli-Palestinian conflict set me apart from other Israeli and Jewish friends, and I constantly felt conflicted and unsettled. Whenever I returned to Israel I found that my old friends, some of whom used to share my views, had moved toward the consensus, which in Israel

"He is just another general like the rest of them," my mother said. "I have no reason to believe that things will be any different." I, on the other hand, was full of optimism, and I had no idea she felt that way.

In the summer of 2000, Barak and Palestinian leader Yasser Arafat met at Camp David in Maryland at the invitation of President Bill Clinton to finalize and seal a peace agreement. Arafat insisted it was premature to hold a summit, but his opinion was ignored and the summit was convened on July 11. It gave rise to great expectations around the world. I, too, was buoyed: I really expected the leaders would finalize the process and it would result in peace; I chose to believe that Barak would pick up where Rabin left off before he was murdered and that he was serious about peace and compromise; and I chose to believe a peaceful resolution in the shape of a two-state solution was inevitable.

As the days went by, word was that all the parties had left to do was to sign on the dotted line. But the talks went on and on, with no sign of an agreement. I spoke to Rami constantly because he knew people that were on the Israeli delegation. "All that is left is to dot the i's and cross the t's, the deal is done," he kept saying. "I have it from people who are as close to the top as you can get."

Then, on July 25, I felt the floor drop out from under me. It was announced that the delegates were leaving with no agreement. I was devastated, as were millions of other Israelis and Palestinians who were hoping for an end to the conflict. President Clinton emerged from the summit and said, "The prime minister moved forward more from his initial position than Chairman Arafat."[1] This was a serious accusation coming from the guy who was supposed to be the "honest broker." He was blaming Yasser Arafat for not being flexible enough. Barak said, "We tore the mask off of Arafat's face," and now we know that Arafat did not want peace after all.

I felt that things did not add up. I had followed the process closely, and I knew that Yasser Arafat had been consistent for years. For the sake of peace he was willing to give up the dream of all Palestinians to return to their homes and their land in Palestine. He was willing to recognize Israel, the state that destroyed Palestine, took his people's land, and turned them into a nation of refugees. He was ready to establish an independent Palestinian state in the West Bank and Gaza—which make up only 22 percent of the Palestinian homeland—with Arab East Jerusalem as its capital.

He was ready to do all this, but he was not going to settle for anything less. He had always been clear about what he saw as the terms for peace.

In the end, it turned out that my gut feeling was right. As accounts of the negotiations began to surface—through articles, first hand accounts, and books like *Harakiri: Ehud Barak: The Failure* by journalist Raviv Druker—it was clear

---

1 Jane Perlez, "Impasse at Camp David: The Overview; Clinton Ends Deadlocked Peace Talks," *The New York Times,* July 26, 2000, http://nyti.ms/zxvZGv.

that what the Israelis had demanded at Camp David was tantamount to total Palestinian surrender. It also became clear that Ehud Barak himself was despised by his own aides and that none of his political allies remained with him due to trust issues. Barak demanded that Arafat sign an agreement to end the conflict forever and in return, he would be permitted to establish a Palestinian state on an area of land that could not be defined clearly because it was broken into pockets with no geographic continuity. Instead of Arab East Jerusalem, he would receive a small suburb of East Jerusalem as his capital. To that Yasser Arafat refused to agree.

In September 2000, frustration and disappointment ran high and the atmosphere was charged when Ariel Sharon who was opposed to the peace process from the beginning decided to march to the Temple Mount in Jerusalem. He did it surrounded by hundreds of fully armed police in riot gear. The Temple Mount, or *Haram al Sharif* as it's known to the Muslim world, is a 35-acre plaza that takes up one-sixth of the Old City of Jerusalem. It is home to the Dome of the Rock, the most iconic structure in Jerusalem, and the Al Aqsa Mosque. This mosque is believed to sit on the spot where patriarch Abraham was going to sacrifice his son. It is believed to be the site of the First and Second Jewish Temples, and it is the place from which the prophet Mohammed made his night journey into the heavens. It is so holy for Jews that observant Jews refrain from entering it for fear of defiling the Holy of Holies. For Muslims around the world, only Mecca and Medina are holier than Jerusalem.

Sharon claimed he was merely exercising his right to visit the place. It was more like an invasion than a visit. The response was immediate and entirely predictable. Palestinians from all walks of life saw this as desecration of holy ground, and massive protests began. Israel reacted with violent force. The unrest spiraled into ever-harsher Israeli repression and massive Israeli military incursions into the West Bank and Gaza. Palestinian-Israelis in northern Israel also protested and they too were met with violent response from the police, who shot and killed 13 civilians. Sharon lit the fuse over this barrel of explosives, and thus the second *Intifada* or Uprising was born.

Then the entire peace process came crashing down, as well as Barak's government. He had serious internal political problems, and he had hoped that sealing a peace deal would save him politically, but in the end he was forced to call early elections. These were held in February 2001, and Barak suffered a humiliating defeat, making his period in office the shortest of any Israeli prime minister. Ariel Sharon, who ran against Barak, won in a landslide. All of Sharon's shortcomings and past offenses were forgotten, and he was now at the helm in the prime minister's seat.

To understand why Sharon was elected, we have to understand how Israel views its generals—and this general in particular. Ariel Sharon, or Arik as he is known in Israel, was larger than life. He was a war hero. He fought in 1948, he headed Commando Unit 101,[2] he fought in 1956 in the Sinai Campaign,[3] and he proved to be a brilliant commander in the 1967 War. He seemed destined to be the IDF chief of staff, but in early 1973 it became clear that he would not get the job, and he was forced to resign. IDF chief of staff is as much a political appointment as it is a military post. The public and the army would never accept another chief of staff as long as he was in uniform, so Arik was forced to end his military career and resign. Following his resignation, my father wrote an article lamenting the fact that the IDF lost "a military genius." [4] He said Arik Sharon would have been a brilliant chief of staff, that he "combined the unique quality of being a brilliant military man, an admired leader and he knew how to organize his command so as to achieve the best possible results on the battlefield."

When the 1973 Mideast war broke out, the only war that was not initiated by Israel and where Israel was caught completely off guard, Sharon was immediately called back to the army. He commanded a reservist armored division and he saved the IDF from a humiliating defeat. He was fearless, and he represented the Israel in which Israelis wanted to live: strong, fearless, no-nonsense. He was the average man's general, who grew up and lived on a farm—not one of those sophisticated generals who hobnobbed with the rich and powerful. The battles he commanded are taught at military colleges around the world, and many of Israel's top commanders served under him as junior officers. Not unlike George Patton, the legendary World War II hero he was often compared to, Arik Sharon was both brilliant and dangerous. In Israel, the feeling was that no one else could bring the security people wanted, and certainly nobody could punish the Arabs as he could—on that he had a solid record.

I sensed disaster approaching and could no longer sit still. Compounded with Smadar's death, these political developments were all too much for me. I had to do something.

The first step, I thought, was finding people with whom I could talk, but how? I placed a few ads in *The San Diego Reader* classified section asking about dialogue groups but got no reply. I searched the Internet, and finally I came across the American-Arab Anti-Discrimination Committee (ADC), and they referred me to George Majeed Khoury, a Palestinian from Jerusalem who lived in San Diego. He and I communicated by e-mail and phone for several weeks, unable to get together because of our busy schedules, until finally we met at his office.

---

2 Unit 101 of the IDF, founded and commanded by Ariel Sharon on orders from Prime Minister David Ben-Gurion in August 1953. It was created in order to better deal with Palestinian refugees infiltrating into Israel. The unit was merged into the regular IDF Battalion 890 in 1954, mainly as a result of killing dozens of unarmed citizens during the raid known as Qibya massacre.

3 The Sinai Campaign also called "The Suez Crisis," Nov 5, 1956.

4 Matti Peled, "Premature Retirement," *Ma'ariv*, July 20, 1973.

I will never forget his warm greeting: "At last we meet!" I'd been apprehensive to meet him, but his warmth put me at ease right away. We sat in the reception area at his office, and he told me about the San Diego Jewish-Palestinian Dialogue Group: "We meet once a month, and we are a young and very active and vigorous group of people. I will have to ask the members if you can join us, but I will recommend that they do."

A few weeks went by, and I heard nothing. I sent Majeed another e-mail, and he invited me to a gathering in his home. When the day of my first meeting arrived, Gila worried that something bad would happen to me: "You don't know these people. What if this is a trap? Be sure to call me and come home as soon as you can." I promised that I would.

At that point, I had not acknowledged having such fears myself, and if I did they were overshadowed by anticipation and the sense that I was about to embark on something new and important. I was so excited driving there that I took a wrong turn, and the half-hour drive ended up taking over an hour.

When I finally reached their house, I saw a sign above the door that read: "Majeed and Haifa Khoury." I stood for a while, looking at the name "Haifa." It was the first time it ever occurred to me that "Haifa" was an Arabic name, and that perhaps the city of Haifa was an Arab city before it was Israeli.

I walked in hesitantly. About a dozen people were there, and I guessed that some were American Jews and others were Palestinian, but at first I couldn't tell for sure who was who. They sat in the living room around a table with the usual Middle Eastern spread—hummus, falafel, tabouli—common to both Israelis and Palestinians. I heard a woman refer to one of the salads, made of diced cucumbers and tomatoes with olive oil and lemon juice, as an "Israeli salad."

Another woman's eyebrows shot up. "Israeli salad? What's that supposed to mean?" she asked sharply. "Are you telling me that we have been eating an Israeli salad all these years?" I felt a bit uneasy by the exchange, but everyone else laughed. It was, in a way, a harbinger of things to come.

Another Jewish woman mentioned that she would soon be going home to visit. "Home? What country are you calling home? Let's be clear about one thing, that country is *my* home." This, too, did not cause any anger or antagonism, but laughter.

Soon we sat around a dining room table and began introducing ourselves. I was the only Israeli—I was almost always the only Israeli. I was quite nervous.

When it was my turn to introduce myself, I looked down and quickly told them who I was and what my views were. I told them about my family and my father, and about Smadar. "I am Zionist, and I believe in the Jewish state. I believe firmly that a Palestinian state should be established in the West Bank and Gaza, with East Jerusalem as its capital."

"Wait a minute." Doris Bittar, one of the group facilitators, pulled out a copy of *Al Jadid*, an English-language magazine covering Arab-American culture. "Are you Nurit's brother?"

It so happened that about a month earlier, *Al Jadid* had published a story about a movie called *The Bombing*. The movie, by the French producer Simone Bitton, described the suicide attack in which Smadar was killed. Doris knew of Nurit because she had just read the story in *Al Jadid*.

I had no idea our story had been written about, but everyone in the room seemed to know about it. People were stunned when I said that I was the uncle of the little girl in the film. The fact that I just happened to be there at the meeting that day felt like serendipity.

This is the first time I am in a place where Jews and Palestinians exist as equals, I thought. There are no occupiers and occupied, we are all citizens with equal rights and protections under the law. The fact that we were able to talk and to look each other in the eye made a huge difference; in fact, it may be what made this possible. Had we been living back home, we would never have met like this.

It was also the first time I sat in a room with Palestinians of all ages and backgrounds to talk about our shared homeland. In many ways, I had more in common with the Palestinians than with many of the Jewish-Americans in the group. The things that characterize American Jewish culture—New York Jewish humor, Jewish delicatessen food—were completely alien to me. On the other hand, traditional Palestinian warmth and hospitality, Arabic food, and photos of our shared homeland put me completely at ease. I didn't even mind seeing the map of Israel with Palestine written all over it, something I thought would trouble me since my people had fought so hard to win it back. Perhaps the fact that we—the Palestinians and the lone Israeli—had actually lived in the Middle East and had memories from the same land created an almost instant bond. I loved every minute of that evening. Nurit later said that meeting Palestinians gave me a taste of home. She was right. I finally found a piece of home in America.

The meeting had started at seven, and I expected it would last an hour or two at most. When I had not returned by ten, Gila became worried. Neither of us had been to the home of a Palestinian before, and we knew none of the people involved in the group. She was seriously afraid for my life, and she called my cell phone to make sure I was okay. I told her everything was fine.

The meetings of the San Diego Jewish-Palestinian Dialogue Group were held once a month, and everyone was polite and respectful as they told their stories. From the Palestinians, I heard stories of displacement and ruthlessness I had never imagined possible. However, we were not there to argue, we were there to listen and to share our experiences. As we became more comfortable with one another, we began approaching more dangerous ground and topics that went beyond the realm of "safe" dialogue.

Majeed referred to his life experience by saying, "I was ethnically cleansed twice!" First, when he was a child. "Because of the constant bombing of our neighborhood, we were forced to leave our home in West Jerusalem." Then, while he was attending the American University in Beirut in 1967, the Six-Day

War broke out and he was not permitted to return to his family, who now lived in East Jerusalem. His criticism of the top echelon of the PLO, many of whom he knew personally, was scathing. His "R"s rolled with rage: "They are corrupt crooks and criminals!"

One day, after attending meetings for several months, I got word that Manal Swairjo, one of the women in the dialogue group, was going to speak at a local synagogue on Sunday morning. Rabbi Moshe Levin of Congregation Beth El, also a member of our group, had invited her to speak. It was a risky move by the rabbi. He headed one of San Diego's most prominent synagogues, and to invite a Palestinian to speak while Sunday school was in session and so many people were present was no small matter. I later heard that he took some serious criticism for doing that.

Manal is a remarkably accomplished woman, a PhD, a world-renowned scientist, and a captivating speaker. She has a tremendous smile and beautiful green eyes. "I was born and raised in Kuwait where my father, a refugee from Majdal (now the Israeli city of Ashkelon), was a teacher," she told those gathered. "My father was a young boy when the town was taken by Israel, and his family was forced to move to a refugee camp in the Gaza Strip." I had not known this and, I am sure, neither did the predominantly Jewish audience.

In an answer to a question she said, "In Kuwait, we were taught Hebrew, and we were told that we had to learn it because Hebrew was the language of the enemy." Hearing that sent chills down my spine. "We even learned to say it in Hebrew: *Ivrit hee sfat ha'oyev.*" When she repeated those words in Hebrew, spoken with an Arabic accent, I did not know what to do with myself. I was flooded with thoughts and emotions, a combination of pain and surprise. Frankly, I was deeply insulted. She was drawing a connection between my language, this language that like a thread links me to the Hebrew culture, the language of the great Hebrew writers, both ancient and modern, and her fate as a Palestinian. Immediately, I thought of the poets Bialik and Lea Goldberg, the prophets of the Old Testament, and the immortal author of the *Song of Songs*. How could my language be associated with any enemy? Soldiers and Jewish settlers in the West Bank I can see as enemies of the Palestinians, along with a few Israeli politicians. The Hebrew language was the very heart and soul of Hebrew culture. *Did that mean that I, too, was the enemy?* I felt that I was suddenly associated with things I thought I was detached from. This was not the last time someone said something that shook me to my core, but it was the first real kick in the gut.

I wrote to Manal immediately, not to argue so much but to express the strength of the thoughts and emotions I experienced when I heard those words. She said she had no idea her words would have such an effect.

Years later, after Manal's daughter was born, her father came to San Diego to visit. Gila and I went to see her, and when Gila met Manal's father it was an emotionally charged moment. They both realized they came from the same place; Majdal, now the city of Ashkelon, just a few kilometers north of Kibbutz Zikim,

where Gila was born and raised. They had grown up seeing and loving the same landscape, and it affected them both deeply. Manal's father kept saying through his tears that we "were good people" and that he felt no resentment toward us. "This was not your fault."

Some time later Manal and I talked about it. "This was the first time I ever saw my father cry for Palestine," she said.

My journey and my transformation were becoming more intense. Soon I had to face my moment of truth—although it turned out to be the first of many such moments, moments without which dialogue is just plain talk.

We were at a dialogue meeting at Majeed's house. Majeed was explaining a point when he said, "The Palestinians had barely 10,000 fighters, but the Haganah and the other Jewish militias combined were triple that number if not more. So when the Jews attacked, the Palestinians never had a chance." That was the most outrageous version of history I had ever heard: that the fighting forces of the Jewish militias in 1948 were superior to the Arabs' and that the Jews attacked.

My father and all of his friends had fought in that war. I'd heard first-hand stories about the sieges, the fierce attacks, and the touch-and-go battles where our forces were outnumbered and won only because they had the wits and the moral high ground. My mother had told me that during the siege of Jerusalem, they'd had to share half a tomato for meals and dash to the wells to get water while bombs fell and snipers shot at them. In the Negev where my father fought, it was the few Israelis fighting the huge Egyptian army.

I was fully convinced that with my background I knew more than anyone else about this aspect of the conflict and that what Majeed was saying made no sense. In a way it even dishonored the story of the creation of the Jewish state, a story in which the few defeating the many is a crucial element. If what he said was true, then it de-glorified much of the story.

That could easily have been my breaking point. I could not explain why Majeed would be perpetuating this insane notion that Israel was not a "David" defending itself against the Arab "Goliath," but I wasn't ready to dismiss him as a liar.

I could not dismiss him because by now trust had been built between us. This trust allowed me to let go of the safe comfort of "knowing" so that I could explore the unknown territory of the "other." This was very difficult, but I felt that even if what he said was not the truth that I knew, I would have to explore it.

I didn't say anything right away because I didn't want to start arguing. Instead, when I got home that night I called my brother Yoav, who taught political science at Tel Aviv University.

"Yes, what your friend said has merit. If you want to know more, read a few books by Benny Morris, Ilan Pappé, and Avi Shlaim." These three "New Israeli

Historians" had all recently rewritten the history of the establishment of Israel. I did exactly as Yoav advised. Over the following weeks and months I read all the books by these authors. And the more I read, the more I wanted to know. They had corroborated what Palestinians had been saying for decades. In fact, they corroborated what most of the world had known for years: that Israel was created after Jewish militias destroyed Palestine and forcibly exiled its people. This was a rude awakening for me. I recalled watching the Israeli TV series *Tkuma*, or *Rebirth*, that came out in 1998 to commemorate Israel's 50th independence day. In one chapter dealing with Israel's War of Independence, a veteran commander of 1948 was asked if it was true that the Haganah forces burned down Arab villages. He slowly looked up at the camera, waited a while, and then said, "Like bonfires." This meant a whole new paradigm through which to view the Israeli-Palestinian conflict.

The purpose of dialogue is to eliminate the barriers between two sides through listening and empathy—which, I've learned, is easier said than done. The willingness to accept another's truth is a huge step to take. It is such a powerful gesture, in fact, that contemplating it can make you want to throw up.

At first I felt like a baby learning to walk, realizing little by little that it was OK to let go of the comfort of holding onto what I "knew" to be true. It opened the door to a discussion most Israelis are fiercely protective about—which is, what did the Zionist forces really do in 1948? Once I had taken a few steps into that unknown, I found confidence, and to my surprise I found that there was something even more secure to rely on than the myths of heroism and redemption I'd heard during my childhood. Many if not all of these myths were created and perpetuated by the new Jewish state, which wanted to substantiate the David versus Goliath image and painted my people as heroes who rose from the ashes to reclaim their historic homeland. For me, the only thing stronger than that myth was trust—the trust that was already in place between members of the dialogue group. Without that there could have been no progress. The group was not about accusing but listening and telling personal stories, and that was what allowed me, for the first time in my life, to learn that the Palestinians had a narrative of their own and that it was different from the narrative I had been taught. In fact, it was 180 degrees different.

This was an excruciatingly painful thing to learn, and it was possible only because Doris and her husband Jim Rauch were brilliant facilitators. Doris is an Arab-American artist of Palestinian and Lebanese descent. Born in Baghdad, she grew up in New York and picked up quite a bit of the Jewish-infused culture of that city. She has dark hair and warm dark eyes. There is a constant expression of motherly concern on her face, and when she laughs or smiles she lights up the room.

Jim is Jewish-American, and an accomplished economics professor at the University of California, San Diego (UCSD). He is quiet and methodical and sharp as a razor. Everyone felt comfortable with Doris and Jim because they clearly respected both cultures and possessed a unique ability to bring people together. They were excellent facilitators who didn't interject their own issues. Many of the meetings took place at their beautiful home in San Diego, and it was mainly their dedication that allowed the group to thrive as, month after month, they put their heart into the difficult task of making the dialogue work. From my perspective, it was a tremendous success.

Over time, the dialogue phenomenon grew and San Diego had three or four active groups that emerged out of our group, including one that I initiated. I received addresses and names of people who might be interested from Doris, and I called them to see if they were serious about participating in a dialogue group. It turned out to be another dedicated group. Before long, however, I realized that I made a better participant than facilitator: I wanted to be an active contributor to the conversations and to express myself fully—not to be unbiased and somewhat colorless, which was what a good moderator needed to be. So I relied on others in the group to facilitate the meeting.

Pretty soon word got out that there were Jewish-Palestinian dialogue groups that were active in and around San Diego and that they had something positive to say. This excited some people and alienated others. The local papers and TV stations took an interest in us, and the *Christian Science Monitor* did a major story about us.

But crossing the line to understand the "other" point of view was not seen as a positive step by everyone. Jewish and Palestinian members talked with great pain about people in their respective communities, sometimes even close friends, who had shunned them because they were meeting with "the other side."

"They told us we are not welcome anymore, because we meet with terrorists," said one elderly Jewish lady.

"We were told we should be ashamed of ourselves," said one Palestinian.

I was asked to participate in panel discussions with other members of the group. We were invited to speak at synagogues, mosques, and churches. Civic organizations and service clubs asked us to speak. We would sit together on the stage and take turns telling our stories. That was when I realized I had to learn to hold back my tears when talking about Smadar. Then we would take questions from the audience. From time to time, two of us would be invited to speak, and so I had opportunities to share a podium with Majeed, Doris, and Manal. I noticed that we gradually moved from representing opposing points of view to presenting a shared vision.

In 2002, Israeli television's Channel 10 decided to produce a documentary on Israelis living abroad. Yehuda Litani, a friend of Nurit and Rami, came to San Diego to interview a Palestinian doctor who lived there. When Nurit heard that Yehuda was coming to San Diego she told him that I lived there too, and he decided to do a chapter about me as well.

Gila was pregnant with Tali when he came, and we all became very good friends. He and his cameraman followed me around for about a week, shooting scenes of me teaching classes at the dojo and on the beach in Coronado. He came to a meeting of the dialogue group and he conducted extensive interviews with Nurit and my mother. The result was a 40-minute documentary about me that touched on my family, my father, and Smadar, plus my work with Jewish-Palestinian dialogue groups and my karate training. At the end of the documentary, Litani commented that I made an effective goodwill ambassador for Israel, and he lamented the fact that I no longer lived in Israel.

Indeed I felt I was finally doing something—but it was just the beginning.

Chapter 8:

Two Flags

My involvement went to the next level when I formed an unlikely partnership with Nader Elbanna. On the surface, Nader and I have very little in common. He is a devout Muslim and Palestinian Arab, and I am a casually secular Israeli Jew. We are of different generations: He was born in 1946, and I was born 15 years later. And different cultures: he had a traditional Arab upbringing, and I had a liberal Western upbringing. Politically and socially he is a conservative man, and I am a progressive liberal.

Our life stories are products of the same drama, the drama of Israel-Palestine. And yet they are very different stories. The resurrection of an independent Jewish political homeland, which was the proud centerpiece of my family's story, was the cause of the destruction and devastation of Palestine, which made up his family's story. Though we both lived in exile, I did so by choice and could return any time I wished, while he was exiled by force and not permitted to return.

We were brought together by fate, perseverance, and deep affection. Like brothers born to the same mother, we are sons of the same homeland. Had we remained in our homeland we never would have known each other, yet our exile brought us together.

I met Nader's son, Jamil, before I met Nader himself. In 2002, Doris invited Jamil to a meeting of the dialogue group. I remember we were at Majeed's house that evening when Jamil introduced himself and told the group, "I was born and raised in Jordan, completed my education in the U.S., yet my father brought me up to be a proud Palestinian."

As I watched and listened to him I couldn't help thinking: This educated, well-mannered, well-dressed young man, who was born and raised in Jordan and educated in the U.S., still identifies himself as a proud Palestinian. That impressed and unsettled me at the same time, reminiscent perhaps of stories I had heard about Jews who for centuries lived in exile, yet remained connected to their identity and their homeland. Later that year, I met Nader. This time we were at the home of Doris and Jim, who by then had become known as the mother and father of the San Diego Jewish-Palestinian Dialogue Group.

Nader was dressed in a coat and tie. He was helping himself to food, when I approached and introduced myself. He told me his name was Nader, which he pronounced "Nayder," as Americans would say it, as in Ralph Nader.

"You must mean Nader," I said using the Arabic pronunciation of his name, which is more like "Nadehr."

"How do you know?" he asked.

"I am an Israeli, and I know how the name is pronounced."

He abruptly turned away and left the room, wasting no time on niceties. I was surprised. It was the first time anyone I met through the group was less than cordial and friendly.

As the meeting went on, Nader shared his story with the group: "I was born in Nazareth to a Muslim family, and we had Jewish and Christian neighbors." I later learned that his ancestors had come to Nazareth with Ibrahim Pasha of Egypt, who conquered Palestine in 1831. The family had a cemetery of its own in Nazareth, where generations of the Elbanna family had been laid to rest.

Nader continued: "In 1948, we had to leave Palestine, to leave our beautiful home in Nazareth, and were forced to live in a tent in Zarqa, in the desert." Nader was two-and-a-half years old when his father, acting as any responsible father would (and thousands of other Palestinian fathers did), took the family across the Jordan River, intending to return once the fighting was over. They ended up in a refugee camp in the city of Zarqa, north of Amman, Jordan. During that time however, Palestine was destroyed, its people were scattered, and the state of Israel was founded. The new state did not allow any of the Palestinians who left to return to their homes and land. They were to remain refugees forever.

Nader lifted himself by his own bootstraps and began a career in the Jordanian military, eventually graduating as an officer from the Royal Jordanian Military College. He remained in the Jordanian army until September 1970,[1] when he retired from military life and became a businessman. He decided to bring his family to the U.S. in 1988, around the same time that Gila and I did. He has six children, and his two youngest boys are about the same age as my boys Eitan and Doron.

At one point during the meeting, Nader said something that really caught my attention. "I was a captain in the Jordanian army, and I fought in the battle of Karame." *In Karame! On the other side!* My brother Yoav was in Karame; a lieutenant at the time, he commanded a tank platoon. I was not sure my Jewish-American friends could fully appreciate the significance of this historical battle.

It was a milestone in the relations between Israel and the Palestinian resistance, particularly Yasser Arafat's Fatah movement. The battle began on the night

---

1 Ongoing clashes between Jordanian forces and Palestinian *fedayeen* led to a full civil war in September of 1970, the result of which was the expulsion of the PLO from Jordan. Palestinians who served in the Jordanian army refused to fight against their Palestinian brothers and were discharged from the army.

of March 21, 1968. At the insistence of Israeli Defense Minister Moshe Dayan, a major Israeli army offensive took place in the village of Karame, east of the Jordan River. Fatah headquarters were located in the village, and Yasser Arafat was based there with a few hundred Palestinian fighters, or *fedayeen*. In what was the first open battle between the Jewish army and the Palestinians since 1948, Israel mobilized more than a hundred tanks, the entire 35th Airborne Brigade, Special Forces commando units, several air force squadrons, and an entire reservist infantry brigade. The massive Israeli forces were too cumbersome. The tanks got stuck in mud, delaying the attack and ruining any element of surprise. Arafat, who was barely known to the world until then, was informed by Jordanian intelligence that a large-scale Israeli military attack on the town was underway. During the battle that ensued, the Palestinians suffered heavy loses but they held their ground, surprising the Israeli military with their audacity. The Jordanian army, in which Nader served as a young officer, got involved in the fighting, supporting the Palestinians and defending its sovereign territory against the invading army.

The U.S. was vehemently against the attack. The U.S. ambassador to the United Nations, Arthur Goldberg, said that actions such as this, on a scale so out of proportion, "are greatly to be deplored." The battle achieved mythic proportions in the Arab World and on December 13, 1968, *Time Magazine* did a story about Fatah, and Arafat's face appeared on the cover, bringing his image to the world for the first time. The title on the cover was, "The Arab Commandos – Defiant New Force in the Middle East."

In Arabic, Karame means "dignity." For Israel, the battle of Karame has become synonymous with humiliation.

Nader ended with his personal narrative of the battle: "My best friend, Ibrahim al Shahshir, was hit by a phosphorous rocket shot from an Israeli tank, and he died slowly as I held him in my arms."

When the meeting was over, I wanted to go up to Nader, but I was not sure what to say. So I walked over, told him that my brother had also fought in Karame, and gave him my lapel pin. It had the Palestinian and Israeli flags side by side, one of the few such pins I still had from the days of my father's activism. When my father wore it, displaying the Palestinian flag was illegal in Israel. It meant a great deal to me, and I wore it to all the dialogue meetings. Later Nader would say, "At first I thought Miko was a spy sent by the Mossad, and I was sure that I would have to fight him that night. Then I saw he was wearing a pin with the Palestinian flag. I had never seen, nor did I ever think I would see, an Israeli wearing a Palestinian flag."

Several months later, Nader's daughter Rania came to a dialogue meeting. She is tall and thin and wears glasses and a *hijab*, the scarf that devout Muslim woman wear over their head. With her quiet demeanor and traditional Muslim head covering, it was hard to anticipate what she would be like.

"When I decided to become a devout Muslim, I learned I had to put aside my prejudices." She spoke quietly and articulated her thoughts clearly. "Islam drove me to get to know the "other" and to be a better listener. So I decided to reach out and meet Jewish people and Israeli people, which is why I am here. I think it made me a better person." Rania's words took many of us by surprise. None of the Jewish-Americans in the group had ever met a Palestinian woman who was also a devout Muslim, and neither had I. She was also the only one among the Palestinian women who wore a hijab.

A few more months passed before I saw Nader again at another meeting. He mentioned that he was a member of the Rotary club of Escondido, a city in north San Diego County. I had joined the Coronado Rotary club several years before. I had no idea what Rotary was when I joined, but I quickly learned about the tremendous amount of important work Rotary does around the world. Even with its conservative reputation and my less-than-conservative views on just about everything, I made many friends and colleagues in the Coronado Rotary club and throughout the Rotary world.

When I learned that Nader was a member of Rotary too, it gave me an idea. We were both from the same land, we both participated in Jewish-Palestinian dialogue in San Diego, and we were both members of large Rotary clubs. We had important stories to tell, and I knew his manner of speech was capable of moving audiences deeply. So I made a proposal: "Why don't you and I start speaking together at Rotary clubs?"

Initially, he was skeptical, but he was also a little receptive. Although it took time, eventually trust grew between us, and Nader became more confident in expressing himself and his identity as an American who is a Palestinian and a Muslim. We began speaking at Rotary clubs all over San Diego County (there were 33 in the area), and we were a hit. We became known as the Israeli and Palestinian Rotarians who saw a bigger picture and managed to get along despite their obvious differences. We ended up spending a lot of time together, and we started to become friends.

"You must bring your family to visit us in Coronado," I said to Nader one day. He was hesitant at first. I think he was not completely comfortable because he did not know what to expect. He had never been to the home of an Israeli family. The fact that Israelis had destroyed his country and driven his family into a refugee camp in the desert was no small thing. It took a leap of faith to place his family at the "mercy" of another Israeli family.

Eventually he agreed. As Nader likes to tell the story, "We came to Coronado to visit and share lunch, planning to stay no more than two hours." At around 1 p.m., he and his wife Afaf and their two younger boys, Sami and Yusef, arrived. Afaf, a devout Muslim woman from a very conservative background, and Gila, a secular Israeli girl from a kibbutz, hit it off right away. They went off talking, and I took

Nader to show him a video I had just seen about Palestine. The boys disappeared with Eitan and Doron, only to come out from time to time and announce, "We're hungry." We all had lunch and the two hours turned to four, and four to six. We kept talking and the kids kept playing. We all went for a walk on the bay.

"Look." I pointed to our kids, who were way ahead of us on their scooters. "Israeli and Palestinian kids who don't even know they are supposed to be enemies."

Nader looked at them and sighed. "They are the future."

Before we knew it, Gila and Afaf were talking about preparing dinner. "After dinner we really must go," Afaf insisted. It was nearly midnight when they got up to leave, and then the boys emerged from the playroom. "Can Sami and Yusef spend the night?" I looked at Gila, who didn't seem to mind. "Sure, why not. As long as their parents say it's OK." Afaf and Nader were caught a bit by surprise. It took them a minute or two and finally they gave their consent.

I thought little of it at the time. Our kids have friends spend the night quite often. But it turned out that for Nader this carried a special significance. He never imagined his two sons would ever spend the night at the home of a Jewish-Israeli family.

The year 2002 was marked by the birth of our daughter Tali. Gila's pregnancies were not easy, and so it took me six years before I was able to convince her to have a third child. After yet another difficult pregnancy and painful delivery, Gila gave birth to Tali on September 28, 2002.

In January of 2003, Rotarian friends had invited Nader and I to join a new committee being formed by Rotary district 5340, the district to which both of our clubs belonged. It was called Pathways to Peace and its mission was to highlight Rotary's peace-building efforts. I thought this new committee presented some good opportunities for us, and indeed it did. Rotary is an organization made up of people who take on impossible tasks and make them happen, and those were just the kind of people with whom we needed to be in touch.

By this point, I'd been participating in dialogue groups for a couple of years, and Nader and I had been speaking together for some time. After each talk people would come up to us, often with tears in their eyes: "What you do is so wonderful, how can I help?" Or, "Please keep up this wonderful partnership, you give me hope." And, "Let me know if there is anything I can do." We gave a talk at a Rotary seminar at the Salk Institute near UCSD, and as soon as we were done people came over to us and said, "Where is the pitch? Why are you not asking for money or something that will help you get something started?"

These comments, in addition to the fact that I was beginning to feel restless in my limited peace-promoting roles, made me think it was time to act, to do something beyond participating in dialogue and talk. But what? Nader and I were having lunch at Aladdin's restaurant in San Diego one day when I brought up the subject.

"I feel the same way," Nader agreed. "We need to do more than talk."

Our Rotary district was wrapping up a project to send wheelchairs to the Republic of Malawi, and I said to Nader, "Why not wheelchairs?" I had done some research and learned that there was a desperate need for wheelchairs among Israelis and Palestinians. Gaza alone needed over 20,000 wheelchairs at the time. "Maybe we can do 'Wheelchairs to the Holy Land'?" We agreed to raise money for 1,000 chairs, 500 hundred for Israelis and 500 hundred for Palestinians.

We went with this idea to the Pathways to Peace Committee, and everyone liked it. Mike Bardin, one of the co-chairs of the committee, said, "It's a great idea, but be careful, the devil is in the details," and he was right.

We decided that the majority of the funding would come from individual Rotarians who would contribute directly to the project, which we did end up calling "Wheelchairs to the Holy Land." We spoke at Rotary club meetings for more than a year raising the money. Some people were moved to tears seeing the two of us standing side by side, addressing the issues respectfully as friends and partners. But it wasn't all smooth sailing. Some of the presentations were tricky, and we had to navigate through some difficult questions: Why should we help those Palestinian terrorists, when they can't even help themselves? Why do Israelis get half when clearly Palestinians are in much greater need? It helped that we gave the presentations together. We knew we were walking a fine line and wanted to stay away from politics as much as possible and focus on the human aspect.

On March 22, 2004, I'd just landed at the San Diego airport returning from a trip, when Nader called, sounding very upset. "Go home and listen to the news," he said.

An Israeli Apache helicopter shot three missiles and killed the Hamas leader Sheikh Ahmed Yassin as he was wheeled out after morning prayer at a Gaza mosque. Yassin, an aged quadriplegic, was the founder and spiritual leader of Hamas. According to reports, seven bystanders were killed, including his two bodyguards. An additional 12 bystanders were injured, among them Yassin's two sons. "How can we keep talking while this is going on?" Nader pleaded. "I want you to cancel tomorrow's presentation, I can't do this anymore." We had a presentation the following day that had been scheduled months in advance.

"Tell them how hard it is, tell them how you feel about the assassination of Sheikh Yassin," I suggested. "We don't have to pretend that all is well. If all was well we wouldn't have to do this work." I convinced Nader to do the presentation as planned, and he later agreed that it was the right thing to do. Still, it was not easy for him.

When we spoke at the Coronado Rotary club, my club, a huge crowd gathered to hear us. The club meets at the Hotel Del Coronado and has around 200 members. In an average meeting about 100 members show up, and if the program is a good one then more will come. This time, extra chairs and tables were brought into the hall to accommodate the seemingly endless influx of members and guests. Nader showed up sick, running a high fever. "I will be fine, don't worry, I will never let you down."

The presentation went well. The slideshow worked smoothly, I was feeling relaxed, and the mood in the club was generous and supportive. Then as the Q&A session was wrapping up, a question came straight out of left field: "What do you say about Yasser Arafat?" We had wanted to stay away from political issues as much as possible, and no topic was more politically divisive than Yasser Arafat. Half the world—and, I suspected, most of the people present at our presentation—saw him as a villain. The other half, including me, did not. I stepped back to collect my thoughts; there seemed to be no way to respond without pissing someone off.

Then Nader stepped up to the microphone. "Yasser Arafat," he said, "he is just a man. Sitting in a small room with a cell phone. All he can do is order pizza." He brought the house down. It was our most successful presentation in terms of raising funds.

One local youth ministry approached us wanting to support our project. They were so sincere and enthusiastic that at first it seemed too good to be true. But it wasn't. They put together a "Walk for Wheelchairs" fundraiser for us and raised a total of $8,000, much of which they gave us in bags of change from people of very little means who believed in our cause.

We also applied for a matching grant from Rotary International and were approved for $25,000, which brought us to a total of $84,000. This translated to 1,280 wheelchairs, or four shipping containers. We were very, very happy. We were told that previous Rotary projects like ours had purchased the chairs from the Wheelchair Foundation (TWF), a company that matched donations and arranged for the chairs to be built and shipped.

After we sent the money to TWF, I received a receipt for $84,000 and a note saying, "Thank you for raising money to send wheelchairs to help children in Israel." I called immediately to correct them: "We specifically stated that half the wheelchairs were going to Israel and half to the Palestinian Authority."

It took several e-mail messages and phone calls to realize that this problem was not going away. Someone had decided to thwart the Palestinian half of the project. Regardless of how many times I explained that the whole premise of the project was full equality between Israelis and Palestinians—one dollar for Palestinians, one for Israelis—I could not get through to anyone.

I finally spoke to the company's president, and he promised he would look into it. We were on the phone several times. I was insistent: "We are not going to compromise on this issue. I have an interview tomorrow with the *San Diego Union-Tribune*, and I have no problem telling them your organization jeopardized the project. Hundreds of people gave us their money because we promised equality and fairness."

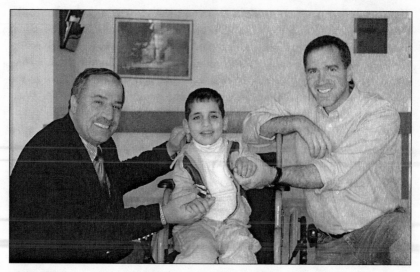

Nader Elbanna and one of the beneficiaries of our wheelchair outreach.

He got back to me that day saying they would go ahead with our project, but his company would only be responsible for delivering the chairs to the nearest Israeli port. It would be up to us to get the wheelchairs into the West Bank. With the help of an American chapter of the Equestrian Order of the Holy Sepulcher, a humanitarian nongovernmental organization (NGO), we secured a home for the Palestinian chairs at the Arab Rehabilitation Hospital in Beit Jala near Bethlehem, as well as someone to pick up and deliver the chairs.

What I told the people at the Wheelchair Foundation was true. In May of 2006, John Wilkens, a senior reporter with *The San Diego Union-Tribune*[2] had contacted me saying he wanted to do a story about our project. It just so happened that we met on Nader's birthday.

I knew that John Wilkens pieces were always major stories but I was still unprepared for what I saw when I opened the Sunday paper: a huge photo of Nader and me posing together and a feature-length story including smaller photos from previous visits to the Middle East that I had given John. I received calls from many Jewish and non-Jewish friends who saw the story and congratulated us for it. One particular moving phone call came from Dr. Stephen Drossman, the doctor who had delivered our children.

But then, in the summer of 2006, Israel launched a large military operation into South Lebanon. This led to rocket retaliation by Hezbollah[3], and the tem-

---

2 *The San Diego Union-Tribune* is now the *U-T San Diego*.
3 Hezbollah is a Shi'a Islamic group based in Lebanon. Its militia is credited in part with forcing the Israeli military to end its occupation of southern Lebanon.

porary closure of Israel's northern port in Haifa. The people at the Wheelchair Foundation wanted to call the whole thing off again. Once more, I insisted we couldn't. Israel had two ports in the south, Ashkelon and Ashdod, either of which would serve our purposes just as well.

In the end, the chairs arrived in Ashdod in December 2006, one month ahead of schedule. The two containers addressed to the Israeli NGO Yad Sarah and the Rotary club of Nazareth had no problem clearing customs and reaching their destinations.

The two containers intended for the Palestinian Authority did not fare as well. The Israeli authorities stated security considerations, and they held the containers for two months. It took the American consulate's intervention and a great deal of persistence, mostly by our good friend Chuck Radloff, who happened to be in Israel at the time and saw to it that the job got done. At last, thanks to Muna Katan, who was instrumental in getting the chairs to their destination and volunteered to pay the $7,000 in holding fees that the Israeli authorities charged us, the two containers reached the Rehabilitation Hospital in Beit Jala. Our mission was truly accomplished.

Chapter 9:

The Fear Virus

In 2003, Nader was granted a U.S. passport and was finally eligible to return to his homeland, as a tourist, for the first time after more than fifty years in exile. Gila and I were in Israel at the time, so we decided to drive up to Nazareth to visit him and meet his extended family.

If anyone had asked me then whether I was afraid of Arabs, or of visiting an Arab city or country, I would have said, "No, of course not. Why should I be?" I was an open-minded person, wasn't I? And my father was Matti Peled, for God's sake—I knew as well as anyone else that not all Palestinians were terrorists. So it came as a real shock when, that summer, I realized just how deeply embedded my fear was.

Driving from Jerusalem toward the Galilee in the north, the scenery was beautiful. The roads were wide, and the Palestinian towns we saw along the way were pretty in their way: minarets rising prominently in the sky; older homes snuggling close together and the more affluent ones featuring the reddish tint of "Jerusalem stone."

However, as soon as we entered the city of Nazareth, a sense of alienation descended upon me like a dark cloud. The street signs and billboards screamed at me in Arabic. I realized I was surrounded by Arabs, and suddenly everything spelled danger. I was sure that we stood out as clueless foreigners. Still, I couldn't have put my finger on it, what it was exactly that I feared. Would they (*they!*) attack us? Was there a mob somewhere waiting to assault Jews? I realize now that, despite my politics, I was indeed afraid, and that this fear existed deep in the recesses of my mind, where I can only guess it was nurtured for years. Moreover, I had to exercise enormous control to prevent it from consuming me.

We looked for the home of Abu Najib, Nader's oldest uncle, and I soon realized I had no idea how to find it in this city that, at the time, was completely foreign to me.

"We have to stop and ask for directions," I admitted to Gila reluctantly.

My wife looked at me. "But who should we ask? Is it safe for us to get out of the car?"

The thought of admitting we were lost and vulnerable in this seemingly hostile environment seemed tantamount to inviting an assault. In that moment, we became the defenseless Jews that we were brought up to be, just like our forefathers in the ghettos of Eastern Europe.

But what choice did we have? "We have to trust somebody or face the absurd prospect of giving up and returning to Jerusalem," I said.

Logic reminded me that I had been active in dialogue groups for a couple of years in California, and there was certainly no reason to fear talking with Palestinians in my own country. But *was* this my own country? Nazareth looked nothing like the country I knew. The buildings were older, the roads were narrower and more crowded, signs pointed to ancient Christian sites, and the conversations that floated above the streets were all in Arabic. It was a dense and chaotic place, mostly because it had had nowhere to expand—the reality in many Palestinian towns because Israel took so much of their land. Regardless, it was not the Israel I was familiar with. Not even the Israeli Police could be found in Nazareth.

I took a deep breath, stopped the car, and asked a young man for directions. He didn't know where the house was, so he started asking people around him.

Great, I thought, now everyone knows that we are Jews and we are lost.

The young man eventually found someone who could direct us to the house. He spoke to us in Hebrew, which in hindsight shouldn't have surprised me because we were in Israel after all. He helped us as much as he could, leaving his shop to come out and point us in the right direction.

We had to stop and ask for directions several more times, and each time it became easier. People were either indifferent to our presence or eager to help us out and make us feel welcome. I couldn't help thinking, *these people are nice.* Which more than anything, showed how different I felt from "these people." It wasn't until much later that I realized the significance of this moment—not so much in terms of overcoming my fears, but in terms of realizing and accepting that I *had* fears in spite of who I thought I was.

We finally made our way to the home of Abu Najib. It was a large house, several stories high, and the entire family was gathered in the dining room. Two older cousins of Nader, seated by the doorway, were performing what Nader told me later were ancient songs to welcome a son back from exile. The celebrations were not for us but for Nader, who had not seen his family in decades. A table was laid with food and children were everywhere.

We were welcomed immediately and made to feel at home, and I could not help notice the absence of the more Western restraints that my culture had adopted and that typically made visitors less comfortable when visiting people for the first time. When the meal was over and the excitement subsided, Nader took us to see members of the Nazareth Rotary Club, one of the oldest and most active Rotary clubs in the Middle East. The club had programs to build health clinics, sponsor Boy Scout troops, and deliver aid to people in the West Bank, among many other projects.

When Nader introduced me, he said, "Do you know who Miko's father is? Matti Peled."

Their faces lit up.

"Abu Salaam!" they said. Father of Peace. "Of course we know Abu Salaam."

Nader looked at me and beamed.

This was the first time I heard my father called by that name. I was aware, of course, that he'd worked closely with Palestinians in Israel and was well known in the Palestinian-Israeli community. But it didn't hit me until then how much of an impact his involvement had really made. Everywhere I traveled, both inside Israel and in the West Bank, I would hear my father referred to as *Abu Salaam*, as people shook my hand with great emotion. I heard stories for the first time about how he vehemently opposed the massive land confiscations Palestinians had to endure, helped those who had legal issues, and spoke out against injustices when people were detained or deported. The truth is that at the time I didn't know the full extent of what my father did for peace and what it meant to so many people.

Gila and I spent the entire day in Nazareth, seeing what the city had to offer. We went to Nazareth Village, a re-creation of what Nazareth was like in the time that Jesus lived. We visited some of the lovely churches and hostels, like Saint Gabriel, that make up the Nazareth landscape. We returned to Jerusalem late at night, and I felt as though a heavy load had been lifted off my chest. It was a relief from the strain of fear.

The next day Nader and his family came to visit Jerusalem and met us at my mother's home in Motza. I showed Nader my father's study, which my mother keeps neat and tidy, where the photos of Dr. Issam Sartawi and David Ben-Gurion still hang side by side.

Once you have developed trust, it allows you to cultivate more trust. You've got to really get out of your comfort zone and meet it halfway. This was true in every case I experienced, from that first trip to Majeed Khoury's house in San Diego, through the visit to Nazareth, and into the next phase of my journey—the occupied West Bank.

Now that I'd become aware of the fear in my life, I wanted to get rid of it once and for all. If there was ever to be peace, there had to be complete trust, and that can only come through individuals reaching across, if not breaking down, the wall of fear. But Israeli security regulations made it impossible to reach out to the other side without breaking the law. Under Israeli law, it is illegal for Israelis to visit any place within Area A, a designation for presumably hostile territories that includes all the main cities in the West Bank (supposedly under complete Palestinian control). It infuriated me that I wasn't allowed to visit people because they lived on the other side of a border neither one of us had any part in creating.

This sign is placed at every point of entry into Palestinian controlled areas: "Entry for Israelis into Area A is Forbidden, Dangerous, and Constitutes a Felony!!"

In fact I was beginning to believe that the security reasons cited by the Israeli officials for the wall and the checkpoints, which were keeping us from visiting and getting to know people on the "other side," were merely scare tactics designed to prolong the conflict.

So when Rami and Nurit said they were making a rare trip to see friends in a Palestinian town called Beit Ummar, near Hebron, I jumped at the chance to join them. They were taking their son Yigal, Smadar's younger brother, who was 11 years old at the time. I asked my eldest son Eitan, who was nine, if he wanted to join us, and he said sure.

It would be my first visit to the West Bank since my military service, and I took the trip against the express concerns of many people who were dear to me. My sister Ossi was furious. "Never mind you taking stupid risks, but taking a child to a hostile place? Have you lost your mind?" Gila and my mother were at a loss: talking about peace and justice was well and good but venturing into "enemy territory," which is how most Israelis view the West Bank, was reckless. In the end I prevailed, and we left for what was to be the first of many visits to Beit Ummar.

We were going to see Khaled and Ali Abu Awwad, two brothers whom Rami and Nurit knew from the Bereaved Families Forum. Because Israel built modern highways leading into the West Bank for the use of Israeli settlers, the drive there was very smooth. Travel on most of these roads is prohibited for Palestinians, however, and it is not until you are quite close to Beit Ummar that you begin to notice the green Palestinian license plates, easily distinguishable from the yellow Israel plates.

When we arrived, Ali was waiting for us on the porch, which was emblazoned with a sticker in Hebrew that read: "It will not end until we talk to one another." Eitan and Yigal played with the other kids who were there, and we just sat and chatted. Beit Ummar is an agricultural town noted for its many grapevines and its specialties of stuffed grape leaves and a grape syrup called *dibs*. It also has hundreds of cherry, plum, apple, and olive trees.

The real process of getting to know one another would take place over the course of several years, and the bonds that tie my family with the Abu Awwad family become ever deeper with each year. Khaled has the quality of being the natural leader of any space he occupies. He has jet-black hair and an olive complexion, and his face is serious and agonized like the hero of a Greek tragedy, but not harsh. The depth of his Hebrew is enviable, and hearing him speak you might think he spent years in the university studying it, but he didn't.

Ali is tall and skinny with curly black hair, an energetic organizer who fiercely believes in principled non-violent resistance to the Israeli occupation. Both brothers spent time in Israeli prisons for their role in the first *Intifada*, the first Palestinian Uprising. Their mother, Fatima Abu Awwad was an admired leader of the *Fatah* cell in Beit Ummar and she spent a great deal of time in and out of prison.

In the fall of 2000, at the beginning of the second *Intifada*, Israeli settlers shot Ali in the leg. While he was in Saudi Arabia getting treatment, and Khaled was visiting him, they got word that their older brother Yusef, 31 years old, married, and the father of two children, had been shot. They were told he was injured, but when they got home they heard that a soldier with whom Yusef had apparently argued shot him point blank and killed him. This took place at the checkpoint at the entrance to Beit Ummar.

A few months later, in February 2001, Israel settlers shot and killed another brother, Saed, 14 years old. Neither crime was investigated, nor was anyone ever brought to justice. Beit Ummar has many similar stories.

We spent all afternoon together in Beit Ummar. Nurit wanted to make sure we got there after lunch but before dinner, so they wouldn't feel they had to feed us. When we arrived, she insisted we were only going to have tea.

Ali looked at Nurit and smiled. "You are going to eat. The question is do you want to eat now or a little later?"

So, as usual, we stayed longer than we planned, and they fed us like kings. Eitan and I had *maqlouba*, a signature Palestinian dish, for the first time. It is a casserole of chicken and rice that is embedded with potatoes and cauliflower, served with savory yogurt.

It was dark by the time we left. We all piled into the car and drove in silence for a while.

"I am so glad we went," I said.

"Yes it was very special," Rami agreed.

There could have been nothing more natural than this visit to Beit Ummar, except of course that we were all supposed to be enemies.

As we passed the checkpoint, Rami's phone rang. Khaled wanted to know: "Did you pass the checkpoint all right?"

"Yes, we're fine," Rami reassured him.

About 15 minutes later, Khaled called again, just to be really sure.

The last time I was attacked and fought hard to overcome the "fear virus" was in December of 2005. I decided to visit the West Bank on my own for the first time. I drove from Jerusalem to Bil'in, a Palestinian village west of Ramallah that has distinguished itself by its commitment to non-violent resistance to the Israeli occupation. In a story shown on Israeli television news at that time, Bil'in was described as a small and impoverished village. They made no mention that it was neither small nor impoverished until Israel confiscated 60 percent of its land to build a Jewish settlement and the Separation Wall. The wall actually ended up separating mostly Palestinians from one another and from their own land and was eventually deemed illegal by an international court.[1] The settlement that was built, Modi'in Illit, offered apartment buildings for Orthodox Jews on Bil'in land at very low prices.

Every Friday since February of 2005, local residents, Palestinians from the surrounding areas, and Israeli and international peace activists have been gathering in Bil'in to protest the confiscation of land. Even though the protests are peaceful, they have been met with heavy-handed treatment by the Israeli army. That includes large amounts of tear gas, rubber-coated bullets, and live ammunition. The more persistence the people of Bil'in demonstrate, the more brutal the force employed against them by Israel's army.

An Israeli peace activist wrote to me and told me about Bil'in and particularly about Mohammed El Khatib, who is one of the leaders of this non-violent resistance movement in Bil'in. She suggested that I speak to him, and she gave me his cell phone number.

I was intrigued; the persistence of the Bil'in people was very moving. So I called Mohammed El Khatib from the U.S. and told him I wanted to visit Bil'in and meet him. I told him I got his number from an activist friend, and he introduced himself as the head of the local council of Bil'in. Though relatively unknown at the time, today his name is synonymous with the Bil'in struggle, which is one of the most important elements of the greater non-violent Palestinian struggle. We spoke on the phone several times, and when I visited Israel in December 2005, I finally had a chance to meet him.

---

1 On July 9, 2004, the International Court of Justice declared the route of the barrier to be in violation of international law because it was built within occupied Palestinian land rather than along the Green Line border. The vast majority of the wall is built inside the West Bank, not along the border.

I traveled to Bil'in in a rental car with the yellow Israeli license plates. I was worried that this made me easily identifiable as an Israeli. If Nazareth frightened me at first, the West Bank was the lion's den—and this time I was alone. Once I passed the last checkpoint and was in the occupied West Bank, the demons began running around in my head like crazy. I had failed to determine where, exactly, I was supposed to meet Mohammed, and I had no idea what he looked like.

I also did not know exactly where Bil'in was. Somehow I had assumed he would meet me as soon as I entered the Palestinian territories, and I was disappointed when I realized I was wrong. As I drove through the winding hill roads, I could see none of their pastoral beauty. Just as in so many storybooks I read as a child, I could only see Arabs lurking behind every curve of the winding road, every rise in the land, waiting to harm me.

At one point I picked up a day laborer who needed a ride to his village, which was on the way. He had a speech impediment and spoke no Hebrew, but he uttered the word "Bil'in" and pointed me in the right direction. I dropped him off where he wanted, and I was driving alone once again.

I called Mohammad several times from the car to be reassured that I had followed the right path. But even with his reassurance, I was scared. Everything I had ever learned told me this trip was a terrible mistake.

The road to Bil'in was full of anxiety and uncertainty.

Finally I stopped by a small house where an elderly couple sat in their front yard.

"Bil'in?" I asked.

"*Hadha Bil'in*," the old man replied. This is Bil'in.

I called Mohammed again, and he said to keep going until I reached the mosque. As I maneuvered through the potholed streets, I saw a lot of graffiti in Arabic, a few posters of Hamas leader Sheikh Ahmad Yassin, and many posters of Abu Ammar (the *nom de guerre* of Yasser Arafat), which I found to be comforting. I never would have thought a poster of Arafat would be a comforting sight. I also saw children, lots and lots of children, in uniforms, with backpacks on their shoulders, going to and from school, some with their arms slung around each other, chatting and laughing.

At last I found Mohammed near his home. He was a young man, the father of three. No sooner did I arrive than his mother brought out a freshly baked pastry topped with fried cauliflower and eggplant for me. We talked for a while, and then he said he wanted me to meet two friends of his.

We got back in my car, and he directed me. We had just pulled off the main road and into an unpaved alley when out of nowhere came two young men. They had dark hair, dark skin, and an unshaven look—in other words, they looked exactly like the young Palestinian men I had been conditioned to see as dangerous. They were Eymad Burnat, the filmmaker, and Iyad Burnat—two brothers who have built their reputations by courageously facing off against the Israeli army in countless protests. They were among Bil'in's resistance leaders, principled young men and fathers, equally dedicated to justice for their people and to non-violence.

The four of us walked together toward the edge of town where the Separation Wall was being constructed. Since there was no army present at the time, we ventured into the "seam zone"—the area between the wall's route and the Green

Mohammed El Khatib is one of the leaders of the non-violent resistance movement in Bil'in.

Line—an area prohibited to Palestinians. It is interesting, by contrast, that Israeli law allowed any Jew in the world, whether an Israeli citizen or not, to live on that land.

We managed to walk all the way to the settlement of Modi'in Illit without being stopped and saw some of the huge apartment complexes being built on Bil'in's land for a planned Orthodox Jewish community.

The sheer size of the buildings struck me. This was a massive project. Billions had been invested. *These settlements are not going away,* I thought, *and this land will never be handed back to its rightful owners.*

I recalled the idea of land swaps that is often mentioned in Israel as a solution to the building of settlements on Palestinian land. According to this idea, when it comes time to make peace, Palestinians will be compensated for the land taken from them to build Israeli settlements. Israel will give them land elsewhere. Suddenly, it seemed like a totally insane notion. Families from Bil'in would be given land somewhere miles away, probably in the Negev Desert, in return for these choice ancestral lands right next to their village. I found it hard to believe that anyone really took this seriously. Was there a single Israeli who would agree to take a land swap like that?

Mohammad insisted we talk to some of the residents, who were either moving in or had already done so. Many had only recently immigrated to Israel and barely spoke Hebrew. Mohammed, on the other hand, spoke Hebrew quite well. I couldn't help but think it ironic that these new immigrants, who could barely converse in Hebrew, had rights over these lands that the Palestinians were denied, simply because they were Jewish. Quite unbelievable!

We walked up and down the streets, moving farther from Bil'in and deeper into the settlement area. I felt uncomfortable, worried that these guys would get in trouble.

Their courage inspired me. They were the ones taking the risk, and if they didn't care, I sure wasn't going to stop them; I had come to support them.

After several attempts at striking up a conversation with the new residents of this neighborhood, none of whom spoke Hebrew, we found an immigrant from Britain who did understand. We introduced ourselves, and he asked if we wanted to see his apartment, apologizing that it was not yet furnished because his young family had just moved. He seemed to have no problem inviting me, along with two young Palestinians from the nearby Bil'in, into his home.

"Do you know where the real-estate developer got the land?" Mohammed asked the settler.

"Yes," he said, "we saw the bill of sale. It was purchased from the people of Bil'in at a fair price."

"Who showed you the bill of sale?"

"The mayor of Modi'in Illit."

"I'm head of the town council of Bil'in, and I can tell you that no one has sold this land, it was taken by force."

"Well, that's what the mayor told me."

"I will tell you what," Mohammed said, as he took out his cell phone. "I have his number, let me call him."

Mohammed rang him, but the mayor of Modi'in Illit didn't answer.

I marveled as I watched Mohammed asking all these questions, completely relaxed, knowing that even though this was Bil'in land, he could be arrested and held for an indefinite period if soldiers showed up and found us there.

Now I was becoming curious. I asked the resident, "How much did you pay for the apartment?"

"Only $80,000, which is why we moved here from the nearby town of Modi'in." Modi'in is only about a mile or two away but is still on the Israel side of what used to be the border. This was a four-bedroom luxury apartment, with easy access to Jerusalem and Tel Aviv.

It was all strangely pleasant and civil given the bizarrely charged circumstances. I suppose because the man ultimately had no qualms about his rights this land. We thanked him for graciously letting us into his new home and walked back toward Bil'in.

As we were leaving the settlement, a security guard gave us a suspicious look, clearly wondering why these Arabs were wandering around the neighborhood. I challenged him in Hebrew: "Is there a problem?" He walked away mumbling something about "damn peaceniks." I was afraid he might call the army and turn this into a scene.

Walking back to Bil'in, we could see Palestinian day laborers with their heads hanging low going home from the settlement construction site.

"What do you think of these Palestinians who are building the settlement?" I asked. I don't know what I was expecting, but Mohammed's response both surprised and comforted me.

"They have no choice because they need to feed their children," he said, "and since Israel confiscated their land there is no other work available to them."

But as these laborers walked past us, it was clear they were not proud.

Considering that the Jewish settlements in the West Bank symbolize, more than anything else, the declining possibility for Palestinians to gain freedom and independence, Mohammed's explanation was worth noting. There were, and probably still are, national resistance movements that would not look so kindly on their own people participating in an act that obstructed their very struggle for freedom. In other places, they would be punished for collaborating.

Back in Bil'in, the four of us talked more about the situation. Mohammed was emphatic: "We completely refuse to participate in any violent resistance." He had just returned from Jordan, and he was kept for eight hours at the border crossing by the *Shabak*, Israel's internal intelligence service. "They try to get us to react with violence, but they won't succeed," he continued, "and we will not give up the fight either."

The army is answerable to no one and the residents of Bil'in have no recourse, no law that protects them or their property. Still, non-violence was like a religion for these men.

I knew that violent resistance, or terrorism—for which the Palestinians had become known around the world—represented only of a fraction of Palestinians. But until then, I was not aware of the prevalence of more peaceful responses. Khaled and Ali from the Bereaved Families forum had spoken of non-violence and now I was hearing about it again. In fact, the bulk of Palestinian resistance has always been non-violent, but the violent armed struggle is what receives media attention. The vast majority of Palestinians in Israeli prisons were convicted of non-violent political resistance. What makes the Bil'in non-violent movement unique is their persistence even in the face of violent Israeli measures.

We were all getting hungry and Iyad and Eymad asked to use my car to go buy groceries for dinner. Everything I'd been taught as an Israeli told me that lending a rented car with Israeli plates to a couple of young Palestinians in the West Bank was a breach of security of the highest order. These guys might seem nice now, but did I know who they really were? Wasn't it the perfect opportunity to take advantage of a naïve Israeli like myself? What if they disappeared, leaving me stranded here, where I might be killed? What if they use the car to plant a bomb? It was not an easy decision.

Letting go of my fear and placing my trust in these committed young activists was not a choice, it was a mission. I had driven all the way to Bil'in to meet them, and I had spent the entire day with them. They were the type of men who would make any nation proud. They were husbands and fathers of young children, and they deliberately and consistently refused to engage in violence, just as they refused to accept the injustice imposed on them by the Israeli occupation.

Another companion in Bil'in, Iyad Burnat and I walking to the weekly protest.

I gave them the keys to the car. Half an hour later they returned with meat, vegetables, and yogurt, and soon we were feasting on kebabs, roasted veggies, bread, olive oil, and salad.

By the time we finished dinner it was getting dark, and I still had to drive back to Jerusalem. They pointed me in the right direction, and off I went, frightened once again, still involuntarily recalling stories of Palestinian mobs killing innocent Israelis. I told myself that these guys would not put me at risk. They knew I'd be safe, or they would not have let me drive alone.

Along the way, I picked up a couple young schoolboys who asked for a ride. I wanted to fight the urge to run away and to embrace the fact that I was there. If these Palestinian boys were not afraid to get a ride from an Israeli, why should I fear giving them one? They rode with me for a couple miles and thanked me as they got out of the car at their destination. And as I continued to drive through the dark streets of Bil'in, mostly empty by now because of the late hour, I was comforted by their thanks, and by the trust I had in my new friends from Bil'in.

Chapter 10:

The Commanding General's Order

In April 2007, Nader and I went to visit the institutions in Israel and the West Bank that had received our donated wheelchairs. Nader flew to Amman, Jordan, where he has a home, and I flew to Tel Aviv. We planned to meet in Jerusalem.

It was going to be our victory lap. "Wheelchairs to the Holy Land" had succeeded: We had served children on both sides of the conflict, and we had overcome a lot to get the project done. But there was a tremendous gap between my perceptions and reality. Instead of a victory lap, the trip evolved into a long journey that led to a sobering discovery. I arrived in Jerusalem right after the Passover Seder, and I spent a few days with my family before going to meet Nader. It was Easter, and my sister Ossi suggested that we go see one of the most terrific and rare sights taking place in Jerusalem that year.

Ossi, the younger of my two sisters, has always been quiet, smart, and very funny. She and I became friends relatively late in life, probably because I was six years younger than her. She studied and became quite an expert on Eastern Christianity. In particular, she knows a lot about Christian iconography and visiting the various churches in the Holy Land with her is an enlightening experience.

Every four years Easter is celebrated by all the Christian denominations on the same day, and 2007 was one such year. Ossi, her husband Haim, and I ventured into the Old City at 10 p.m. to see what is called *Sabt al Nur*, or "Saturday of Light."

The Old City is contained within ancient walls, and within its narrow streets and alleyways are kept the ancient traditions of Christian, Jewish, and Muslim faiths. It is both a spiritual place, with its churches and mosques and synagogues, and also very earthly, with stores that offer freshly butchered meat, freshly picked fruit and vegetables, sweets, herbs, clothes, fabrics, and knick-knacks of every kind. I have a favorite route that I take every time I visit the Old City, and every time I discover something knew.

On that particular night, when Ossi and I went, young and old, men and women, pilgrims from around the world converged on this small city and marched holding torches, singing and celebrating the resurrection. I had never seen so many people in the Old City, and it amazed me that in all the years I had lived in Jerusalem I had no idea that this took place. We went from one church to another to see how each denomination celebrated the occasion that defined their faith, the resurrection of Jesus of Nazareth.

We began with the Church of the Holy Sepulchre, where old women climbed steep staircases to be close enough to kiss an image of Christ, and priests performed ceremonies in all languages. On the small roof, hundreds of Ethiopian pilgrims huddled together as their priests prayed and performed their indigenous Christian ceremonies. It was moving to see such devotion, and also quite frightening to see how crowded the spaces were and how little was set up in the way of public safety.

By 2 a.m. we came to the glorious Russian Orthodox Church, whose golden onion domes set it apart on the hill across from the Temple Mount. After the service, the congregation exited the church, and the priest made the famous announcement: "*Cristos Anesti*" (Christ has risen), and the crowd replied: "*Alithos Anesti*" (He has risen indeed). Here the priest announced it in every conceivable language, and the crowd responded in their respective native tongue.

I have spent a great deal of time in Jerusalem, and she never ceases to amaze me.

When it was time for Nader and me to meet, I felt worried. I have heard from many Palestinian-American friends how the Israeli authorities harass them when they enter Israel, often holding them for hours before letting them through. I also knew that Nader made a trip from Jordan to Israel with his family six months earlier, 18 people in all including sons and daughters-in-law and grandchildren, some of them babies. As they traversed the bridge into Israel at the northern crossing, the Israeli security officials took their passports and detained them for the entire day.

The Israeli authorities provided them with no explanation, no food or water, and no courtesy. Their passports were returned to them at the end of the day when the crossing was closing. They were all exhausted, and by this point no public transportation was available, which meant they were stranded. Eventually they were able to call a minivan driver who transported workers at the crossing. They paid him several hundred dollars to come back and take them to Nazareth. In the past, when Nader and I crossed together, he was allowed to go through with no delays, and I had good reason to believe that with an Israeli citizen beside him again he would not be harassed.

Nader is a strong and resilient man, but this was more harassment than anyone should have to endure. So I suggested to Rami that he and I take a short trip to Jordan, spend a few days with Nader in Amman, and then all three of us could travel to Israel together. With Rami and I present, I was certain that things would go more smoothly.

Crossing from Israel eastward into Jordan is more than just crossing a river. The Jordan River is the gateway to the East and to the Arab world. My mother had served in the British army and was able to travel all over the Arab world. Stationed in Cairo, she had traveled as far as Beirut and Damascus. My father had visited

With Nader at Fatah Headquarters in Ramallah. Fatah was considered a dangerous enemy for as long as I could remember, but now I was there with friends.

Naguib Mahfouz in Cairo several times, and now it was my turn to get to know the larger neighborhood.

Israel and Jordan have had peaceful relations since 1995, but you can tell that the relationship between the two countries is still strained. In the huge immigration terminal on the Israeli side of the border hangs a larger-than-life photo of the late Jordanian King Hussein bin Talal lighting a cigarette for the late Israeli Prime Minister Yitzhak Rabin. This casual, friendly gesture demonstrates the close relations that existed between the two men. The emptiness of the terminal bore witness to great expectations that had not materialized.

This would be my second trip to visit Nader in Jordan. The first time, he met me at the northern crossing of the Jordan River and took me to see the ancient Roman city of Jerash before heading south to Amman, where we spent most of the time meeting his friends.

Rami, too, was excited about the idea, and we left with a sense of adventure. As soon as we arrived in Amman, Nader met us and took us to have lunch at Jabri's, a popular local chain restaurant that serves great food and sweets. Then we spent some time at Nader's house to rest and talk for a bit. In the evening, we walked around Amman as much as we could and ended up at the Del Mondo Café. We drank coffee, Nader and Rami ordered hookahs, and we sat and talked for hours.

Nader pointed to the people in the café. "Look around you," he said. "When I lived here 20 years ago you would never see women in a café like you do today."

I reflected on what he said and added, "And look at the three of us, two Israelis and a Palestinian sitting together in an Arab capital, drinking coffee, without a worry in the world. That too was not possible 20 years ago."

I really wanted to see Saladin's famous castle at Ajloun in Northern Jordan. So on Friday morning, the day we returned to Israel, Nader went to the mosque to pray and then we took a cab to Ajloun. It was a cold and cloudy day with a light rain, which made the scenery on the way to Ajloun hauntingly beautiful and the scene at the castle itself even more dramatic. The village of Tishbi, where the prophet Elijah was born, is just behind the castle to the east. Mount Tabor rises to the west, and on a clear day one can see the Sea of Galilee. The castle itself is magnificent, typical of castles built all over ancient Israel/Palestine[1] during the Crusader period. It overlooks the hills and valleys extending for miles around.

From Ajloun, we proceeded to the border to enter Israel. The closer we got, the more tense we all felt. As we entered the terminal, I glanced at Nader. He appeared nervous, his face pale, his lips dry. I could tell that visions from his previous experience were still fresh in his mind.

At passport control, I handed the girl behind the counter all three passports together, Nader's U.S. passport sandwiched in between our two Israeli ones. "Are you together?" she asked.

"We are," I said.

"There is a problem with his passport, he should sit down and wait. Does he speak Hebrew?"

"No he does not, what is the problem?"

"His name raises a red flag," she said, "and it may take a very long time. We have to wait for an OK from headquarters, and it is late."

Rami demanded to know the nature of the problem. "We are not leaving without him," my brother-in-law said. No sooner did he finish his sentence than a young man with an unshaven face, dressed in jeans and t-shirt, came out to see us.

"His name raised a red flag, we can do nothing until we hear from headquarters." His Russian accent was heavy. It takes a special kind of arrogance, or ignorance, for someone who is new to a country to keep an older person (who was born in that country and whose ancestors were born in that country), out. I said nothing.

We told him who we were, we told him who Nader was, and we told him we were not leaving without him. "He deserves a red carpet VIP treatment for his work with Rotary and the wheelchair project, not to mention the unnecessary

---

1 Palestine and Israel are the same place, and with time I found that I myself began using both names when speaking about our shared homeland.

hassles you guys had put him through six months ago. You would do well to take that into consideration."

Rami could tell that I was beginning to lose my patience. "Miko calm down," he whispered. Then he turned to the young man, who had not yet identified himself. "You have no right to treat people like this without an explanation. You owe him an explanation and an apology." Now he was losing his cool.

"My hands are tied. We have to wait for word from headquarters. It may take a long time."

"We will wait right here until you clear it up," I said.

He disappeared into his office. The girl behind the counter came out with her backpack slung over her shoulder, her work-day concluded. It was getting close to 8 p.m., when the crossing closed. Ten minutes later the young man returned with Nader's passport.

"The red flag had been removed from Nader's name. This will not happen again," he promised.

The entire time Nader sat there quietly. He was unable to communicate with the authorities, and Rami and I had no intention of letting them get away with harassing him. As it turned out we were delayed only 30 minutes.

We took a cab to Nazareth, where we spent the night. In the morning, we met with members of the Rotary Club of Nazareth, who showed us the facilities where the wheelchairs had been distributed, and that night we headed off to Jerusalem. The next morning, Nader and I drove to Yad Sarah, or Sarah's Hand, an important charity in Israel that lends medical equipment to people in need for free. When my father was dying, we decided to care for him at home, and Yad Sarah provided the wheelchairs and other necessities free of charge and for as long as they were needed. It felt good to be giving back by providing them with new wheelchairs.

At Yad Sarah volunteers do most of the work, and most of them are deeply religious Orthodox Jews. As we toured their building, I saw Nader looking around at the people. "There are many orthodox Jewish people here," he observed. I realized this was the first time Nader had ever been around Orthodox Jews.

"Yes, religious people are known to volunteer to do charity everywhere in the world," I told him. We spent an hour touring the facility before heading to Beit Jala to see the wheelchairs at the Arab Rehabilitation Hospital.

Beit Jala is adjacent to Bethlehem, and I had not been to Bethlehem in at least 20 years. A friend took us there, driving down a road that did not require passing through a major checkpoint—instead there was a small roadblock with soldiers waving cars through. My friend dropped us off at Muna Katan's office, and she and her father took us to Bethlehem for lunch. After lunch, Muna's father drove us around for a while, and he showed us the wall that surrounds this ancient city. The ugly concrete structure was built around the city by Israel to separate Palestinians from lands that Israel wants to settle. There is graffiti all over the wall, a combination of art, poetry, and statements of resistance. Nader and I asked to step out of the car to get a closer look.

"Go ahead," our host said, though he opted to stay in the car for fear Israeli snipers might start shooting from the watchtowers above us.

At last Muna's father took us up to Beit Jala to see the hospital, and we thanked him for his hospitality. Dr. Edmund Shehadeh, the general director of the hospital, met us and gave us a tour of the facility. It is an immaculately clean and well-kept modern facility, and almost completely dependent on donations, making its existence at once crucial and miraculous.

We saw patients in the red wheelchairs our project had donated and we all posed for pictures together. We sat with Edmund in his office for a while. He pointed to the tracts of land being confiscated by Israel to build settlements, particularly the settlement of Gilo just south of Jerusalem, which we could see from his office window. You could also see the work being done to expand the wall and tunnels to allow Israeli settlers to travel from Israel to the settlements in the West Bank without having to see or interact with Palestinians.

Upon leaving, we were not sure which way to go. My friend was unable to come get us, so we took a local Palestinian taxi that could only take us as far as the checkpoint but not beyond it, since most Palestinian cab drivers in the West Bank are not permitted to enter Israel. As our taxi approached the checkpoint leading to Jerusalem, we realized that it was not the same way we had come, and a saga began that we did not expect.

This was Checkpoint 400, or Rachel's Tomb Checkpoint, situated near the place where tradition has it that the matriarch Rachel was buried. We asked the cab drivers who were present where to go, and they all pointed in the direction of this checkpoint or terminal. It was a menacing facility—more like a prison than a checkpoint—with high walls and fenced walkways. The place was empty. Nader and I wandered around for a while, not knowing which way to go. We both thought we were in the wrong place. Finally we exited the facility, found some soldiers, and asked them how to get out to go to Jerusalem.

"Go right in, and they will show you," they responded.

So we entered the structure again, as they suggested. All we saw were metal revolving doors with green and red lights, but not a single living soul. It was so quiet it felt eerie. I was very uncomfortable, and Nader began cracking jokes to diffuse the tension. We entered through the metal doors and found ourselves in a large hall with stalls with darkened windows.

A disembodied voice summoned us over a loudspeaker: "Come forward." We approached a window, and through a small crack we could see there was a frowning female soldier sitting behind it. She took Nader's American passport and handed it back to him. I was relieved. Then she took mine. I used my Israeli passport, as the law requires. We waited for some time, then a door opened and a soldier with a semiautomatic called me in to another section of the facility. He had my passport in his hand.

"Come with me."

"Why, what's the problem?" I asked.

"You've violated the commanding general's order that prohibits Israelis from entering Area A." I had entered Bethlehem, which is in Area A, and while I was aware that Israelis were not allowed into Area A, I had no idea what it meant to be "caught." I was completely overwhelmed by size of the facility and by the fact that a soldier with a loaded semiautomatic was holding my passport.

I was taken at gunpoint into the office of the checkpoint commanding officer— a simple man wearing the markings of an officer on the shoulders of his stained shirt, his buttons strained by an overinflated gut. As I entered the office, he quickly removed his feet from the desk.

"What's the problem?" he asked, as the soldier handed over my passport.

"This man violated the commanding general's order not to enter Area A."

The commander looked up at me. "Do you have any idea how serious this is?" He began to lecture me on the severity of my actions. "I was in Beit Jala at the hospital as part of a mission to deliver wheelchairs to Israeli and Palestinian—" I tried to explain the nature of our mission.

"I'm not interested!" He cut me off abruptly. At that point I'd had enough, and I became focused very fast. "How dare you sit here and lecture me, commanding this monstrous facility and enforcing a brutal, illegal occupation. You are a criminal and a shame to your country. Now I demand my passport back so that I may proceed to Jerusalem."

I was abruptly ordered out of his office. I sat in the corridor with an armed soldier facing me for a couple hours. Meanwhile Nader was out there somewhere with no phone or money or the slightest idea where to go. I called Rami to tell him what had happened and where we were, so that he could come for Nader. As it turned out, Nader was resourceful enough and had already found a way to contact Rami. The two of them were now concerned about me.

"Here sign this." Another officer came by and handed me a document.

"What is this?"

"It is a document saying we didn't harm you or take anything from you."

"Where is my passport?"

"We will return it to you shortly."

"Fine, I'll sign just as soon as you return it."

After another long wait, two armed soldiers came for me. They had my passport.

"Come with us."

"Where are we going?"

"To the police headquarters in Jerusalem for questioning."

As we approached the police car, one of the soldiers turned to me. "Why didn't you tell them it was all a mistake? You'd have been out by now. People do this all the time."

By then it was after five, and rush-hour traffic was terrible, which meant we had a long ride ahead of us.

"Pretty bad traffic," I offered, trying to start a conversation. The officer in charge barked at me, saying I was not permitted to speak.

But the silence only lasted a minute or two. "So, how is life in America?"

I guess they do want to talk. I was calm by then, and I wanted them to listen.

"Take a look at the date of issue of my passport," I said.

He complied. "September 5, 1997."

"Exactly. I bet you don't remember what happened the day before that? Well I will never forget. The passport was issued the day after Smadar was killed." I proceeded to tell them about Smadar, and about my father and my family. I told them about the Bereaved Families Forum, the Israelis and Palestinians who meet regularly to find ways to end the violence. They became quiet. When they realized I was a member of the "holy order," they suddenly became polite and friendly.

"Yes, but why would you want to help those stinking Arabs? Don't you know they could have kidnapped you, and then we would have had to launch a rescue operation," one of them said in a sincere tone.

"Really?" I said. "I am not a soldier. I was invited to visit. I had a meal with friends and then I was shown around a magnificent rehabilitation facility. They thanked me for providing them with much-needed wheelchairs. Here, on the other hand, I am being held at gunpoint and my passport has been taken from me. Which seems more like kidnapping to you? And my Palestinian-American friend is seeing all of this, and what do you imagine he is thinking about how my people are treating me for doing this charitable work? Do you think this reflects well on Israel?

"You guys talk to me about the commanding general's order. Let me ask you about another general. Have you heard of General Matti Peled? He was one of the commanders of the Six-Day War. Here is what he said would happen forty years ago." I told them about my father and what he predicted would happen if the occupation continued. When we reached the precinct, everyone but a few police officers had already gone home.

"We need an investigator to question this man."

The cops took one look at me and realized I was no hardened criminal. "Why? What did he do?"

"He violated the commanding general's order by entering Area A."

"Is that all? Release him and forget it." But these guys were determined to complete their mission. "It's nothing personal," they said.

At last an investigator was found. I was questioned, reprimanded, and told that if I were caught in Area A again, I would be fined or even arrested. Just as he was finishing up with me there was a knock on his door. Rami and Nader stood in the doorway smiling at me.

"Are you OK?"

I was glad the ordeal was over and I was very glad to see them there. But I was not OK. My own people had arrested me for doing something good. My disillusion with Israel had sunk to a new low.

Chapter 11:

Who Will Speak for Gaza?

In early 2008, I ate lunch with Rob Mullally, a great friend and fellow Rotarian, at a restaurant in San Diego's Old Town. We had just come out of a meeting of Rotary's Pathways to Peace Committee, where I had announced that Nader and I were going to Gaza.

Rob was dismayed. More than dismayed. What he said, precisely, was: "Miko, why the fuck are you going to Gaza?"

It's not so much that he was surprised, because he knew me well enough by then to know that I was very committed to doing something on the issue of Palestine. However, he couldn't help but be concerned. Gaza was difficult if not impossible to enter, it was controlled by Hamas—which wouldn't appreciate an Israeli Jew poking around, not even a well meaning one—and Israel could decide to strike at any time. In other words, things in Gaza were so volatile that it was not the most prudent thing to do. Rob was thinking of Gila and our children.

In the greater scheme of things, I knew that many Rotarians had accomplished more difficult feats—going into remote areas of Africa and Asia to immunize children against polio, starting microcredit lending projects for women in male-dominated societies around the world, and building schools for girls in Pakistan and Afghanistan. So it didn't seem like such a stretch for Nader and me to go to Gaza for a few days. I wanted an opportunity to use our Rotary connections to bring in much-needed medical supplies, to build bridges that would allow for an ongoing relationship to develop, and to open a crack in the walls that surrounded Gaza.

Personally, I also saw it as an opportunity to try, in some small way, to defy the Israeli domination over Palestine. And my experience exiting through the Bethlehem checkpoint convinced me that the best way to defy Israel was to defy the laws that supported that domination. Israeli law prohibited Israelis from going to Gaza.

"I'll tell you why, Rob," I replied.

"Israel is getting away with murder, and it's making me sick to sit around here and do nothing. Innocent people are being killed, children are hungry, there is mass unemployment and poverty, and it's happening an hour's drive from Tel Aviv. None of this was caused by a natural disaster. It was caused because Israel deliberately created these conditions, and no one in America says a thing. The literacy rate in Gaza is more than 90 percent, and it can become a haven for commerce, education, culture, and stability. If we could only get Israel's boot off their neck, if we could only defy the occupation. And I think that Rotarians can help me do this. That is why I am going to Gaza."

What I told him was true. The situation is so severe in Gaza that it makes domination of the West Bank seem practically benign. Israel's restrictions on travel and movement and the import and export of goods, plus the occupier's complete control over land and sea, have created a siege that is choking one and a half million people, including 800,000 children. Gaza has essentially been turned into an enormous concentration camp. On top of that, Israeli military incursions have left countless civilians, including children, maimed and traumatized, both physically and emotionally, and usually without access to treatment.

But the history of Gaza demonstrates what the future could hold should it be free. Ancient Gaza was a prosperous trade center and a stop on the caravan route between Egypt and Syria. The city was occupied by Egypt around the fifteenth century B.C., and the Philistines settled the area several hundred years after that. Gaza became one of their chief cities.

In the Old Testament the Philistines' presence in Gaza marked the city and its occupants as the traditional enemy of the Jewish people. For example, the Philistines caught and killed the great Jewish hero Samson; the young David killed the giant Philistine Goliath with a sling and stone; and King Saul, the Israelites' first king, fell on his sword after being defeated by the Philistines in a war where his beloved son Jonathan was also killed.

During the days of the Roman Empire, Gaza was a center of learning and culture. It is even believed that as a young boy, King Herod the Great attended school in Gaza, which was known for its superior education institutions. During that time, Gaza was one of the largest and most prosperous cities in the region. It is also believed to be the site where Mohammed's great-grandfather is buried. Under Islamic rule, the city became an important Islamic center.

In the twelfth century, Gaza was taken by Christian crusaders, and although Christians did not hold it for long, Gaza and its surrounding area developed into an important center of Christian monastic life and learning. When the British came to conquer the Holy Land in 1917, it took them three attempts and thousands of casualties before they were able take the city.

After the establishment of Israel in 1948, thousands of Palestinian refugees were driven from their homes and into Gaza, thus creating the "Strip" around the city of Gaza. These refugees and their descendants make up the majority of the population of Gaza today. Since that time, Gaza has made a name for itself as a persistent center of resistance, and the people of Gaza have paid a heavy price for this. Since the early 1950s, Israeli commandos have conducted "punitive" operations against the people of Gaza—in spite of the fact that the people of Gaza never had an army and never posed a military threat. Although there were incidents where Palestinian *fedayeen* attacked within Israel, for the most part all the refugees wanted was to collect their crops and feed their families and ultimately to return to their homes.

When President Jimmy Carter published his book *Palestine: Peace Not Apartheid*, Nancy Pelosi was speaker of the House of Representatives and she decided to join the crowd of Israel supporters and publicly denounce the book. In an advertisement published by the Anti-Defamation League, Pelosi stated, "It is wrong to suggest that the Jewish people would support a government in Israel or anywhere else that institutionalizes ethnically based oppression." In fact, Israel was a staunch ally of South Africa during the apartheid years, and Israel used ethnically-based oppression for decades to achieve its goal of creating a Jewish majority in Israel/Palestine. Nowhere has this oppression been more evident than in Gaza.

In *The Tribes Triumphant*, arguably one of the best books ever written about the Middle East, journalist Charles Glass illustrates his travels through the Levant with a rare intimacy. He visited Gaza countless times and stayed there long enough to know the place well. In one of the most moving passages in the book, Glass describes children in Gaza on their way to school in the morning:

> ...in smocks of blue or grey, little girls with white fringe collars, boys leading their younger brothers...with canvas bags of books on their backs, hair brushed back and faces scrubbed....Thousands and thousands of children's feet padding the dusty paths between their mother's front doors and their schools... Gaza is a children's land...beautiful youngsters so innocent that they could laugh even in Gaza.[1]

While I was studying in Japan I got to know many Israeli travelers, and most of us were young enough to still have memories of our military service fresh in our minds. One of the guys was as an officer in Israel's naval special forces, a captain in the revered Naval Commandos. He told us once how he and his unit would patrol the Gaza coast aboard their naval warships. They would come upon Gazan fishing boats and from time to time they would single out a particular boat, order the fishermen to jump into the water and blow up the boat. Then under gunpoint, they told the fishermen to count from one to a hundred and then when they were done to start over again. They would make them count over and over again until one by one the fishermen could no longer tread water, and they drowned.

The young Israeli officer said this was done, as he put it, "...to set an example, and teach the Arabs who was boss." I thought I was going to throw up when I heard this, but over the years I heard many similar stories from Israeli soldiers.

In an article I published about Gaza, I mentioned this story, and a few days later I received an e-mail from Charles Glass. In addition to publishing *The Tribes Triumphant*, Charlie is an award-winning journalist. He was ABC News's chief

---

1 Charles Glass, *The Tribes Triumphant: Return Journey to the Middle East* (London: HarperPress, 2006), 216.

Middle East correspondent from 1983-93. He also worked for *Newsweek* and *The Observer*, among many other publications. He's best known for a 1986 interview with the crew of a hijacked TWA flight on the tarmac of the Beirut airport. In 1987, Charlie was taken hostage by Shia militia and was kept prisoner in Beirut for 62 days. He was the only Western hostage in Lebanon known to have escaped. He relayed the entire story in his book, *Tribes with Flags*, which is the precursor to *The Tribes Triumphant*.

In his e-mail to me he wrote,

> Dear Miko, Great piece. I hope it is published everywhere. It reminded me of the story that *The Chicago Daily News*, for whom I was writing in Lebanon in 1974, killed when I wrote it. The Israeli navy was blowing up the fishing boats of kids off Tyre, and they had to swim back to town. I met the kids and saw the boats, and I wrote the story. At age twenty-three, I was innocent enough to believe it would be published. I learned then something that was taught to me again and again over the years: you cannot write even simple facts about what Israel was doing if your editors cannot accept that Israel would do such things. I don't know if they didn't believe the story or they wanted to protect the image, but it happened with just about every American news agency I ever worked for. Anyway, well done. Warmest wishes, Charlie.

When Tzipi Livni was serving as Israel's foreign minister, she defended the Israel Defense Forces' operations against Palestinians in the Gaza Strip as necessary for the advancement of peace negotiations. *Ha'aretz* newspaper reported that Livni said she would expect people not to make a comparison between Israeli civilians harmed by terrorism and Palestinian civilians harmed during Israel's defense operations. I was confused. Ms. Livni saw no problem with Israeli forces killing Palestinian civilians, including children, but it was not permissible to criticize Israel for doing this. How did Israelis turn away so completely from the values I thought we all held so dear?

As I prepared for the trip to Gaza, my dear friend Samir Kafiti, Bishop Emeritus of the Episcopal Diocese of Jerusalem, put me in touch with Dr. Suheila Tarazi, the general director of Al-Ahli Hospital in Gaza.

Dr. Suheila and I had communicated by phone and e-mail over several months, and I told her about our plan to come to Gaza and bring a few small useful items with us—to test the waters, so to speak. Because of the tight siege, nothing could come in and what little was allowed was scrutinized by Israel in a manner that seemed completely arbitrary. I had heard stories from medical teams that were not permitted to bring in their equipment, of expensive machinery that had to be left behind and was ruined because Israel would not allow it in, with little or no explanation.

Suheila gave me a list of items, and since we were planning to travel through Egypt, we decided to purchase these items there with the help of Egyptian Rotary members. We were hoping it would lead to a point where we could deliver more significant items in the future.

Nader and I embarked on our trip in November 2008. I contacted members of Rotary in Cairo, Egypt, and Nader contacted Rotarian friends of his in Amman, Jordan, and they all agreed to help us. I flew to Jerusalem and then traveled to Amman, where I met Nader. That evening we had dinner with Jordanian members of Rotary, and the next morning we left for Cairo.

At the airport I felt anxious, but just as things seemed to be going well (security checks had gone fine, and the flight was leaving on schedule), I spilled an entire cup of hot coffee all over my laptop and my lap. A young Jordanian airport employee came up to me as I scrambled to recover my laptop and what was left of my dignity. He asked me, "Are you OK?" And then he got me another coffee, free of charge, while a second young man cleaned up the mess. Luckily I had on a dark grey suit, so the coffee stain didn't show. I had to laugh; I guess I was in good hands in the Arab world.

We soon boarded our plane, and an hour and 10 minutes later we were in Cairo. Mahmoud Ayoub, a retired Egyptian diplomat, Renaissance man, and member of a local Rotary club, met us at the airport appearing as determined as we were to see our project succeed.

He took us to our hotel in his tiny car, negotiating the city's notorious traffic like a mouse maneuvering through a herd of buffalo. We settled in our room and I stepped out onto the balcony to see the Nile and take in the sights and sounds of the city.

Cairo is known for its thousands of minarets, many of which date back hundreds of years, and most of which seemed within sight of our hotel room balcony. The Nile, which more than anything symbolizes Egypt's vast history and enormous size, was flowing right in front of my eyes. I was in an Arab capital—in many ways, it is considered *the* Arab capital—and I loved it. In this old hotel, I felt like an actor in the movie *Casablanca*, or some other 1940s movie set in the Middle East.

Nader's daughter Rania was also in Cairo with her husband, Dr. Nahid Hassaniya. Nahid, a native of Gaza, works in the U.S. as a pediatric cardiologist. He came to Cairo with a team of U.S. cardiologists to teach for a few weeks.

That night Rania joined us for dinner with members of Rotary who graciously hosted us at the Cairo City Club. The next day we went to a local distributor to pick up the equipment that we had agreed to take to Gaza. But when we arrived, we found that it had not been ordered, and that we would need to wait at least a day to receive it. I had to remind myself that things moved at a different pace in the Middle East. There is a saying in both Hebrew and Arabic about all delays having a good reason. In Hebrew it is, *"Kol Akava letova,"* and in Arabic it is, *"Kul Ta'akhir fiha khir."* Besides, for the most part, things were going very well. Nahid

Nader, Nahid, and I linger before leaving for Gaza.

had family in Cairo, and we were invited to wait at their home in the neighborhood of Medinat al Nasser. While there we learned that a relative of Nahid's would be marrying the famous Egyptian megastar and singer Hamada Helal, and we were invited to the wedding. But if everything went according to plan we'd be in Gaza at that time.

It was five in the evening when the equipment finally arrived. It came in a large van with a driver and guide, all provided for us by our Rotary friends in Cairo. Traveling from Cairo to Gaza freely without a guide is not permitted, and one has to have a guide who is certified by the government. Neither the guide nor the driver we had spoke any English, but they were experienced and they knew the roads and the laws.

The late hour meant we would have to travel mostly by night and I wasn't crazy about this, but we decided not to delay any longer. We said our farewells and set off to Gaza. By midnight we had crossed the Suez Canal. We kept driving until we reached the coastal town of El-Arish, 25 miles from the Gaza border, where we spent the night.

You know you are in the Arab world when you are awakened at dawn by the call to prayer. This morning was no different, and having been so awakened I went outside to watch the waves at this rather empty and unknown corner of the Mediterranean. Not a soul was in sight, and the horizon was sharp and clear, but inside me, I felt a storm brewing. I was anxious about what the day ahead would bring; I wanted more than anything to get to Gaza. Only a few short miles from where I sat, a tragedy of immense proportion was taking place, and if Israeli authorities had their way, I wouldn't be able to do anything about it. Rather than drive the 45 minutes from Jerusalem to Gaza, I had to travel around the world to Cairo and then from there go on this long journey overland, and still there was a serious chance that I would not be permitted to enter.

Just as Israel prohibits Israelis from entering Area A in the West Bank, they also prohibit us from entering Gaza. The difference is that Gaza is completely sealed off and there are no side roads through which to enter. The border is sealed tight by Israel and it takes months to get a permit to enter from the Israeli side. So for me this was the only chance to enter, and I had bet heavily on succeeding.

During breakfast, I realized that we were not the only ones at the hotel who were trying to reach Gaza. Practically everyone else was trying to get there, too; some had been waiting for several weeks. Apparently the border had been closed for that long, with no explanation and no sign of opening any time soon. We knew this sort of thing happened often. Indeed we feared this exact scenario because we'd been warned that there would be nothing we could do about it.

At eight in the morning we drove toward the border city of Rafah, passing through several Egyptian security checkpoints along the way. The closer we got to Rafah, the longer the soldiers seemed to take examining our passports, and the more nervous and on edge they seemed. At one point they got into a shouting match with our guide.

Finally we neared to within five kilometers. I had been much closer to Gaza many times while in Israel, but this time it was more significant—this time I was hoping to get into Gaza. We drove through Rafah in silence until we reached the border. As I looked at the gate I remembered that Dr. Suheila told me it would take a miracle for us to get in. I never believed in miracles so fervently in my life as I did at that moment. We had come such a long way, and now we were a few hundred yards from Gaza.

To the right of the gate, a platoon of Egyptian riot police sat idly in the shade. They were remnants of attempts by Gazans about six months earlier to break into Egypt to buy food. Otherwise the place was quiet and desolate. Our driver stopped the car 50 yards from the crossing and Nader and I took our bags and walked up to the gate. A young Egyptian soldier wearing a uniform several sizes too big for him and holding a long rifle told us it was closed. Nader asked to see a superior, but the soldier said, "No, you can see no one." At that point a plainclothes intelligence officer, whom we secretly called "the weasel," came to inquire who we were and what we wanted. Then he repeated what the young soldier had said: "The crossing is closed, and you have to leave."

We refused to take no for an answer. Instead, we made a flurry of phone calls to our friends in Cairo, whom we hoped had connections in high places. They called us back and said there was no one to talk to. The border was closed and no one knew why or for how long. We stayed anyway and made more phone calls. Finally the soldiers suggested that we go to the Egyptian *mukhabarat* (intelligence service) headquarters, not far from the border.

We drove through dirt roads littered with garbage to an unmarked building surrounded by a wall in the middle of nowhere. We asked the sentry to call an officer whose name had been given to us by the people at the border. He disappeared inside only to reappear a few moments later and tell us we had to leave. Nader insisted. The sentry disappeared again. After a few moments, a guy in plainclothes opened the door and said we had to leave. Nader asked to use the restroom, and the man pointed to the wall and suggested we relieve ourselves there.

Our guide and driver were in shock at the lack of courtesy displayed by these officials. They knew we had come all the way from America to help people in Gaza and that we had medical equipment to deliver. They were as appalled as we were by the fact that the Egyptians were no more helpful than the Israelis, and they took the insult personally and on behalf of all Egyptians. In their frustration they looked for ways to assist us. It was a moment of clarity for me: I could see that if Egyptians had a say in their country's governance, as opposed to being ruled by a dictator, things would be better for the entire region. As it stood, the Egyptian government appeared to be committed, along with Israel and the U.S., to maintaining the siege on Gaza.

At last one of them said, "I used to work for the Belgian Embassy. Maybe if I call them, they will help."

We realized we were getting nowhere, and I was concerned that if they did let us into this building, we would never come out. I was beginning to imagine what it would be like for me as an Israeli in an Egyptian jail, a thought that terrified me, so we drove away as quickly as we could. We stopped at a small hut on the edge of town that sold tea and coffee, sat in the shade, ordered tea and called Cairo again. We were conspicuous in our suits, and I felt most uncomfortable. Our friends in Cairo said they would check for us once again, and in the meantime we should wait. So we did. We sat there until it got late and we had to return to our hotel in El-Arish.

The following morning we were determined to try again and were met by the same resistance, but this time another plainclothes officer came out to talk to us. They told us he was a colonel. As he and Nader spoke, curious soldiers, policemen, "the weasel," and a host of other onlookers who seemed to come out of nowhere surrounded us. Nader and the colonel talked for a long time. Then the colonel took our information and said he would return with an answer.

A few more hours passed and I grew nervous. The thought of the Egyptian jail came back, and I was about to tell Nader we'd better give up and head back to Cairo or we'd surely be arrested. At last we saw the colonel and his retinue heading toward us. He said there was no way we could enter Gaza. After hearing yet another passionate and compelling argument from Nader, the colonel said plainly, "I can't let you in, the Israelis are watching us."

What the officer was saying may or may not have been true, which is that the Israelis were preventing him from letting us enter rather than his Egyptian superiors. I had no doubt that Israel demanded the border closed, and that the Egyptian government complied. I just think the demands were made at a much higher level.

Throughout this whole ordeal, I sat quietly on the side, hoping no one would pay attention to me. Although I was carrying my U.S. passport, it stated clearly that my place of birth was Jerusalem. I obviously didn't have an Arab name, so it wouldn't have been easy for someone to conclude I was an Israeli. At one point the weasel noticed me and came up, trying to talk to me in his broken English. He looked at my passport and noticed the place of birth. "Falastini, Falastini" he remarked, using the Arabic for "Palestinian." He assumed that since I was born in Jerusalem that I was Palestinian. I smiled and pretended not to understand.

Frustrated but not surprised, we finally gave up. It was hard not to feel defeated. It was obvious to me that I was up against a force that was not going to be easy to defy. My desire to do something had to be tempered with the realization that in my desire to defy Israel I was going to fail more times than succeed. I decided I was going to get in the game, to speak out and to act more than ever before. Whatever voice I had I was going to use it and whatever strength I had I was going to muster it. More than anything I needed patience, because this was gong to be a very long battle. Still we could not have done more and for me the most difficult thing was to call Suheila and let her know we were returning to Cairo. She thanked me for trying and wished us all better luck in the future.

We drove in silence back to Cairo. When we arrived, exhausted and depressed, it was after 9 p.m., and I remembered that we had been invited to the wedding of Hamada Helal, which was taking place that night. It seemed like a small silver lining, and if nothing else it might be uplifting after the disappointments of the past few days.

The wedding was—unbelievable. Inside the wedding hall, lights dangled from the ceiling like fireflies, a dim, enchanted light. All of Cairo's elite was present—as well as all of the biggest names in Arabic music and film. I recognized practically no one, but Nader was jumping on chairs like a child to get a good look and snap pictures. The music celebrities were not just there to be seen, they performed as well. So it was an all-night marathon of Arabic music.

At one point I looked at Nader's watch and noticed it said 3:30. I told him his watched must have stopped, and he corrected me: "It is 3:30 a.m."

"Remember where we were when the day began?"

Nader nodded. "It was a crazy day." He said the party would probably go on until nine or 10 a.m. and that this was typical of weddings in Egypt. We didn't last quite that long. At 4:00 a.m., we finally gave in and went back to our hotel to get some sleep.

The following day was a Friday; Nader went to pray, and I relaxed at the hotel. I stood on the balcony again, taking it all in. Later I phoned Mahmoud, and together we went to Cairo's famous market, Khan El-Khalili. Then we walked around old Cairo and visited Al-Azhar, one of the oldest universities in the world, and the magnificent Al-Azhar mosque.

From Egypt, Nader and I flew back to Amman, and then I returned to Jerusalem. I took the equipment with me and left it at the Episcopal Diocese. Several months later, Bishop Suheil Dawani was able to enter Gaza and delivered it all to Al-Ahli hospital.

Three weeks after we returned home, it became clear why the border with Gaza had been closed.

On December 27, at 11:25 a.m., Israeli air force jets began carpet-bombing Gaza. The Israeli daily newspaper *Ha'aretz* reported that on the first day of this attack, called Operation Cast Lead, over a period of eight hours the Israeli air force dropped 100 tons of bombs on Gaza. Considering that a one-ton bomb can destroy an entire city block, and Gaza is a small place and very crowded, one can only imagine the devastation and the casualties. This was the beginning of 21 days of abject hell. Israel attacked with massive air and ground forces against an area and a population that had no military force. Israeli pilots dumped hundreds of tons of bombs, and for the people of Gaza there was nowhere to hide, no way to defend themselves and, with the border shut, nowhere to run. To make things worse, Israel claimed that notices were given to the local population that the attack was imminent and that people should leave areas that were going to be bombed. One can only imagine a mother or father sitting for days anticipating this onslaught, yet knowing full well that there was no escaping it. It was in preparation for this massive assault—apparently in response to rockets fired from Gaza into Israel—that the Gaza border had been closed.

Only hours after the bombing began, it was reported that close to 500 people were killed, including dozens of children. During our attempt to enter Gaza, I had called Suheila several times and she had constantly been encouraging me and thanking us for our efforts. After the attacks began, I wasn't able to call her but I managed to get a few e-mail messages through. In one exchange she described how helpless she and the other doctors felt. Everything was destroyed, broken, or shattered, and there was no electricity. It was early on in the assault when she wrote to me of a six-year-old boy who was wounded and brought to the hospital. She wrote to me: "We were unable to save him."

By the end of the 21-day attack, 1,400 people were killed, thousands wounded and maimed, and many thousands more left homeless with nowhere to turn. In an article published in *The San Diego Union-Tribune*, I wrote: "As I sit and view the reports, photos and live videos streaming in from Gaza I find it impossible to make sense of it all."

I recalled being taught a story from the Old Testament, where Abraham the patriarch argued with God over His decision to destroy the cities of Sodom and Gomorra: *And Abraham stood before the Lord. And Abraham drew near, and said: wilt thou also destroy the righteous with the wicked, perhaps there be fifty righteous within the city, wilt thou also destroy and not spare the place for the righteous that are therein? ...and the Lord said, if I find in Sodom fifty just men within the city, then I will spare all the place for their sakes.*(Genesis 18:23–26)

One has to admire Abraham for his tenacity. Stepping near as he did to confront the almighty and argue with God for the sake of a principle that he held dear, the principle that human life is sacred. Abraham wanted to get a real commitment from God, that He would indeed spare the city for the lives of innocent people.

Who was there to speak for the people of Gaza? There can be no doubt that among the 1.5 million people residing in Gaza there are more than 50 righteous men and women. After all, there are 800,000 children in Gaza.

After our return, Nader and I were invited to give a talk at the University of San Diego Joan Kroc Institute of Peace and Justice. During my remarks I, mentioned that the latest assault on Gaza was not isolated but rather part of a continuous Israeli campaign against Gaza, a campaign that by that point had been going on for more than six decades. Every few years, the Israeli army found a reason to conduct a brutal attack on Gaza and leave behind as many casualties as possible, beginning as early as 1953 with the infamous Unit 101, led by Ariel Sharon. What happened shortly after our failed attempt to cross the border was a continuation of an ongoing war, a war that aims to complete the ethnic cleansing of Palestine. I heard stories of people who drove to the Gaza border to sit on lawn chairs and view the bombing.

During the lecture, members of the Zionist community who came to hear us were appalled that I would criticize Israel at such a time. "It is a question of values," I tried to explain. "Some people believe that killing innocent civilians is morally acceptable. I think, and my Jewish roots teach me, that even if the devil himself resided in Gaza, as long as a single child resided there too, the city had to be spared."

I felt betrayed by my own people, I felt ashamed of the country I used to be so proud of. As Nader and I flew over Egypt on our way back to Amman, I told him that I couldn't help thinking that Gaza is a problem that is very easy to fix. "Look at the vast desert below us, nothing we can do will change it. But Gaza is not like that, in Gaza there are educated people who can work and be productive and contribute. They don't need us to do anything but open the gates and take down the barriers."

My people, my friends, were holding the keys to the gate and would not let anyone enter. After this trip, I started to think a little differently about what real

peace would look like. I started to think that a complete removal of all the barriers between Israelis and Palestinians was the only hope—indeed that it was
inevitable.

Chapter 12:

Abu Ansar[1]

After my experience at the Bethlehem checkpoint in April 2007, Nader and I went on to travel to Ramallah and then to Haifa to meet people in what turned out to be a marathon tour with very little time to rest. Once we were done, Nader returned to Amman, Jordan and I decided to stay in Israel/Palestine and attend the Annual Conference on Non-Violent Joint Struggle, also referred to as The Bil'in Conference. It was the second time the village Bil'in hosted a conference dedicated to the ongoing non-violent popular resistance.

I was searching for more direct forms of political activism. The wheelchair project was both important and interesting, but I realized that humanitarian work was not going to bring about a solution. Also, I was beginning to diverge from what my father and other Zionist Israeli progressives saw as the solution—that is, the two-state solution. I was beginning to see that the issues that made up the conflict could only be resolved through a state where both peoples live as equal citizens.

Obviously this was not going to happen without a fight, and the only fight to which I would dedicate myself was a non-violent one. That was why I wanted to learn more about what was happening in Bil'in. I also felt very strongly about the need to continue to defy Israel's laws pertaining to the occupation.

I was excited that I happened to be in the country when the conference was taking place. I took a taxi from Jerusalem to Bil'in, and there were already many people there when I arrived. The event was being held under an enormous tent in the village school courtyard. As I entered the courtyard, I immediately saw Dr. Omar, Bassam Aramin, and a few other friends standing around and talking. I knew Dr. Omar through the Bereaved Families Forum. He was general director of the Palestinian health department and Nader and I met him in Ramallah during our trip with the wheelchair project. I met Bassam during a meeting of an organization called Combatants for Peace.

After we greeted one another, Dr. Omar asked me who I was with and who was going to take care of me while I was at the conference. I told him I had come alone and that I was not concerned because I was sure to meet people I knew. He

---

1 Ansar was the name given by Palestinian prisoners to Ktsiot Prison in the Negev Desert.

With Dr. Mustafa Barghouti in Bil'in. He was, at the time, a member of the Palestinian cabinet.

turned to a friend standing next to him and introduced him as Jamal Mansur, or Abu Ansar. He had a large body and a prominent mustache and stood about six feet and two inches.

Dr. Omar turned to me. "I have to go, but he will take care of you, he is our good friend from prison."

Then he took my arm, turned to Jamal, pointed to me, and said in Arabic, "*Hadha habibi, habibi, habibi!*" In other words, I was a special guy and a close friend. Jamal had a house in the village and was staying there for the entire conference. He spoke excellent Hebrew, and he took good care of me, making sure I was comfortable at all times. I found him to be a warm-hearted, well-mannered gentleman. He introduced me to all the dignitaries at the conference, and indeed there were many. He took me to meet Fadwa Barghouti, the wife of the famous imprisoned Palestinian leader Marwan Barghouti. We sat with her for a while and talked.

I said, "I hope your husband will be released soon, his country and his people need him."

"I hope he is released too, but for his family and his children, who need him too."

Then, Dr. Mustafa Barghouti[2] arrived. At the time, he was a member of the

---

2 "Barghouti" is a very common Palestinian surname; none of these men are closely related.

Palestinian cabinet. As dignitaries came and went, people would form lines to walk up and say hello. I couldn't help noticing that every time Jamal walked up to greet some dignitary, people would step aside and allow him to go first.

Jamal has large hands and he uses them affectionately, placing them on people's shoulders or knees when he speaks. We sat in the back of the huge tent and divided our time between listening to the various speakers and just chatting with each other. I understood that Jamal and Bassam and Dr. Omar all knew one another from the time they had spent in Israeli prisons, but I never knew what the charges had been against them. As we talked throughout the day, the complex world of Palestinian prisoners—a world I knew nothing about—began to unfold.

"Abu Ansar, why were you imprisoned?" I asked at one point.

"Please call me Jamal. Well, we were young and foolish and we did stupid things. It doesn't matter now."

I decided to let it go for a while. When Jamal would introduce me to people, each time he said the same thing: "He is the son of General Matti Peled, the Israeli general who met Yasser Arafat in Tunis. His sister's daughter was killed in an attack in '97."

Israeli and Palestinian societies are similar in many ways, but in one way they are virtually identical. In both societies, there are two groups of people who are holy-like, untouchable: the warriors and the bereaved. Those who fought for the cause and those who sacrificed loved ones. Whenever I give a lecture or write about

Jamal Mansur, or Abu Ansar, and I at the Annual Conference on Non-Violent Joint Struggle in Bil'in.

172 | The General's Son

the Israeli/Palestinian issue, I am always introduced as the son of General Peled and the uncle of Smadar Elhanan; it is as though these two aspects of my personal story give me the right to speak.

Jamal's introduction usually brought a response along the lines of: "Of course I remember General Peled, Abu Salaam. He helped me so much when the Israeli authorities wanted to deport me." I heard that sort of thing being said over and over throughout the day by so many people, and I still hear it each time I meet Palestinians in the West Bank.

Then Jamal would also add, "He and his Palestinian partner Mr. Elbanna just completed a project to bring 1,000 wheelchairs, 500 to Israelis and 500 to Palestinians."

When lunch was served Jamal took me to sit with his friends. After lunch we helped ourselves to coffee and then we went to sit by ourselves again.

"Jamal, why were you in prison?" I asked once more.

"I was young and foolish; I was 16 years old. One day, Israeli soldiers came to our village, Bil'in, where I grew up and imposed a curfew. The curfew meant no one could leave the house. It was a hot day and my little sister was thirsty and my mother wanted to step out to fetch clean water, but the soldiers wouldn't let her. Each time she tried they just said no. The day progressed, and with it the heat. There was a bucket near the house with water that was used to wash vegetables. The water was dirty with soil and shrubs. The soldier pointed to it and said, 'Here, she can drink this.'" Jamal paused for a moment. "She was just a little girl who was thirsty, how do you say no to something like that?

"So my mother took the water and tried to strain it through a cloth and give it to the little girl. But she cried because she could not drink the dirty water. I couldn't just sit and watch this sort of thing. Then I decided I have to join the resistance to fight."

"So what happened that you were arrested?" I pressed him. He was clearly reluctant to tell me what happened, but a bond was beginning to form between us, one that would become stronger over the years.

"One night I was told we had an operation. Three other members of the cell and I were sent on a mission. It was to kill two armed Israeli soldiers who were guarding a branch of an Israeli bank in Ramallah." As I listened to the story, I couldn't help wondering why these soldiers were guarding a bank in the first place. My guess was that they were young and inexperienced and were carelessly placed in this predicament by their superiors much like I had been so many times during my service. Jamal, with three others, snuck up and killed the two soldiers.

"How did you kill them?"

"Two of us took one soldier, and two took the other soldier, and we stabbed them to death with a knife."

My entire childhood and much of my adult life I loved and admired the IDF. I used to say that I could recite the army ranks before I knew my alphabet. Now I was hearing about two soldiers, two young men wearing the uniform I respected so much, being stabbed to death. How did I feel about it? I was saddened that two young men lost their lives, and I was saddened that a good man was brought to a point where he chose to take a life. But I felt no special affinity to these soldiers because they were Israeli or because they were IDF soldiers: The state that they served had abused its power and for that abuse, these soldiers had to pay with their lives.

In the end, two soldiers were dead, the young men who killed them spent years in prison, and all of this benefited no one. It advanced no cause and it improved the lives of not one person. Surely humanity was capable of more than this.

After carrying out the attack, Jamal lay low for a while. He went back to work in Tel Aviv, and six months later he was caught.

"At first they tied me up so that I was completely bent over," he recounted to me. "They gagged me and took me to a remote spot by the beach in Tel Aviv. They beat me for hours under the cover of darkness. It was so bad that I prayed they would just throw me into the sea and let me drown." Jamal has nerve damage in his back and legs from the beating. In his youth, he had been an athlete and had practiced karate. Today, he can do nothing but walk, and he doesn't walk very fast.

He continued: "Then the Israeli authorities blew up my father's house." Jamal was sentenced to life in prison, but was released in 1985 as part of the Ahmed Jibril prisoner exchange: 1,150 Palestinian prisoners were released from Israeli prisons in exchange for three Israeli soldiers who were held by the Popular Front for the Liberation of Palestine (PFLP) in Lebanon.

Upon his release, as the prisoners were leaving the bus, Jamal was called by one of the Israeli officers and was immediately placed under administrative arrest. This meant imprisonment without charge or trial. He was put back on the bus and sent to jail for six more months. They did this to him twice, adding a year to his jail time. "I told my wife not to wait for me and not to expect me to return," he said. "If I come back she will know when I arrive. Otherwise the disappointment is to hard to bear."

During his years in prison, Jamal developed a reputation as a man of character, a man that could be trusted. Both the prison guards and the prisoners trusted him and he often acted as liaison and peacemaker.

Jamal and I have been friends ever since that day in Bil'in. He's been instrumental in helping me travel throughout the West Bank, and over the years he has introduced me to many excellent people I otherwise would not have met. We would walk through Ramallah and stop at a shop or an office or a corner neighborhood store. He would gesture toward a fellow and say, "We were in prison together." After which, he would introduce me to his friend. Then we'd all sit and have coffee or juice, and I never felt more comfortable and welcome than I did in these random meeting with Palestinians who had fought and paid dearly for the sake of freedom. Most of them moved on with their lives after prison but didn't lose their desire to see better days. They managed to create the semblance of normalcy in this cramped and confined existence Israel permitted them. We would spend half an hour or so before going to the next place to meet another friend.

At first I would only go to Ramallah by taxi and with a driver I knew personally, but before long I began taking a Palestinian bus from Arab East Jerusalem. Thanks to Jamal I became comfortable traveling alone in the West Bank, wandering the streets of Ramallah or Bethlehem or even the Deheishe Refugee Camp. Like this, I saw yet another aspect of Palestinian life that most Israelis don't imagine: the relative normalcy. Because the day-to-day details of our lives are the same: children returning home from school, licking ice cream and laughing; young girls busy texting on their cell phones; people going about their life as people do everywhere. This was how I became convinced, beyond any words or ideology, that we are similar and that we can prosper together once we overcome the bitter, brutal regime of Zionism. That Israeli and Palestinian people can create a new political reality within the framework of one state, one democracy in which they live as equals. It was a clear departure from what my father believed the solution would be, indeed from what most people think the solution will be, but it took into consideration aspects of Palestinian life of which my father was not aware.

Thanks to Jamal, I have also learned a good deal about the lives of Palestinians in prison—a topic largely ignored by Israelis and the outside world. He has described to me in detail the prisoners' system for mentoring new inmates and maintaining order.

"The older prisoners would be responsible for the new, younger prisoners. They would give them books to study and teach them about the routine in the prison. The *Fatah* prisoners, who were the majority of the prisoners, had a routine in place and that routine dictated how we conducted our lives and gave us structure."

Swearing and fighting were not allowed. When someone broke the rules, the prisoners themselves administered trials and penalties.

"Once there was a prisoner that was very hotheaded," Jamal recalled. "I came and talked to him. I told him to stay calm, that fighting was not permitted, and he needed to learn to work things out and get along with the other inmates. But he didn't listen." This prisoner got in a fight and pulled out a knife on a fellow prisoner. Jamal told me that the penalty was to break the two or three fingers this prisoner used to hold the knife. "It was very hard to do, and no one wanted to carry out the sentence. But the prison authorities did not care for us, and we had to keep the order or we would have complete chaos."

The prisoners had daily study sessions mandated by the prisoners themselves. Time was allocated for exercise, lectures, and political meetings. "We held elections on a regular basis to elect our representatives and people who carried out different roles in the prison. We also had elections where we decided on issues that pertain to our lives and to the general Palestinian political life outside the prison."

Dr. Maya Rosenfeld, a research fellow at the Harry S. Truman Institute at the Hebrew University and an expert on the social and political history of the Palestinians in Palestine and the diaspora, has written:

> None of the organizations and movements that gained ground in the 1970s and 1980s... was able to implant and sustain equally comprehensive programs and institutions as those that were upheld by the prisoners' organization.

Also according to Dr. Rosenfeld:

> The flagship of the prisoners' movement...was in the sphere of education. Education programs...(history, languages, sciences) and studies of political theory and ideology were introduced through the fostering and indeed through the enforcement of daily schedules that allocated special time slots for individual studies, instructed reading, and group discussions...political meetings for the discussion of current (external and internal) affairs and so forth.[3]

The prisoners studied Hebrew, Israeli history, the development of Zionism, and other national movements. Prisoners that I met, Jamal included, all spoke excellent Hebrew and English and were better acquainted with the writings of major Israeli and Jewish figures than most Israelis I know.

Another former prisoner told me, "The books were brought in from outside by other prisoners. From time to time the prison authorities would search our rooms and confiscate our books. When that happened, those of us who had already read the books would teach them orally to the other prisoners."

After he was released, Jamal worked as a translator for the PLO headquarters in Jerusalem, the Orient House. His boss was Faisal Husseini, one of the most admired Palestinian leaders and a member of the Jerusalem nobility, as it were. He was the son of Abdel Kader Husseini, the Palestinian leader who was killed in the battle of The Kastel in 1948. The Orient House was later closed by Israel because its activities were deemed illegal. Jamal honed his Hebrew there and developed excellent skills as a translator.

---

3 Maya Rosenfeld, "The Centrality of the Prisoners' Movement" in *Threat: Palestinian Political Prisoners in Israel*, ed. Abeer Baker and Anat Matar (London: Pluto Press, 2011), 11.

Unfortunately, Jamal is not permitted to enter Israel under any circumstances. So, for years now we have had the same routine. I call him from Jerusalem as soon as I get to my mother's house. We set a time to meet and then I take the bus from East Jerusalem to Ramallah, where Jamal waits for me. We meet with hugs and kisses on the cheeks. Since we are great friends, it is always at least four kisses. Then Jamal takes me to see people, places or events he thinks would be interesting.

The stories about the life of prisoners continued to fascinate me. They reminded me of stories relayed by Nelson Mandela in his memoir, *Long Walk to Freedom*, and I wanted to know more. I knew that Bassam Aramin too was arrested and a leader of the *Fatah* prisoners while he sat in prison. I met Bassam several times with Jamal and over time I got to know him well. He and my nephew Elik were involved together in Combatants for Peace and over the years our families became close.

I will never forget the first time I saw Bassam. It was in A-Ram, a town between Ramallah and Jerusalem, and there must have been close to 100 people present, most of them former Israeli soldiers and former Palestinian resistance fighters. They were in the process of forming an organization dedicated to reconciliation called Combatants for Peace. I noticed one Palestinian gentleman, around 35 years old with a heavy limp, walking around looking quite serious. I thought, what is it about this man that makes him stand out? Was it his limp, his severe countenance, or the fact that he was impeccably dressed in a suit and tie in the midst of a crowd of mostly jeans and t-shirts? When everyone was seated, he walked up to the head of the table and sat down.

When he rose to speak, he made his remarks in Arabic and another Palestinian member of the group simultaneously translated into Hebrew. At one point Bassam stopped talking, gave the translator a stern look, and said something to him in Arabic. It turned out the translator misrepresented what Bassam was saying. The translator apologized and Bassam made the correction, restating his point in perfect Hebrew. Bassam spoke about the need for an ongoing, relentless struggle against the Israeli occupation, and about the criminal treatment of Palestinians by the Israeli government, and he made it amply clear that he believed the struggle should be executed through non-violent means.

It turned out the limp was a result of childhood polio. "When I was a child growing up there were four other boys in my class in school who had polio and they ended up with a limp or some other form of physical disability. I used to look at them and think to myself, how sad it must be for them to have that terrible limp. I never thought that I had a limp, too."

When I had the chance, I asked him why he was arrested, and about his life in prison. "We called ourselves freedom fighters," Bassam told me, "but the outside world said we were terrorists. We began by throwing stones and empty bottles at the army. Then, one day we came across some old, discarded hand grenades and we decided to throw them at the Israeli army jeeps. Two grenades exploded but no one was injured. The soldiers came after us and we tried to run, but I could not run very fast with my limp, and they caught me. So in 1985, at the age of seventeen, I received a seven-year prison sentence.

"In prison we were treated like heroes by other prisoners, but our jailers taught us how to continue hating and resisting. On October 1, 1987, I was among 120 prisoners, all of us teenage boys waiting to go into the dining room, when the alarms suddenly went off. About a hundred armed soldiers appeared and ordered us to strip naked. They beat us until we could hardly stand. I was held the longest and beaten the hardest. What hurt me more than anything was that the soldiers were smiling the entire time."

Bassam spent years as an underground leader within the prison, and prison authorities suspected he was engaged in illegal political activities. So he was moved from prison to prison to see if this would disturb his leadership. "They kept asking if I was the leader and I said no. I am just a little guy with a bad limp, what kind of leader can I be? I showed no emotion when they moved me around from one prison to another, and I said nothing. Finally the prison authorities gave up and returned me to my original cell."

"Believe it or not…" He paused as I was listening to his every word after dinner one night at my house. "That day, when I returned to my cell, I was even happier than the day I was released from prison." Bassam had concealed all of his correspondence with other prisoners and prison leaders under the floor of that original cell.

Both Jamal and Bassam have an abundance of calm and patience that never ceases to amaze me. In encounters with Israeli soldiers, they keep their cool and often engage them in the sorts of intelligent conversations that these young sol-

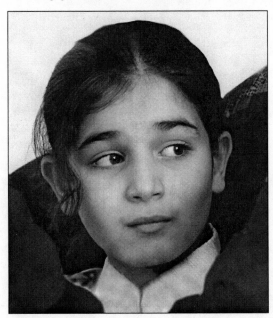

Bassam's 10-year-old daughter, Abir.

diers probably never imagined they would have with Palestinians. Their caring and empathy are far stronger than any anger they might be carrying. Both display a desire to reach out and help the "other side" see through the veil of fear, a fear they know the young soldiers feel as they sit in their posts watching out for the next suicide bomber.

Bassam's most painful moment would come two years after I met him. On January 16, 2007, as Bassam's two daughters, 10-year-old Abir and 12-year-old Arin, were walking home from school, an Israeli soldier took aim and shot Abir in the head. Arin would later describe how Abir suddenly flew out of her hand and lay bleeding on the ground.

I don't recall how I heard the news, but I was under the impression that Abir was seriously wounded, and that there was hope. I immediately called Bassam at the hospital to ask how Abir was doing.

"She just died," he said quietly.

I was so overwhelmed by emotion I did not know what to do or say. Once again I found myself separated by oceans from people I love when I needed to be beside them.

Chapter 13:

Defiance

It was Friday, December 10, 2010—my 49th birthday—and I had been staying with Khaled's family in Beit Ummar for a few days. I was there because I wanted to experience the occupation from the inside, and Khaled and his family were gracious enough to host me for the week. Ali said he wanted me to come with him to Nabi Saleh, another Palestinian village where weekly protests were taking place following Friday prayer. I had been to protests in Bil'in as well as other places, and so I was glad to go. Ali and I drove from Beit Ummar to Nabi Saleh, which is northwest of Ramallah.

Nearly half of Nabi Saleh's valuable agricultural land had been seized for an Israeli settlement called Halamish. Near the village there is a natural spring named *Ein Al Kus* (Bow Spring). In 2009, settlers from Halamish had taken control of the spring and its surroundings and prevented Palestinian access to it. Since then, the people of Nabi Saleh and the nearby village of Dir Nizam had been protesting the theft of the spring, the theft of their lands, and the occupation in general, every Friday afternoon.

The shortest route from Beit Ummar, which is near Hebron in the southern part of the West Bank, to Nabi Saleh, which is close to Ramallah in the central part of the West Bank, goes through Jerusalem. But most West Bank Palestinians are not allowed to enter the city or even drive through it, so if you are a Palestinian or driving with a Palestinian, it takes forever to commute between these two places. We had to take a detour road, a huge eastward loop through the desert. It is a steep winding road that goes through Wadi Nar in the Judean Desert and then winds back up north toward Ramallah once you bypass Jerusalem. It took us almost two hours to take a trip that would otherwise have taken no more than thirty or forty minutes. In June 2010, AP reporter Ben Hubbard wrote this about the trip: "Wadi Nar means 'the Valley of Fire,' a place where brakes fail, clutches burn up, engines stall and people die. The ride up and down the canyon walls is among the worst routes Palestinian motorists must use to circumnavigate the towns, army posts and well-maintained highways built for Israelis."[1]

---

1 Ben Hubbard, "Separate roads push West Bank Arabs to the byways", *The Guardian*, June 13, 2010. Archived at http://www.guardian.co.uk/world/feedarticle/9215464.

But it was well worth the drive. Nabi Saleh lies in a spot surrounded by roll-ing hills and olive groves, the epitome of everything that is beautiful about the Palestinian landscape. As you approach the village, you go past the pre-military Jewish preparatory school and then the settlement of Halamish, both of which are eyesores, constructed with no regard for the landscape.

Ali is chronically late, even by Palestinian standards, so although he drove like a madman, by the time we reached Nabi Saleh the protest had begun and the Israeli army had blocked the main road to the village. We were bummed. Ali is very serious and passionate about the development of a non-violent resistance throughout the West Bank, but often he is his worst enemy and he was very upset with himself for being late. "Ali, in Hebrew we say, '*Kol Akava Letova*'," I said.

"We have the same saying in Arabic," he replied, quoting: "*Kul Ta'akhir fiha khir*,"—every delay happens for a good reason. Then Ali remembered that there was a back entrance to the village, which was another 15-minute drive.

When we reached the other side of the village, there was an army roadblock there as well. Three soldiers gestured for us to stop. I could tell they were reservists because they were older and pretty unkempt.

"Closed military zone," they said. "You have to turn back." *Indeed!*

Ali and I stepped out of the car to talk to them. They were clearly reservists, and their commanding officer, a captain in the reserves, who was a short, pleasant-looking chap with a beard, told us we couldn't enter.

Ali tried a few lines on him. "What's the matter?" he asked. "We just want to visit friends, and we always visit here, and we were never stopped before."

The officer smiled and said, "You wouldn't want to go there anyway, it's a war zone."

"War?" I asked. "You call this a war? A war means two armies engaged in battle. Is there another army present? Do they have tanks and warplanes? Are they well armed? Surely you aren't referring to the boys throwing rocks as an army." I didn't wait for him to reply, before adding: "Besides, if you weren't here, there would be no rocks. They would march with their flags and then go home."

Other soldiers began crowding around, all of them reservists and far less patient than their commanding officer. "This is a closed military zone, and you are in violation of the commanding officer ordering you to leave," one said. "Are you refusing to follow the order?"

"I thought he was in charge," I said, pointing to the young officer, who was too young and friendly for his own good. "Besides," I continued, "neither you nor your officer has the authority to declare this area closed. This is Palestinian land so why don't you all go home and let us and the people of Nabi Saleh exercise our right to protest in peace?"

"But why are you even here, what are you protesting?" the officer asked in a very friendly tone.

"We are here to protest the occupation and theft of these people's land," I said. "Why are you here?"

"This place is no different from Tel Aviv or any other place in Israel. Jews are allowed to live here if they want, and we are charged with keeping them safe," the officer said.

This exchange went on for some time until finally the conversation looked like it was reaching a boiling point. Ali began talking to the other soldiers too, and he mentioned that Israeli soldiers had killed his brother at a checkpoint similar to this one.

"Well, if we killed him then he must have deserved to die. Israeli soldiers do not kill without good reason," one of the soldiers replied.

I was chomping at the bit to bring up Jenin or Gaza or a thousand other examples where Israeli soldiers had killed countless innocent people for no good reason. But this was not the time or the place. Our objective was to get into Nabi Saleh and I didn't trust myself to keep my temper under control. I suggested to Ali that we leave. I didn't want any problems with these soldiers because we still had another option for getting to the village. As we were turned away to get into the car, I stopped and looked at the soldiers, now a group of seven or eight. I pointed at Ali and said, "You have no idea who this man is, but believe me when I tell you that one day you will all go on your knees before this man and beg for his forgiveness."

We got into the car and turned around.

We drove back about 300 yards, so we were out of the soldiers' sight, parked the car among the olive trees, and walked through the olive grove under the soldiers' noses to the village. We walked in silence for about ten minutes, until we saw Bassem Tamimi waiting for us. Bassem is about 5'8", with slightly graying light brown hair, a mustache, and light blue eyes. He is a good-looking man and he was wearing jeans and a black leather jacket. He was very friendly, and I was struck by how calm he seemed. Ali introduced us and we all walked back up to the road and toward the village.

As we entered the village itself we saw a group of Magav[2] soldiers firing tear gas grenades from massive launchers. They paid us no heed as we walked right by them, made a right turn, and walked up a hill to Bassem's house.

Ali told me that he and Bassem knew one another from prison, and Bassem was a highly respected man in the village and in Palestine in general. Calm and collected, he had the look of a guy who wouldn't be easily unnerved. We sat on his porch and had tea while his two young children played outside.

The house sits on a hill so we had a good view of the small village whose 500 inhabitants had decided it was time speak their mind. On the dirt road right by the house were four Israeli army reservists, one of whom was an officer; they had

---

2 Magav is the acronym for *Mishmar HaGvul*, which means "border patrol" in Hebrew.

just erected a small makeshift barrier from large rocks they had gathered. A few minutes after they were done an army Jeep approached, wanting to drive through, so they had to dismantle the barrier to let the Jeep pass. As they bent over to move the heavy rocks, their guns slung forward and hit their heads. They were a miserable sight to see, not at all the daring and fearless soldiers one might expect from an army that claims to be one the world's finest. It took great deal of restraint on my part to keep still and not tell the soldiers how stupid they looked. But, since I was a guest, I didn't want to cause any trouble.

Bassem soon invited us into the house to eat. His mother cooked and he served us eggs, fresh baked bread with freshly picked herbs, and an assortment of salads. As we sat down to eat, his cell phone rang. Ali smiled as he listened to Bassem talk. I asked Ali what was so funny. He said the regional Magav commander was on the line. "He is asking Bassem in Arabic to tell the *shebab* (the youth who were protesting) to stop because it was Friday, and he wanted to go home for the weekend."

An Israeli military commander calling a Palestinian resistance leader, begging him to stop protesting so he could go home to Friday dinner? What kind of House of Crazy was this?

The commander called several more times, but every time Bassem said calmly, "When the soldiers leave the village, the protest will stop. Not the other way around."

After we were done eating we walked down toward the main road. There were quite a lot of people there, watching the protest, including young children who were stuffing their little pockets with rocks. The older kids were throwing rocks and the soldiers were shooting. They fired mostly tear gas and from time to time you could hear that they turned to rubber-coated steel bullets and live ammunition. At one point, one of the young Palestinians picked up a tear gas grenade that had been shot at him and threw it back at the reservists while it was still spewing gas. The Israeli soldiers were terrified. They began running wildly in all directions, tripping over the rocks, their guns dangling from their shoulders and helmets bopping on their heads. I thought, thank God for them that they don't have to face a real army.

I could clearly hear shots being fired from somewhere above us. I looked around and I noticed that the commanding officer, a lieutenant colonel, was standing a few hundred feet away. I shouted to him in Hebrew "There are children everywhere! Stop shooting!" He looked at me for a long minute, then looked away and started walking back toward his Jeep.

Just then a woman wearing a black *hijab*, pants, and a black shirt ran past me. She had an intent, almost mesmerized look, and she was holding a very large rock in her hand. She ran toward the lieutenant colonel and hurled it at him as he was walking away.

As the rock sailed toward the back of his head, my heart stopped. If the rock hit the officer, the repercussions would have been horrendous. The soldiers would have had a field day shooting everyone in sight. Luckily, it missed him by a few inches. I was relieved and furious at the same time.

"At least get the children out of here!" I shouted.

With all the commotion, the officer was oblivious and had no clue that he had been in danger. He went to his Jeep, sat in it for a while, and every so often would come out shooting in the air and then return to the Jeep. I kept calling him and the others to stop shooting. Then the Jeeps would speed by, screeching up and down the road, and the rocks would fall on them like a hailstorm.

I looked at Ali as all this was going on. "Don't you feel like throwing rocks at the soldiers?" I asked him. Ali, like many other Palestinians I've met, strongly disapproved of the rock throwing. "It only serves the occupation," he said. But unlike several towns where rock throwing was frowned upon, the *shebab* there had not yet bought into the non-violent aspect of the protests. They reacted to the army's presence in their village by throwing rocks and, frankly, I couldn't blame them.

It was getting late and we still had a long drive to get back to Beit Ummar. It didn't look like this would end any time soon, so we ventured back, rocks and tear gas canisters flying above us in every direction, until we reached the car, still parked in the olive grove. I was never so relieved in my life as when we entered that car and drove off.

I couldn't get the day's images out of my head: Jeeps screeching through the tiny village and rocks coming down on them like a hailstorm. Right or wrong, brave or foolish, I had to admit to myself that on a simply visceral level, seeing the Jeeps get blasted with stones felt good. I felt no sympathy for the soldiers, none whatsoever.

As we drove away I really felt I could use a beer. I asked Ali if we could stop somewhere for a beer because there is no alcohol in Beit Ummar, and drinking is frowned upon in many places throughout the West Bank. So we stopped at a gas station on the way and sat for a bit while I had a beer. Back in Beit Ummar that evening we went to Yusef's apartment. Yusef was Khaled and Ali's older brother who was killed by soldiers at the checkpoint in Beit Ummar. His widow and her children, along with Seham, Ali's older sister, were all there. We had dinner, then we had tea, watched music videos on television, and relaxed for the rest of the evening. I was worn out by the long trip and the day's events. But there was more to come.

Just prior to coming to Beit Ummar, I had learned that in Beit Ummar, too, there were weekly protest marches. By that point I knew of about half a dozen towns and villages that had joined the popular resistance movement. I felt a strong bond with Beit Ummar, both because of the bond between my family and the Abu Awad family and also because I personally loved Khaled and Ali and their family and it hurt me physically to see what was being done to them. So I wanted to protest.

The day after the trip to Nabi Saleh was a very windy, almost stormy Saturday and Khaled took me to meet Yunis, one of the men behind the popular resistance. Yunis and I walked together from his house to the main road, trying to look casual so as not to attract the attention of the soldiers who were manning the checkpoint at the entrance to the town. We walked into an orchard where we met about twenty other protesters—Israelis, Palestinians, and foreign nationals—some who had come from other parts of the country. We began walking as a group towards the main road leading to Hebron, several people carrying flags and one person with a megaphone. Yunis told everyone in English that we were to stay on the side of the road and not disturb the traffic, and that this protest was completely non-violent so no stone throwing under any circumstances.

We reached the main road and less than two minutes after we began to walk an ocean of fully armed combat soldiers appeared as though out of nowhere. "Get in formation already, hurry up" I heard one of the sergeants calling his men. In no time there were two rows of soldiers pushing and shoving us, and several officers were running around as though this was some battlefield. I immediately began to argue with the soldier in front of me and insisted that they stop pushing us and leave us alone, but to no avail. I began to tell them what they were doing was illegal and then mocked them for showing up dressed for combat only to push around a few peaceniks with a flag. My voice grew louder and the pushing got harder. "Get him out of here" I heard one of the officers, a tall army major, yelling at the top of his lungs as two soldiers grabbed me by the shirt, shoved me away from the rest of the group and placed me by an army Jeep. I stood there for a while looking as the soldiers proceeded to push the protesters first one way, and then another. Finally I began walking back toward the group as they were being led across the busy road and up a steep terrace towards the orchard where we all met initially. As soon as I was near the group I noticed several army majors and at some distance I could see the brigade commander, a lieutenant colonel. He was an Ethiopian immigrant with a small physique and I remembered reading a story about him in an Israeli paper: He was considered a success story, one of few Ethiopian immigrants who succeeded in the brutal environment of the IDF. I began to call to him and tell him he was a criminal and that he and the other officers were a shame to their country and to Jews everywhere. The major who ordered me removed the first time then came to me, and grabbed me himself, shouting, "He's under arrest for incitement, get him the hell outta here, now." Once again two soldiers dragged me to the Jeep but this time they proceeded to handcuff me. At one point a young blond soldier with a ski mask covering his face approached and stood very close to me. "Cowards and criminals always cover their face when they do dirty work," I said to him. He yelled at me to shut up and I was placed inside the Jeep, the door slammed in my face, with a single young soldier to guard me. A few moments later the major opened the door, warning, "Now you will pay for this!" "No," I said. "You will pay when you are brought before the war crimes court at The Hague. You are not soldiers! You are a sad and pathetic excuse for soldiers. My father was a general and I can tell you that you are a sorry sight for an officer." He slammed the door again and we drove off. Suddenly the Jeep came to a screeching halt. The door opened, "Which general is your father?" It was the major. He was so curious he couldn't contain himself. "He was a real officer not like you, in fact he warned that the IDF would deteriorate and people like you would emerge as officers. You are a shame to all Jewish people. Oh, yes, and my father was Matti Peled."

He slammed the door a final time, and off we went to the Hebron police station in the settlement of Kiryat Arba.

Kiryat Arba is an Israeli settlement built in Hebron, one of the first ones built in the West Bank. It is a ghetto, albeit one that Jews impose on themselves, and the Hebron police station is a small ghetto within a ghetto. To enter the settlement, we had to pass through a fortified checkpoint and weave past large concrete blocks and an electronic gate guarded by sentries. As we rode through this very strange town, we drove past groups of religious Jewish kids and mothers with baby carriages to the police station, where we had to go through a sentry post and electronic gates all over again.

"Fuck these settlers," I heard one soldier say to the other. "They treat us like shit here and we have to protect them."

As I saw all this I began to think to myself, *Palestine's landscape is the kind that beckons you to open doors and its people are hospitable and always welcome you with open arms. It is a land of hospitality and kindness.* Yet the settlers and their protectors have chosen to impose themselves on this land and its people, to take the land by force and close themselves within fortified ghettos, called settlements. Kiryat Arba, just like the other settlements in the West Bank, is an open wound in an otherwise peaceful and welcoming land. How or why people choose to live like this is beyond me.

The soldiers hustled me into the police station, where they were supposed to hand me over to the police. But the station commander, a short, athletic-looking police officer with cropped white hair and an air of self-importance, was adamant that he wouldn't take me.

"I can't arrest this man without the officer who arrested him present. He has to be here in person to give a statement."

"They said they'll send a fax from the brigade headquarters," replied one of the soldiers, caught between the police and the army.

"Tell your commanders that this is a democracy," the station chief said. "This man has rights. We have to follow the letter of the law or I will be forced to release him."

The soldiers were baffled. The exchange between the two authorities, the army and the police went on for hours, each side unwilling to budge while I sat in the middle, very calmly watching this unbelievable spectacle.

Finally, the station commander came out of his office, clearly exasperated, and explained in slow, simple terms to the soldiers, "Look, he is an Israeli citizen and he has rights. It's not a Palestinian that I can just beat up and throw in prison."

One of the soldiers turned to me. "It seems that the law is on your side," he said.

The hours passed, and I somehow knew the major wouldn't come. Finally it was over. One of the soldiers said they were releasing me and he asked where I wanted to be dropped off.

"Back to Beit Ummar where you picked me up."

"It is a hostile place and you will not be safe there," he said. "Why don't I release you in here in the settlement in Kiryat Arba and someone can come and pick you up from here?"

"Thank you," I said. "But my friends in Beit Ummar will be expecting me."

I did not expect them to agree but there we were off again in the Jeep, leaving this ghetto of fanatics behind and returning to Beit Ummar. I called Khaled, and he said he'd wait for me at the entrance to Beit Ummar by the checkpoint. I then called Mazen just for fun. I enjoyed dialing my Palestinian friends from this fortress on wheels, which is exactly what the army Jeep felt like. It ensures that the soldiers see nothing but wires and a hole big enough to fit a gun barrel and shoot. The beautiful Hebron hills and olive trees do not enter through their windows, and neither do people's faces.

When we reached Beit Ummar, the soldiers warned me again, "This is hostile territory, and no one can guarantee your safety here." I thanked them again and walked peacefully into Beit Ummar. The look of surprise on the soldier's face was equal to the look of surprise on the faces of the Palestinians standing around at the entrance to the town as I emerged from the belly of the armored beast. The storm had subsided by then and it felt good to walk in the cool air.

In the summer of 2011 I went to back Beit Ummar to protest again, and again I was arrested. This time we marched towards the settlement of Karmei Tsur that has been eating up Beit Ummar land for years, and now was in the process of expanding and taking yet more land. We marched among cultivated terraces of fruit trees and dirt roads. The soldiers were more brutal this time and there was a new deputy brigade commander, an army major, in command. We were ordered to turn back and within minutes the pushing began. As I was walking away I got shoved really hard by a young soldier, and as the terrain was hard enough to balance, I turned and told him to back off. Within seconds, the deputy brigade commander was in my face. He placed me in a choke, grabbed and twisted my arm, severely spraining my thumb, releasing just as I thought he was going to fracture it. He then asked for my ID and charged me with attacking an army officer and placed me under arrest. "I want four men watching him, he assaulted an officer," he yelled. Another one of the commanders, an army captain, came with four soldiers and stood around me. "Your CO is a liar, you really should report him and quit your posts," I told the captain and soldiers as they stood around me. I showed them my swollen thumb: "Look at this, who do you think assaulted whom? Do you really believe I assaulted a fully armed combat soldier, not to say a major in uniform?"

"Shut up, we saw you assault him," the captain replied. "And him!" he added as he pointed to a young red-headed soldier. "Hey, he assaulted you too, didn't he?"

They soldier just looked down and walked away.

"Your major and your captain are liars! You should report them both and quit this despicable work!" I yelled at the young red-headed soldier. "Is this what you signed up to do when you joined a combat unit?"

I was held at the same spot for some time while the protesters, all 20 of them, dispersed. "I can't believe it takes so many fully armed IDF combat soldiers to subdue 20 unarmed protesters. When did the Israeli army become so weak and cowardly?" I asked as loud as I could. I then suggested to the soldiers that one day they will all return to apologize to the people of Beit Ummar at which point one of the soldiers begged his officer to let him "show me not to talk like that."

I was taken to the Jeep where the commanders stood around all sweaty and dusty. "By the looks of the dust and sweat one might think you were all real soldiers in combat. But you know what you did today was not combat," I told them. "It was sad and pathetic and all you got was me. This was no heroic battle, and you are certainly no heroes." The deputy commander then had me searched, took my iPhone and erased the video and photos I took, looked through my bag and generally tried to show he was in command. "You are a sorry sight for officers," I said.

Once again, I was taken to the Kiryat Arba police station—and this time an officer did show up to place the charges. It was not the deputy commander, who by then had my passport, but the captain. He told a tall tale about how I attacked him, resisted the arrest and forced him to wrestle me and forcibly take my ID out of my shirt pocket. "What pocket?" I asked the investigator as I showed him my pocketless shirt. The captain also said I called him a Nazi. "Too bad he is not here to say this to my face," I told the investigator who then told me that they always charge protesters that they arrest with calling them Nazis.

All of the ridiculous charges were easy to dispute, although by the time I was questioned the officer left and I could not confront him. Some of my exchanges with the soldiers were caught on video and put on YouTube. In the end, I had to sign a document promising I would not return to the region for a period of 14 days. I was returning home to California a few days later, so it mattered little and I signed the document. I was released, but this time the soldiers flatly refused to take me back to Beit Ummar. I was dropped off on the main road to Hebron, outside of Kiryat Arba, and waited until friends from Beit Ummar came by to pick me up.

Somehow, through all this madness, I stayed relatively calm—something I find hard to explain. Perhaps it had to do with the soothing Palestinian landscape.

PART IV

Hope for Peace

Chapter 14:

The Next Generation

On a sunny winter morning, the view from my childhood bedroom in Motza is breathtaking. Every leaf of every tree and shrub seems delighted to feel the sun after a long, cold night. The view is a tapestry of shades, from yellow-green to the deep dark of evergreens. There are flowers embedded in this composition, coral and fuchsia. And the clean blue Mediterranean sky. It's hard to look away.

I am able to return to this spot only three or four times each year and only for a few weeks at a time. When I do visit Israel/Palestine, I am busy meeting people and crossing over to the Palestinian side of the wall, and it feels like I am consumed with activity. But, when I am there at my mother's house, the house I grew up in, I try to take in as much of the moment as possible.

It's not easy leaving my life in Coronado—my karate school, Gila and our three children—even for just a few weeks. Gila is busy running her own business, an acupuncture clinic. Usually a lot of planning goes into my departure, so that things continue to run smoothly. Over the years my staff of instructors and administrators have learned that this is my reality: I live in one place and my heart is quite often in another.

And while it's true that these trips are often motivated by activist missions, I also travel because I like to visit my mother and see the rest of the family as much as possible.

Although in her eighties, my mother Zika keeps a busy, healthy schedule. She sleeps well and exercises by swimming and taking yoga classes. The real secret to her health is her garden, the earth into which she pours her heart and which, in return, yields magnificent blossoms every day of the year, even on the hottest and driest days of the Jerusalem summer. She does this by conserving water and recycling every drop so that she can give it to her plants. She's in her garden every day first thing in the morning, digging her hands deep into the fine earth around her house. The plants and birds seem grateful. In the early hours of dawn, as the sky turns from black to purple, you can hear the birds sing their morning songs, as though praising the beauty Zika has created for them—and for the rest of us—to enjoy.

It was my mother who instilled in me a love of children, and it's largely thanks to her that I decided to make a career out of working with them. Nothing compares to the satisfaction of engaging children. But for years my career had unfolded far away from the conflict in Israel/Palestine. I thought it was time, now, to bring these two parts of my life together—to merge teaching and activism.

Teaching karate to children means providing them with structure, discipline, and high expectations. When taught correctly, karate will also instill an independent spirit. Thus another form of defiance opened up to me: I would teach Palestinian children karate.

Plus I wanted to see how Israeli control over Palestinian life had affected children. I wanted to see and interact with kids in the West Bank, in places like the Deheishe Refugee Camp, or the town of Anata, where playgrounds and parks were scarce. I wanted to hear Palestinian children, listen to them, and to get an idea of how they viewed their lives and their future. So I looked for opportunities to teach karate in those very places.

It was the summer of 2007 when my sister Nurit had actually come up with the idea for me to teach in Palestine. Wael Salame, a good friend who we knew through Combatants for Peace, had boys who practiced at a Tae Kwon Do club in Anata, just north of Jerusalem, and Nurit told him about me and between them they set the whole thing up.

The truth is, I had no idea what to expect. I knew for a fact that Palestinian children had a great burden to carry, far more than children should have: fathers or brothers locked up in Israeli prisons usually with no visitors allowed, family members killed in the conflict, neighbors and friends whose homes were lost to settlement activity or destroyed by the army. Not to mention irregular supplies of water and electricity, severe travel restrictions that impacted their ability to reach school every morning, night raids by Israeli soldiers who stormed their homes at all hours. And the list goes on. One could only assume that their parents and teachers, who loved and cared for them, had given them the tools to cope with their impossible and abnormal surroundings.

I took Eitan, who was 13 at the time, and Doron, who was 11, and their cousin Yigal, who was 14, along to Anata to practice as well. When we arrived at the Tae Kwon Do club, we received a warm welcome from Wissam, the instructor, and there were more than 50 kids, all lined up and ready for practice. There were boys and girls practicing together, and they were completely comfortable with each other, which I am always happy to see. While there is a stereotype that karate is a boys' activity, girls usually really enjoy and excel at it, and I always encourage girls and women to take classes alongside boys and men. The students at the Anata club were serious, polite, and eager to learn, all signs of a good martial arts school.

Practice went on for about an hour and a half. After practice, we all relaxed for a while and talked. Eitan began chatting with one of the kids. I heard him ask: "Do you like going to the beach?" Coming from a southern California beach town, it was a natural thing for him to wonder.

The boy took Eitan to the window and showed him the separation wall being built just outside the gym where the class took place. Even though Anata is part of

Jerusalem, the wall and the checkpoint prevent its residents from traveling freely. "We can't go to the beach," he said. "We are not allowed."

When practice was over we had dinner in Anata at Wael's home, and when we were done the adults had coffee and the kids played soccer on the small balcony adjacent to the house, because there was nowhere outside for them to play. On the way home, at the Anata checkpoint, my sons noticed a Palestinian boy not much older than them being taken in by the soldiers.

Doron, frightened by what he saw, asked, "What did he do?"

"I am not sure." I was not able to reassure him.

Jamal introduced me to a karate club in Ramallah that is run by a friend of his named Nidal. Nidal has been practicing and teaching for many years and has built a fine student body and a very nice, traditional Japanese dojo. I have visited there several times and taught classes and Nidal, Jamal, and I always have a good time together. In the summer of 2010 I went to Nidal's karate school with Doron, and Nurit came along, too, to watch. The class was full, and it was extremely hot. As the class progressed, the heat became unbearable, and with it my thirst. I was thinking of asking Nurit for a water bottle when I remembered then that this was the month of Ramadan.

During this month Muslims refrain from eating or drinking from sunrise to sundown. It was about four in the afternoon and the fast was not going to be broken until seven that evening. I looked at Doron and I could see his mouth was dry

Doron, standing third from left and I standing next to him, with Sensei Nidal at the karate club in Ramallah.

too. The students did not show any signs of weakness, and they were all cheerful and completely focused on karate. Still, their faces were red, and they were hot and sweaty, so I stopped the class for a moment and asked them to sit down.

"*Meen Minkum Sayyim?*" I said. Who among you is fasting?

I could see that even Nidal was surprised when they all raised their hands.

"Wow! You guys are very special kids. There aren't a lot of places in the world where kids would come to karate class and work so hard in such heat without food or water. Especially water!"

I looked at Doron again and I saw that he knew what it meant when all the kids raised their hands: that we, too, were not going to drink till sundown.

During class I gave the kids the same talks I do when I teach at my own karate school in the U.S., but with a little extra: always be respectful, believe in yourself, use your head. I also mention the fact that I can go to Jerusalem and Tel Aviv and travel freely in this country, but they cannot.

"This is your country, your home, and you should be allowed to travel freely as I do, as every Israeli child does. Karate teaches us to overcome insurmountable obstacles, and you will find a way out of the injustice in which you live, and do it without having to sacrifice your young lives. You will have the freedom to live, study, work, and travel anywhere you like. Just remember to believe in your abilities and don't be afraid."

There is always silence when I say these things. The first time I said something like this to Palestinian kids, it was actually not at a karate class. I was at Jamal's house. His older daughter mentioned that she wanted to attend dental school, and we talked about languages. I said that I thought it would be useful for her to be able to converse freely in Hebrew and English so that she could treat patients in cities around the country. "The occupation will not last forever, and you will be able to practice in Haifa or Tel Aviv and so Hebrew would be useful when you treat Israeli patients." She looked very surprised at my assumption that the end was in sight. "*Insha' Allah, Insha' Allah,*" she said. God willing. And her mother repeated, "Insha' Allah."

I do believe that Israelis and Palestinians will live free side by side one day. And even if we become two separate states, why could a Palestinian doctor not practice in Israel, or vice versa? I felt this was an important thing to say in front of Palestinian children. I wanted to state with complete certainty that things will change for the better and to encourage them to believe it and to act in accordance with this belief. The overwhelming force of the Israeli army can make anyone feel hopeless. And the fact that the world does little for Palestinians can lead to a sense of helplessness. I have always thought that change will come from the bottom up— not from any outside source, but from these children. But someone has to paint the picture, and so I do that whenever I can.

In late 2010, I called my friend Mazen Faraj from the U.S. and I told him that I wanted to visit Deheishe Refugee Camp near Bethlehem. Mazen was born and raised in Deheishe, and he still lives there with his family. I asked if he thought I could teach karate there. Mazen did not hesitate to endorse the idea and quickly moved to make arrangements for me.

Once again, I left my cozy existence in Coronado and traveled to my troubled homeland. I called Mazen again from Jerusalem, and we decided to meet by the Everest Hotel in Beit Jala where the Palestinian branch of the Bereaved Families Forum has their office.

It was a sunny December afternoon and I sat out on the balcony waiting for Mazen. The office is located on a hill, and so I had a full view of the occupation. Israeli military vehicles, covered in protective wiring, drove fast and nervously with their blue lights flashing. I could hear the loudspeakers from the army base nearby and police sirens in the distance. And I could hear the sound of new homes going up in the Israeli settlement of Har Gilo.

Mazen arrived a few minutes after I did. I spent most of the afternoon sitting on the porch talking with him. He had set up a visit to the Deheishe Refugee Camp for me, and I was going to teach karate there over the next few days. Mazen is energetic, and he knows how to get things organized.

Sitting on the porch—while he lit one cigarette with another and I sipped Arabic coffee—we went from small talk to politics and then to his story and the story of his family. His older brothers had participated in the first Intifada and sat in jail; they are all principled men who hold respectable positions. Mazen himself belonged to the PFLP and had been arrested by Israel for that reason. He told me of the torture and beatings he endured during his interrogation.

"What kept me from breaking during the interrogation and torture was the knowledge that, like my brothers before me, it would be known that I did not break during the interrogations and I did not talk."

He lit another cigarette, cursed in Arabic, and then said, "Not a night goes by without nightmares from the torture I received at the hands of the Israelis."

Mazen's father, Ali Faraj, 62, was killed in April 2002 during the second Intifada. He went out to buy food for the family and while he was gone, the Israeli authorities imposed a curfew on the camp. Being gone from the camp he didn't realize the curfew was in effect and when he returned, an Israeli tank fired at him and killed him. Then, the Israeli authorities immediately arrested Mazen and kept him under administrative detention for several months. He was targeted because he was the youngest of all his brothers, and the only one who was not yet married. Therefore it was assumed he posed a threat and might try to take revenge.

It was soon time for lunch and the two of us drove to his house in Deheishe. This was my first visit to any refugee camp. In the decades since it was established, Deheishe has become a bustling, disorganized, and overcrowded little town. Its 13,000 residents live on one-quarter of a square mile. All of them are either from or are descendants of people who were from villages around Jerusalem that were destroyed when Israel was established.

My friend Mazen Faraj on the right with Eitan at Deheishe Refugee Camp.

We had lunch and coffee at Mazen's house with his wife and two daughters (I later brought Eitan with me to visit them as well), and then Mazen took me to the Phoenix House, or *El-Feneiq*, a spacious community center that offers kids in Deheishe free after-school activities and camps when school is out. Young college kids who volunteer conduct the activities. Since there are no parks or playgrounds and no swimming pool, putting together activities for kids takes creativity and a lot of dedication. The volunteers I met there, young men and women, had both.

"Why is there no pool?" I asked one of the volunteers who showed me around the center.

"We have no water."

I did not understand.

"All the water supply is controlled by Israel and sometimes the authorities shut the water supply and the camp goes for days without water. You cannot have a pool when you don't even have enough water to drink and wash." Then he smiled: "But we have a very nice gym where we can have the karate class."

For karate to work you need the right environment, a dojo, a place dedicated to training the mind and body. There is no dojo in Deheishe so I too had to be creative and I created one in the gym at *El-Feneiq*. Using both my limited Arabic and some assistance I told the children that they need to remove their shoes and socks before the lesson began. They did remove their shoes, but as children usually do they threw them all over the place. Then, rather than begin the class I asked them to come with me. I removed my shoes and placed them neatly against the wall. I told them that where my shoes go may seem like a trivial thing, but it creates an atmosphere of attention to detail and order, and that brings comfort and calm to the class.

"And keeping the dojo tidy is an important part of karate," I added.

Once the shoes were in place, I assembled the children and proceeded to introduce myself and ask them their names and ages. Then I told them that the first thing we learn in karate is respect, *ihtiram*. In karate respect for others as well as for ourselves, is of the utmost importance. That is why we bow, listen to one another, use our heads and our words to resolve conflicts and solve problems. As I was saying this, I couldn't help thinking of the irony in saying this to people who live under an occupying power that respects none of these things.

Then we began the lesson. As the children lined up I explained how to stand, and as I was explaining a girl who had practiced karate before called out the names of the different positions in Japanese. "*Musubi-dachi*," she said softly, revealing that she knew the term for standing with our feet together. Then I showed them how to kneel down. "*Seiza*," she said this time. She knew how to execute the moves and knew the commands of the various techniques in Japanese. It was good to have her there, and she was a great little helper for me and for the class. An hour had gone by quickly, but it was getting late in the day and dark outside, so I had to wrap things up. I promised we would start earlier the next day.

When I arrived the next afternoon, I saw a long row of neatly placed shoes in the corridor by the gym. More than 35 kids sat quietly on their knees in *seiza*. They were ready and they had taken in what I had previously taught them. The volunteers were visibly proud of the kids, and so was I. Half the class had been there the previous day and the other half was there for the first time. I welcomed all the new students, and I asked those who were there for the first lesson to share with the others what we had talked about.

"Never smoke, it gives you cancer," was the first comment.

"Don't hit others and avoid getting hit yourself," was the next comment.

"Be respectful to yourself and people around you."

"Do your best and do not give up when things get hard."

On and on they went. I was in a daze. These little guys really internalized the lessons and were able to recall them accurately.

I noticed a pile of small exercise mats in a corner of the gym, and I knew exactly how we would end the class that day. There is nothing kids love more than to wrestle. I had them do lots of running and relays and then sat them down and explained how all fighting in karate is done, and wrestling especially. We begin with *ihtiram*—respect, which in karate is expressed by bowing before and after

Karate wrestling in Deheishe.

each match. I made a point of demonstrating how even a student who is a lot smaller than I can take me down. I used Kusai, a particularly talented and serious 11-year-old who came to every session.

"Knowing how to use your strength against a larger, seemingly stronger opponent is a big part of karate training," I told them. This also applies when one is fighting to resist a larger and more powerful occupying power, and I made sure that this point did not get lost on the students and volunteers. While there is an aspect of karate that exhibits conformity, in reality, the history of karate is filled with defiance and rebellion. Karate is about beating the odds and developing an independent spirit. I wanted to share that sense of defiance with these kids. Not that they needed my help, because they could be plenty defiant on their own—but to help channel that energy and demonstrate that the relative normality in which they exist is in fact not normal, and that they should not be afraid to rebel in a responsible, non-violent manner.

When I was done teaching, Mazen picked me up and I returned to the Forum office. From there, Khaled drove me to his house in Beit Ummar, where I would be spending the next five days. Khaled, wearing a dark suit and a serious expression as always, had clearly not eaten all day, distracted by a million and one things. He drove through dirt roads and narrow alleys because most of the wide paved roads are off limits to Palestinians. I watched him as he absentmindedly sucked on one cigarette after another.

I have noticed that Khaled doesn't just smoke his cigarettes. He chews on the filter for a while, and then inhales deeply like a man hungry for air. Then he blows out the smoke that has been thinned out because he's absorbed so much of it. He chain smokes as though sucking in the freedom denied to him by the Israeli invasion into his life, his family, and his country.

Living in the West Bank among Palestinian friends, I began to realize that the Palestinians' suffering goes on no matter how dedicated they are to peace and reconciliation. Dedication to reconciliation and willingness to reach out does not provide Palestinians immunity from the daily struggles with Israeli soldiers, the humiliation or the cold, discriminatory administration of Israel's occupation regime. In Khaled's case, if not for sheer luck or the grace of God, on November 13, 2004, he would have lost yet another family member to Israeli violence, his son Mu'ayed.

It happened two days after Yasser Arafat died. That was the day Arafat's funeral took place in Ramallah, and smaller ceremonies and observances were held all over the West Bank for those who couldn't make it to Ramallah. It was a solemn day for Palestinians and many others around the world. The Israeli army was supposed to keep a low profile and allow Palestinians to mourn the death of their leader.

But in Beit Ummar soldiers in an army Jeep decided to go screeching through town. Residents were leading a peaceful procession of mourning and a symbolic funeral, and as one may expect, the Jeep's presence ignited the atmosphere. A few young people threw stones at the Jeep, and the soldiers responded by firing live ammunition. The result was two casualties: Jameel Omar, a 19-year-old student who was killed immediately, and Mu'ayed Abu Awad, Khaled's 15-year-old son, who was shot by a 5.56 caliber bullet to the hip. Mu'ayed lay on the ground bleeding badly, and the soldiers stood around him, preventing an ambulance from evacuating him.

Khaled was in northern Israel at the time, in a room full of Israeli high school students. He and an Israeli member of the Bereaved Families Forum were there to speak about reconciliation. They explained that the cycle of violence has cost too many lives on both sides and must be stopped and that real dialogue should take place. Suddenly they were called outside the room and informed that soldiers had shot Mu'ayed.

The presentation ended abruptly, and as they turned to leave, Khaled stopped at the door. He turned to the students, who remained shocked in their seats.

"Whatever happens, even if the worst happens, even if I have lost my son, we must never lose hope. We must never stray from the path of reconciliation."

Back in Beit Ummar, Mu'ayed looked like he would soon bleed to death, and his friends decided to evacuate him under fire. A few guys distracted the soldiers by hurling stones, and as the soldiers chased them, others managed to get Mu'ayed into the ambulance that took him to the hospital in Hebron, some 10 miles away. By the time he arrived his condition was too severe and the doctors in Hebron were not able to help him.

When word got out that Khaled's son was injured, people at the office of the Bereaved Families Forum in Israel began searching for someone who could help save the boy's life. In what turned out to be a joint Israeli-Palestinian effort, Mu'ayed was transported to an Israeli ambulance that took him to Hadassah Hospital in Jerusalem, where adequate facilities and the best-trained doctors could treat him. On the way, Israeli army medics tried to stabilize his condition, but by the time they reached the hospital his blood pressure was zero.

Mu'ayad was rushed into the operating room just as Khaled, breathless and sick with worry, arrived. At last, close to midnight, after long hours, the doctor came out of the operating room. "Had he arrived 10 minutes later, he would have died. Thank goodness, we were able to save him and save his leg."

Many Israeli and Palestinian friends came to the hospital to be with Khaled and Mu'ayed during the difficult weeks of Mu'ayed's recovery and rehabilitation. I called several times from the U.S. and spoke to Khaled, and I was relieved to hear that the worst was over.

None of this has provided Khaled and his family immunity. In January of 2010, Israeli soldiers came to Khaled's house in Beit Ummar at two in the morning, banged on the door, and threatened to blow up the house if the family didn't open up immediately. They then threw everyone out of the house, including young and terrified children. They ransacked the house leaving a trail of destruction, and when they emerged the soldiers singled out Muhaned, Mu'ayed's twin brother, and took him away. After spending 12 months in prison without being charged, Muhaned was finally tried and sentenced to a total of two years in an Israeli prison. Meanwhile, Khaled's entire family was denied entry into Israel and thus prevented from visiting Muhaned.

Over the years, Bassam Aramin, father of ten-year-old Abir, who was shot by an Israeli soldier, became known for his dedication to reconciliation and his relentless activism for Palestinian freedom. He coined the term "Palestinian Bar Mitzvah"[1] to describe the horror most young Palestinians have to endure at the hands of the Israeli soldiers. He wrote an article with the same title after the Israeli army put his son Arab through a real-life nightmare. This nightmare, Bassam later wrote, which took place less than two years after his daughter Abir was killed, is the daily bread, the rite of passage of every Palestinian boy.

It happened on a Friday in July 2008, when Bassam's older son Arab, 14 at the time, asked to go on a rare excursion with friends to the Sea of Galilee in the north. For days he had begged Bassam to let him go. At first Bassam refused, insisting that

1 Bassam Aramin, "The Palestinian Bar Mitzvah," *Electronic Intifada*, July 21, 2008. http://electronicintifada.net/content/palestinian-bar-mitzvah/7624.

he was too young to be traveling so far from home without his parents. But, finally he gave his permission, on the condition that Arab would remain in constant phone contact with him throughout the day.

Arab traveled by bus with about 45 people, mostly teenagers and families with children, all of them legal residents of Israel. Arab called to check in after the bus was underway, and everything was going fine.

The day was a huge success, and around 11:00 that night Arab called to say that they would be home in half an hour. When an hour later they had not returned, Bassam became worried and he called, wondering why they were late.

"There are a lot of soldiers here," Arab whispered into the phone. "The police stopped the bus, we don't know why, and we're in Jerusalem—the soldiers are telling us not to talk on the phone, I'll call back later."

Bassam later described the situation in his article: "In the industrial neighborhood of Wadi al-Joz in Jerusalem, Israeli troops on motorcycles, along with police and army units, were stationed on the path the bus was taking from Tiberias back home to Anata. When the bus drove by, the soldiers demanded that the driver stop."

Arab later said to his father, "At that moment all I could think of was Abir."

"We are from national security," the soldiers told the passengers, and they ordered the young men, about 10 of them, to begin taking off their clothes in the bus, in front of the women and girls. Then they took these young men off the bus one by one and had them lie down on the ground, which was littered with stones and broken glass. This puzzled Arab, and later he asked his father about it: "How can they ask the men to undress in front of the women? They don't have morals!"

"Humiliation by forced nakedness didn't just happen to your friends: it is a method used by the Israeli military. When we were in their prisons without any way to defend ourselves, our guards would take sadistic pleasure in seeing us naked, in humiliating us," Bassam explained.

Arab, being smaller and younger than the other boys, stayed on the bus with the women and children. Then a female soldier got on the bus and demanded: "Bring the dog." At that point, another soldier boarded the bus with an attack dog and began terrorizing everyone.

It was hours later when Arab was finally able to again communicate with Bassam, who later said, "There are no words for the state I was in during those hours, waiting for his next call and dreading it would not come. Then at 2:30 a.m., a call came."

"We are at the Moscobiyyeh," Arab told his father, referring to the main police detention center located by the Russian Compound in Jerusalem.

"Why are you being detained?"

"They didn't tell us anything."

"Go up to the solider and tell him, 'You have to talk to my father, he does not know where I am'." Arab replied that he was scared to do so; they'd already beaten many of the kids there because they had talked, and talking was not allowed. "You are a brave boy, you shouldn't be scared of the soldier. Talk to him in Hebrew." Over the phone Bassam could hear Arab go up to the soldier and say, "Please, can you talk to my father?" But the soldier told him to shut his mouth and hang up the phone. "If your father wants to see you, tell him to come here," he said.

Bassam was beside himself, yelling as loud as he could: "You murderers! Where is my son? Do you want to kill him like you killed his sister?" Bassam told Arab to turn on the speakerphone so the soldier could hear what he was saying.

"Dad, don't be afraid. I am okay. They are going to let us go in a bit like they said; I'll talk with you soon." And he hung up.

The soldiers finally let the group go at 3:00 a.m. Arab arrived home 40 minutes later, exhausted but alive and uninjured. After telling his father the entire story, Arab then asked for something Bassam found very surprising. "I want you to take me with you when you go to one of your lectures in Israel so I can tell the Israelis about the practices of their soldiers on that night."

"Are you serious?"

Arab has always questioned Bassam's willingness to talk with Israelis. But he insisted, "They have to know what happened so the parents of those soldiers can forbid their children to act that way toward women and children."

When I learned of what happened to Arab, I felt a need to relay the entire story to Gila and the children. I couldn't let my children grow up oblivious to the fact that this kind of injustice is taking place. So during our Friday night family dinner I told them about this and soon we were all crying. Eitan and Doron, who love Bassam dearly, were speechless, and so was I.

Israel has tested men like Khaled, Bassam, and Mazen, and thousands of others, and still they are dedicated to reconciliation. The experiences they have suffered at the hands of Israel are not unusual but rather typical stories of the Palestinians I have met. Yet they do not allow the actions of the Israeli military to get in the way of their important work.

I have returned several times to teach karate in Anata, Ramallah, and Deheishe, and each time, as I look at the children and youth that come to my class, I have a better appreciation for who they are and what they have to go through just in order to survive. The pain I feel when I leave them and travel freely around this country that is at least as much theirs as it is mine—if not more—only grows stronger with each visit.

Chapter 15:

Abu Ali Shahin

"What made your father change?"

People constantly ask me what it was that made Matti Peled change from a general who was known for his hawkish views and who demanded war in no uncertain terms, to a man determined and dedicated to achieving peace. His insistence that Israel act decisively against Egypt in 1967 and his call for a preemptive strike were part of his legacy, and his harsh words to the hesitant prime minister in the meeting just prior to the war were never forgotten. But his dedication to peace and reconciliation and his dovish opinions in the late part of his life make it hard to believe that during his military service he contributed significantly to Israel's military buildup, and indeed in those years he was no liberal dove.

My father had his own way of answering that question in interviews and articles. "When Israel's strategic objectives called for war, I supported the war, and when peace was possible, I called for peace," he used to say calmly and then add, "There is no conflict here whatsoever." It was a rational response befitting him.

It never occurred to me, nor did I ever have reason to believe, that there was one decisive moment or event that affected him enough to change his thinking. He was not like that, affected by emotion. That's what I thought, at least. So as far as I, or the rest of the family, was concerned there was no need to investigate the issue further or dig deeper to look for his motives.

The weekend after my first stay at Deheishe Refugee Camp to teach karate, I called Jamal to see if he was free the following week. He said there was someone he wanted me to meet in person—a man named Abu Ali Shahin. "He is the man who created the order that guided our life in prison, he was our leader, and he has a lot of respect for your father. In fact, he visited your father's grave several times, and he wants to meet you."

The name didn't mean anything to me, but I was curious to learn about this man. So the next day I took the bus from East Jerusalem to Ramallah, where I met Jamal. We drove together to pick up a few friends of his, all men who had spent years in Israeli prisons, each with a story that could fill volumes. We arrived at a spacious apartment building in Ramallah, where a diminutive old man with white hair, glasses, and a white beard welcomed us at the door with hugs and kisses and then invited us into his study. I asked if it was all right for me to film him. I was

Abu Ali Shahin, Fatah commander and leader of the Palestinian political prisoners for more than two decades.

not sure what he was going to say, but I had a sense it was important so I wanted to record it. He said it was fine and walked out of the room. When he returned, he had a checkered black and white *keffiyeh*, the symbol of *Fatah*, slung over his shoulder. This was Abu Ali Shahin, Fatah commander and leader of the Palestinian political prisoners for more than two decades.

"This is the first time I am speaking in Hebrew since 1982," he said with a smile. And thus began a long, captivating story from a man who at one time was one of Yasser Arafat's closest assistants and on Israel's most-wanted list. But more than that, he knew something about my father that I had never heard before.

"In 1948, during the war, my father was killed," he began.

I later learned that Abu Ali was born in January 1939, so he was not yet 10 when this occurred.

"He commanded the forces that defended our village, Beshshit,[1] and was killed in the battle. After the battle our village was destroyed and we ended up at Rafah Refugee Camp in the Gaza Strip. My father was killed in battle, but war is war, you expect that a man may be killed. But in 1967, just days after the end of the Six-Day War, the Israelis massacred my entire family, killing citizens, not fighters."

---

1 Also known as Beit Seit, or the House of Seth (a prominent prophet in the Muslim tradition and the third son of Adam and Eve according to Jewish tradition). Beshshit was a village of close to 20,000 between the towns Yibna and Isdud, today's Yavne and Ashdod. It had a rich history that goes back to the twelfth century. The village was destroyed by the Givati Brigade in 1948. Its residents were deported, and most of them were exiled to the Gaza Strip, where they lived as refugees.

Abu Ali stood up from his chair and began to pour coffee for all of us. He stopped and looked at me. "That is how I know about your father."

I was puzzled. My father had nothing to do with Gaza in 1967. "How was my father involved?"

"I will get to that in a moment. It was no more than a week after the war when an Israeli army officer showed up in our neighborhood at the Rafah Refugee Camp in Gaza, leading a company of soldiers and a bulldozer. The soldiers told everyone to come out of their homes. The officer inspected everyone and then sent the women and the children who were under 13 years old back home. He took all the men and the boys over 13 to another part of the camp, far enough so the families could not see. Then the soldiers lined everyone up against a wall and shot all of them. When they were done, the officer went one by one and shot each person in the head."

"How many people were there?"

"More than 30, among them a 13-year-old boy and an 86-year-old man. After he shot them, the bodies were laid in a row on the ground and the bulldozer began driving over them, going back and forth and back and forth until the bodies were unrecognizable."

"How did you find out?"

"It was in plain view, many people saw it, they saw the bulldozer and they saw the officer go and shoot each person in the head. There are eyewitness accounts.

"My mother ran out when the news reached her, and she was the first to see the men and boys who were killed. She could only tell who was who by the clothes they wore."

I was barely able to digest all of this and I still did not see how my father could have been connected to any of it.

"Were you in Gaza then?"

"No, I was in the West Bank working undercover. A friend came up to me one day and gave me the bad news."

"When it was confirmed to me that this really happened, I felt such intense pain that I thought my heart would explode. I knew at that moment that I could never cause anybody to feel such pain. I don't care if someone is Israeli or Jewish or anything at all, this is such pain that no one should ever have to suffer."

The atmosphere in the room was growing intense. Abu Ali was sitting comfortably in his chair behind a large desk stacked with books and papers while we were on the edge of our seats. Jamal intervened from time to time to clarify if Abu Ali could not find a word in Hebrew, or offer a translation if he asked for one. But it was clear the entire story was new to all of us.

"Abu Ali, I still don't see how my father was involved."

"I am getting to it. Then I was caught and I was interrogated and tortured for five months. During my interrogation I said to my interrogator, a guy named Pinhas, 'Why do you say we are killers? You are the murderers, not us. Why kill an 86-year-old man? What could he possibly do to you, or a 13-year-old boy?'

"Pinhas took an interest in what I said, and he asked for details. When he came back the next day he took down the names of the people who were killed. Then one day Pinhas came to see me with another officer and said, 'You see this man, he will make sure someone will look into the massacre of your relatives.'"

"Did he actually use the word massacre?"

I was dubious, so Abu Ali emphasized: "He used the word *mas-sa-cre!*"

"It wasn't until many years later, 1979, that I learned this officer worked with your father, and I learned what your father did. I was at Shata Prison at the time, and I was talking with an officer from the Shabak [the Israeli General Security Service, or GSS], and he was the first one to tell me that General Peled heard how my family was murdered in Rafah and he went to see for himself. Later I had this confirmed by people in Rafah. Matti Peled came to the camp in person."

I was hearing all of this for the very first time and the entire thing physically moved me. I looked around at the bookshelves to ease some of the tension. They were stacked with books and binders and I remember thinking that this reminded me of the study of a university professor. Clearly Abu Ali was an intellectual of sorts and had a solid political ideology that was firmly based on principle. But why did my father take such an interest in this particular story? To that I could find no answer, other than it was brought to his attention, and he wanted to see with his own eyes what really happened.

There was more.

"Everyone in Rafah talked about the fact that Matti Peled, one of the greatest officers of the Israeli army, a general that was highly respected, straight as an arrow, the man who was military governor of Gaza, came in person, he even drove himself, and visited the homes of the victims. Your father visited my family's home, he spoke to the adults and he consoled the children. People commented how disturbed he was when they took him to see the spot where the massacre took place. Your father also wrote a report to Yitzhak Rabin and Haim Bar-Lev, but they did nothing."

Abu Ali paused and sipped his coffee. He had transported himself, and us with him, to that time and place. What I wouldn't give to have been in my father's office when he heard of this and decided to go to Gaza to see for himself. If I could have been beside him as he reached Gaza and began looking around. He spoke Arabic fluently by then so he did not need the help of an interpreter. He was not naïve, and it surely did not surprise him to see that officers and soldiers were capable of atrocities. I remembered that in his Gaza Report, at the end of his tenure as military governor, he wrote of the lawlessness with which soldiers had conducted themselves before he took command.

"It became known that this changed him from a militant man to a man dedicated to peace. I felt your father was with us and that washed away the anger in my heart completely. Completely!"

I had learned to subdue my feelings well enough so as not to show emotion, but this man, this Palestinian commander, hero, and patriot, was talking about my father, General Matti Peled, who for all practical purposes was his sworn enemy. In fact, this man was for many years close to being enemy number one. This was much more than I had ever heard anyone speak about my father, and it was all said with such respect and regard for him.

Abu Ali then looked at Jamal and the other Palestinians and spoke to them in Arabic. When he was done, I said, "Immediately after the war, while still in uniform, my father said that Israel must recognize the rights of the Palestinian people. He said that if we don't do this, the Israeli army would become an occupation army and would resort to brutal means to enforce the Israeli occupation on the Palestinian people. He said this while still in uniform, and he never stopped saying it and advocating for Palestinian rights till he died."

Jamal and the others looked at me, and Jamal said, "That is exactly what Abu Ali just said to us in Arabic."

I had read about this statement, and I know it was said in a meeting of the IDF general staff right after the war, but now I was wondering whether or not this was after he saw what he saw in Gaza. I read what he said over and over: "If we keep these lands, popular resistance to the occupation is sure to arise, and Israel's army would be used to quell that resistance, with disastrous and demoralizing results." In light of what Abu Ali was telling me, my father's words seem almost prophetic. He was always concerned for the moral fabric of Israeli society and Israeli soldiers. Had he already seen the first signs of brutality and therefore said these things? There was no way for me to find out.

We were all silent for several minutes when Umm Ali, Abu Ali's wife, called us for lunch. We were joined by the rest of his family and friends to a feast of lamb meat, which Abu Ali served us with his bare hands, along with rice and yoghurt. We ate together and then sat in his living room with coffee and fruit. I noticed a larger-than-life tapestry of Yasser Arafat hanging on the wall and next to him portraits of the poet Mahmoud Darwish and Che Guevara.

I was tired, but I wanted to know more. I particularly wanted to know more about Abu Ali's experiences in prison. Jamal told me that the life of prisoners, their routines of study and political activities, were established largely by Abu Ali. How does a man denied everything in the world that I take for granted not only survive and function, but also find the inner strength to continue fighting and contributing to the welfare of others? He had built an entire movement that impacted thousands of people.

What Jamal told me earlier was also corroborated by Israeli sociologist Dr. Maya Rosenfeld:

> The formative nature of the 'prison years' in terms of the contribution to the political education and maturation of the individual, is traced back to the process by which

Palestinian prisoners succeeded in organizing themselves inside Israeli prisons and building what they referred to as an 'internal order' ("*Nitham idakhili*").[2]

Dr. Rosenfeld also writes: "It is rare to find a family in the West Bank or in the Gaza Strip that has not experienced the incarceration of at least one of its male members."

Clearly this is an issue that defines Palestinian society much more than is otherwise known or appreciated. And this man, with whom I just spent almost an entire day, was behind this order that turned the years in prison that so many young Palestinians had to endure into a meaningful, indeed an educational, experience. So after lunch, I asked Abu Ali to carry on with his story about his life and his work in prison.

By the time the Gaza Strip was recaptured by Israel in 1967, Abu Ali Shahin was commander of the Fatah Southern Command, which included the southern part of the West Bank—Bethlehem and Hebron and the towns surrounding them—and the Gaza Strip.

"After the war, Yasser Arafat and I traveled to the West Bank and Gaza together to inspect the Fatah military cells after the 1967 war. We transported arms and moved fighters from Gaza, where they were well trained, to the West Bank, where the fighters had minimal training."

This was unbelievable. Two Palestinian underground military leaders, who were on Israel's top 10 most wanted list, were traveling in areas that were occupied by the IDF and swarming with Israeli troops. If they went from the West Bank to Gaza they had to travel through Israel itself. This means that Yasser Arafat, who was still unknown to the world, but not unknown to the Israeli intelligence, managed to infiltrate under some disguise, probably from Jordan right under the noses of Israeli troops and the Israeli intelligence services, who had also flooded the newly conquered territories. Arafat was then able to somehow travel inside Israel, and then enter another occupied territory as he went into the Gaza strip.

Abu Ali went on faster than I could digest. I had no idea there were military cells active at the time and being trained within areas controlled by Israel. I was still trying to get my hands around the fact that I was hearing all this from a Fatah commander. It was pretty heroic stuff, and I had a million questions I wanted to ask him.

"When were you caught? And how?"

"September 1967. An informant gave me up. I was on the bus traveling from Gaza to Jerusalem. I had my head down on the seat in front of me the entire time so as to keep my face hidden. Then, about five miles from Jerusalem, the bus was

2 Maya Rosenfeld, "The Centrality of the Prisoners' Movement" in *Threat: Palestinian Political Prisoners in Israel*, ed. Abeer Baker and Anat Matar (London: Pluto Press, 2011), 11.

stopped. I still kept my head down, and after a few moments I felt someone hit me on the head so hard I thought my head would explode. I looked up and there were *Magav*, border police, and soldiers. I saw the guy who ratted me out standing by an army Jeep. Later on he was killed in Frankfurt. Someone was sent there for that purpose.

"During the interrogations, they nearly killed me! For five months I was kept alone in a small dark cell, where they tortured and beat me. There was no latrine, so I had to stand in my own excrement. But I would not cooperate, and I did not talk.

"After almost five months of interrogation they took me out, washed me with a fire hose, and said, 'Clean yourself up, you filthy Arab.' They took me to Sarafend, a military base near Tel Aviv, where they placed me in a room by myself. Army Chief of Staff General Rabin, Deputy Chief of Staff General Bar-Lev, and Head of Army Intelligence General Yariv came in."

These were the three most powerful men in Israel at the time.

"General Yariv spoke as the others watched: 'So, you don't want to talk. Who do you think you are, some kind of hero? Don't you know that we brought down Nasser and his entire army? Do you think we will not bring you down as well?'"

One of Jamal's friends asked if it was all right to light a cigarette, which was a little unusual because in Palestine everyone smokes everywhere and all the time. Neither Jamal nor I smoke, and apparently neither does Abu Ali. Jamal asked him to refrain, but Abu Ali did not mind as long as he opened a window. I could imagine that for a smoker to sit all this time without lighting up was hard so I didn't mind either. He opened the window a little and lit up. Jamal wanted to break the tension a bit, so he placed his big hand on me and said:

"Ahlan Ya Miko," (Welcome, Miko.) *"Ahlan fik,"* I replied. This was all quite surreal, I was an Israeli sitting there among these Palestinians, former resistance fighters, and we were all perfectly fine. Abu Ali stood up, calmly poured us all more Arabic coffee into tiny cups. Then he continued: "I thought that I would be killed soon and this may be my only chance to ever speak up. So I looked at these three generals, and I said, 'One day, when we the Palestinians liberate Tel Aviv, and you are caught and become my prisoners, and you are interrogated, will you talk? Will you give up your friends and your comrades in arms?'"

"So you didn't talk?"

"Never! It would be a disgrace to talk. I was a commander, and if I talked during interrogations I would never be able to hold my head up among the other prisoners. Even to this day I have not talked about what I did. And I did a lot. I have written it all down, and it is being kept somewhere outside of the country. After I die they can publish what I wrote and learn about the things we did." I would lie if I said this did not tease my curiosity, but I respected his commitment to silence.

"But," he said, and he raised his finger and looked directly at me, "I never gave an order to hurt a civilian, and I never did so myself. Even the prosecutor at my trial said, 'He is the enemy of the khaki,' khaki meaning the army. All of my operations, and there were many, were against military targets."

As a child, I remember that "Fatah" was the word to describe the enemy. The way I understood things as a child many years ago, they were the vilest, most frightening bloodthirsty Jew killers since the Nazis. I was the son of an Israeli general, and here I was sitting with a Fatah commander from the days when I was a child and a few other Fatah fighters who were closer to me in age. Had the conflict been solved and peace reigned it would have been somewhat romantic to reminisce about the old days. But the conflict was still going on and so was the resistance. Yet, there I was, and there they were—drawn together as though we were now on the same side, hoping for better days.

"What is the point of harming civilians?" Abu Ali asked rhetorically. "If you harm the military, you harm the state. If you harm a civilian what do you achieve? I never acted in vengeance either."

Jamal wanted to make sure I understood the point so he clarified: "Abu Ali never avenged the massacre of his family in Rafah."

I was reminded of a line from the movie *The Interpreter* with Nicole Kidman, where she says, "Vengeance is a lazy form of grief."

"When my interrogations began, I weighed 75 kilograms [165 lbs.] I was in great shape, like an athlete. I used to walk 120 kilometers [close to 75 miles] in a single night with military equipment on my back. At the end of the five-month interrogation, when they finally sent me to jail, I weighed 39 kilograms [about 86 lbs.].

"They sent me to *Ramle* prison, but the prison warden did not want to take me. I was so frail he was worried that I would die on his hands.

"They put me in with common criminals. I remember one in particular, Shmaya Angel." Shmaya Angel was a renowned Israeli crime lord and serial killer. "They thought the Israeli criminals would kill an Arab like me, but that didn't happen. In fact, I developed relationships with all the heads of the gangs inside the prison. We had an agreement on how we would manage the relations between us because we were united in our struggle against the prison authorities.

"Our communication with the other Palestinian prisoners, those who were held in other prisons around the country[3] was a vital piece of our struggle.

"I would write things for the other *Fatah* prisoners around the country. Issues of policy, lectures on history, and other subjects, and the criminals would help me get it out to the other prisons. I wrote in tiny letters on small pieces of paper and then folded them up. Then we would take a thin piece of plastic and wrap it around the paper tightly. The plastic would then be sealed with heat so it was completely waterproof and then someone would either swallow it or insert it in their anus and carry it when they were transferred to other prisons. Once the paper reached

---

3 In violation of international law, Palestinian prisoners are held in various prisons inside Israel, outside the occupied West Bank and Gaza.

the other prisons, Fatah prisoners would receive what I wrote, copy it onto a large piece of paper and read it to the others."

All of this was done by cooperation between Abu Ali and criminal—not political—Israeli prisoners.

"We even had a constitution," Jamal interjected. The world is told that Palestinians are incapable of governing themselves, but these men took the time and trouble to create a constitution while living in prison under harsh conditions that turn even the finest men into animals.

"Abu Ali, did you write the constitution?" I asked him.

"No. The prisoners' constitution and policies were decided through democratic elections. We communicated with all the prisoners in all the prisons around the country."

Abu Ali obviously saw the value of democratic processes, and this again, under conditions that were impossible. He mobilized and empowered people to take action and to affect change so that their voices would be heard. In the early days the "security" prisoners had to fight and negotiate for the most basic rights like beds and covers, decent food, and clean water. Nothing was given to them without a fight, and he created the order that facilitated this, and he did it while instilling democratic values in these young men who were overwhelmed, overpowered, and incarcerated with no law and no government to protect them or care for them.

Why were we demonizing these people, why do we fear them when we should embrace them?

Israelis like to say that if we were fortunate enough to have a civilized people as our neighbors, say like the Swiss, then things would be different, and we could have peace. But I was being exposed to a side of the Palestinians that was truly heroic. And I could see no reason why we can't share this land in peace and indeed perhaps even share a state with a nation that can produce such principled heroism under the harshest conditions.

Abu Ali went on: "That is also the way lessons were distributed and then taught. I wrote books on the history of guerrilla movements and revolutions like Vietnam and Cuba and Cambodia, the history of Zionism and America, the Algerian struggle for independence and so on."

He picked up a cigarette filter from an ashtray and showed it to me. "An entire book was no larger than this."

"When I was in Shata Prison [a maximum-security prison in northern Israel near Kibbutz Beit HaShita] "I was in the X sections, in solitary confinement for 12 years, but still my brain seems to be OK." He laughed.

"But there I was on one side, and a prison guard on the other. He, too, was a prisoner, sitting alone in a small yard. After all, he was human, and he wanted company too. So we would talk, and when he made coffee, I had coffee too. Life puts us in strange positions, but in the end we have to live together.

"After my prison sentence was fulfilled, they sent me to Dahaniya in Gaza for two years." Dahaniya was a town in the Gaza Strip built by Israel for informants and collaborators who, fearing retribution, could not return to their homes. "These were the filthiest people, scum of the earth, and I had to live there for two years. No one was permitted to speak to me. This was punishment for the fact that I wouldn't talk. This was far worse than any prison and I appealed to the supreme court asking to be sent back to prison, but they denied my request. Your father, along with Uri Avnery and others, protested and spoke against this inhumane punishment, but it did no good. I would look at the soldiers and curse them and curse the Israeli army, but I got no response. From time to time the authorities would come and say to me, 'You can do whatever you want, no on will speak to you here'."

He heaved a deep sigh. "I am 72 now. I will be 73 in 10 days. I am still paying for what I did back then, but I do not regret any of it. No, I am a fighter and a commander, and I devoted my life to the struggle. I did what my conscience dictated and I was prepared to die every time I went on a mission."

Then he paused, sat up, and said quietly, "We all belong to this land and need to live together. Not one Arab state and one Jewish state. Judaism is a religion, and I am speaking of a secular state of all its citizens. That is the only way to live here. Being Jewish or Muslim or Christian or atheist, that is a personal choice, not for me to dictate and not to be dictated to me. I don't want a priest or a rabbi or sheikh to govern my life. We belong in this land, and we need to live here as equals."

This was not the first time I had heard someone talk of the "one secular democratic state" as the right solution. It was the part of the Fatah manifesto to create a secular democracy in all of Palestine. In the past, I could not stomach it, but the more I met impressive, intelligent people like Abu Ali, people who were driven by principle, the more I thought that there was no point, indeed no future, in dividing the people and the land. Not to mention the fact that the settlements and the facts on the ground had succeeded in erasing the West Bank as a viable area in which a Palestinian state could be established. My family were all Zionists, and so was I to begin with, but cracks were forming in my conviction that there was a need or even a justification for a state that was Jewish.

Then, Abu Ali began speaking about my father again. "I visited your father's grave nine or 10 times, and each time I brought flowers. The last time was late in 2003. Then they took away my permit to enter Israel so I can no longer travel outside the West Bank."

At that point one of the other guys in the room asked, "Abu Ali, why did you visit the grave so many times? Wasn't General Peled also responsible for our suffering? After all, he too was an Israeli general."

Abu Ali stood up. I looked at him and thought, his small physique can be misleading because when he speaks, men far larger than he listen in silence. "General Peled was no ordinary general," he said, his tone clearly reprimanding. "He changed as a result of something that he saw, and he never looked back.

He was a great man, and he could have been a cabinet member or even prime minister if he stayed and toed the line. But no! He followed his conscience and remained true to it his entire life. I never met him, but felt and still feel a real kinship towards him."

When I got home that evening I told my mother this story. She immediately replied, "Yes, I remember this. Your father was so upset he couldn't sleep for weeks. He wrote to Rabin and to Haim Bar-Lev about it, but they did nothing. This changed him completely."

Chapter 16:

One State, Two States, Three States

Rami and I have been arguing about politics since I was 12 years old. By the sound of our voices then and now, you'd think that our disagreements were unbridgeable, profound, and fundamental. But in reality we agree on almost everything and all of our arguments are of nuance. With one exception.

I came to the realization that establishing a secular, pluralistic democracy that includes all of Palestine/Israel was the best thing for Israelis and Palestinians and that the two-state solution was not a solution at all. My brother-in-law could not disagree more, and when this came up for the first time in the summer of 2007, he and I had yet another shouting match. It is not that we can't speak without shouting; it is just that we can't speak without shouting when we talk about the future of Israel and Palestine.

Rami is a graphic designer, and with his partner Jaki he owns and operates Studio Rami & Jaki in Jerusalem. I always loved sitting with Rami at his studio and

Rami and I discussing current affairs and enjoying each other's company.

designing posters for my karate school, and Jaki, who is also a martial arts enthusiast, would join us from time to time and contribute his creative touches. Over the years we had done this many times, and my school in Coronado is filled with posters that they made for me. I typically go to the studio after it closes and Rami and I sit together for hours working on a poster. Then, when we are done, we go and get a bite to eat. It is truly one of my favorite things to do while I am in Jerusalem.

It was just such a day in the summer of 2007, and Rami and I had just spent hours working on yet another poster. After we were done we decided to try a trendy little restaurant in the Rehavia neighborhood of Jerusalem, one of many places that serve exotic salads and pasta dishes.

We had no intention to get into an argument, but it was inevitable. To begin with, we always, always talk about "the situation" when we are together. Both he and I think about it and talk about it and do everything we can to change it and it consumes a huge portion of our lives. This was always true, and it became even more so in the years after Smadar's death. Rami's point of view was always pessimistic, but after he became active with the Bereaved Families Forum and began meeting Palestinians, he developed a far more positive view of the world.

When I reached the conclusion that a state for Jews in a land where half of the population is not Jewish was not going to work, things changed drastically for me. I wrote an article titled "The Answers Have Changed" that appeared in the online publication "Electronic Intifada" in January 2007.[1] I took the title from a story about Albert Einstein. According to this story, Einstein was on his way to give a particular exam to a class that had already taken the exact same exam. Alarmed at what he saw and thinking it to be the result of the professor's absent-mindedness, an assistant warned Einstein of what he was about to do. The professor just smiled and said, "It's all right, the answers have changed."

My views on the best solution for Israel/Palestine changed largely as a result of my travels throughout the West Bank and having witnessed Israel's immense investment in infrastructure to attract Jewish settlers and thereby exclude Palestinians—to whom the land belongs. It became clear to me that when Zionists talked about the two-state solution they were lying. I became convinced that universal freedom in a shared homeland was the best thing for both peoples. Zionists failed to demonstrate that when they are in power things go well, so my conclusion was that a real pluralistic democracy would benefit everyone.

Rami read the article and said he was saddened that I had lost hope. He was right in that I had lost hope in the Jewish state and in Zionism. But one might also say I became more hopeful, because I realized that Israelis and Palestinians could live together in their shared homeland. I had hope in our ability to live in peace as long as we all had an equal voice in determining our fate, as long as we were governed as equals.

---

1 http://electronicintifada.net/people/miko-peled?page=1.

"Rami," I said, pressing my point, "you know as well as I that no Zionist government will ever allow a Palestinian state to be established in the land of Israel. No prime minister will ever let go of East Jerusalem and the Jordan River valley, which make up over a third of the West Bank. And since the large settlement blocks that take up large portions of the West Bank will not be returned, where exactly will there be a Palestinian state? We have to change the paradigm from a Zionist one that says Jews must have their own state to a paradigm that sees both Jews and Palestinians as equals living together in a state that is neither Jewish or Arab, and governed by an elected government that represents everyone."

My brother-in-law was losing his patience by the minute. "You don't understand anything! Can't you see it will lead to civil war? It will be another Kosovo or Lebanon and the bloodshed will be unstoppable."

But I couldn't let it go. "Or Switzerland or Belgium. If you compare us to other multinational states, ours is not a very complicated issue. We are two nations who are actually very similar."

The cultural similarities between Israelis and Palestinians are illustrated beautifully in an article written in Hebrew by Yael Lerrer, titled, "Is it Possible to Crack the Cultural Separation Wall?"[2] In the article, she describes a woman from outer space who lands somewhere in Israel.

> This woman notices that close to half of the population are Palestinian Arabs and that Arabic is also the mother tongue of more than half of the Jews, or at least the parents of half of the Jews that live there as well... This visitor notices that most Israelis emerged from Arab culture and that Israel sits in the middle of the Arab world and is surrounded by Arab countries. Wanting to know more about the country and its culture, this visitor decides to visit the bookstores, where she expects to find books in Arabic and Hebrew, the languages of this country. In the first bookstore she finds books in Hebrew only, in the second she finds a few shelves in English as well and the third bookstore is a Russian bookstore. 'There are no Arabs here,' she is told, 'here we do not speak Arabic, this is Tel Aviv.' ...The visitor is puzzled. 'A city with no Arabs, with no Arabic, in the middle of an Arab country?'

"In the long run," I told Rami, "the Zionist state is a disaster for Jews as well as it is for Palestinians. It completely undermined, not to say destroyed, Jewish culture and traditions, both European and Middle Eastern."

My father's generation looked at the old, European Jews with disdain. They were considered weak, and with their Yiddish language and culture they seemed pale and subservient by comparison. By eliminating the culture of the diaspora, and attempting to be different from the old European "diaspora Jews," my father's

---

2 Yael Lerer, "Is it Possible to Crack the Cultural Separation Wall?", *Kedma*, July 2, 2006. http://www.kedma.co.il/index.php?id=1061&t=pages.

generation thought they were doing everyone a favor. In fact, Zionist Israel all but destroyed the Yiddish culture.

Both my parents had a lot of respect for Arab Jews and the rich culture they brought with them when they immigrated to Israel. But in Israel that culture was viewed as inferior, and the Jews who came from Arab countries were called Sephardic or Oriental, rather than Arab Jews, and were forced to give up their identity and their culture for fear of being viewed as Arabs. Indeed, Israel's campaign of ethnic cleansing has included destroying, mocking, or ignoring all Arab culture, including that of the Jewish Arabs.

Palestine has a rich Arab and Muslim history, yet hardly any of it is taught in schools in Israel. Very little Arab literature or poetry is translated into Hebrew or taught and the Arab and Muslim historical monuments that were not destroyed on purpose were left in disrepair and were ruined from neglect. There are examples of this in all of the older cities like Yafa and Ramle, Tiberias and Jerusalem, and pretty much everywhere. The word "Arab" is frequently attached to adjectives such as filthy, or is synonymous with stupid, useless, or lazy.

"You are out of your mind!" Rami shot back.

On his Facebook page Rami insists, "I am a Zionist." He likes to see himself as a Zionist even though he clearly abhors what Zionists have done to Palestinians. Few people have such regard for Palestinians as he does and few have developed true, deep friendships that cross the divide as he has. Yet he is determined that we must not give up.

"Don't you see that your naïve plan would never work?" He said this loud enough for the entire neighborhood to hear. "Separation is the only solution! It is like a divorce that has to take place or the couple will kill one another. And in the meantime we have to struggle, we need to convince people in Israel and overseas to bring about change within the framework of two states. What you are suggesting is totally crazy and unrealistic. The two-state is the only solution that has the smallest chance of working."

By this time most of the people in the restaurant, as well as a few passersby, were looking at us. But we ignored them and Rami continued lecturing, as he did when I was still twelve years old.

"One day the Israeli government will be forced to negotiate in a fair manner and allow the Palestinians a state alongside Israel and the settlers will leave the settlements and return to their homes inside Israel."

"But you know just as well as I that we are all settlers, and all of Israel is occupied Palestine. The West Bank is just a small part of the problem. What about the refugees? And what about the right of return? And what about the horrific negligence of the Palestinian communities who are part of Israel now and are Israeli citizens? How long do you think these issues can go on being ignored?"

That did not help my argument and I was clearly not making any progress. In all honesty Rami's resistance surprised me. My arguments in favor of one democratic state for all Israelis and Palestinians made so much sense to me. Plus, I no longer had emotional ties to Zionism—and there was certainly no rational argument that I could see against a single democracy—whereas Rami's argument was guttural; it came from a deeply emotional place. "My father is an 'Auschwitz graduate,'" he says in his lectures, reminding his listeners that his father survived the Auschwitz death camp and that for many Jewish people the wounds of the Holocaust have not yet healed.

"But Miko, can't you see? A solution that calls for ultimate justice is doomed to fail! Both Jews and Palestinians deserve a state of their own, a flag of their own, and a national political identity of their own. And we have no right to deny them these things."

"Yes, they deserve all of these things, but that ship has sailed. Our flag will not allow any other flag to be raised on this land, and you know this as well if not better than I."

Rami's point was that we'd better reserve our arguments and our struggle to achieve an "amicable separation" rather than to entertain crazy ideas of equality. I had heard Uri Avnery, the veteran journalist and peace activist whom I also greatly respect, make a similar argument: "Will they (Palestinians and Israelis) serve side by side in the same army, the same police force, will they pay the same taxes?"

After the argument subsided a little, Rami made a point that he has since repeated many times: "One or two or three states is not the issue." Meaning: We have a long way to go before we convince people either way, so for the time being we should stick to more burning issues.

"I think it *is* the issue," I said. "As long as Israel remains unchanged and the debate evolves around the creation of a Palestinian state in some undefined region, nothing will change. For years Israel has been saying that it is willing to give the Palestinians a few pieces of land on which they may establish some sort of mini state, and somehow, each time it falls apart. The actors know full well that this is an act. The Israeli settlements in the West Bank expand and the horrors of the ethnic cleansing campaign continue to terrorize the Palestinian people day in and day out."

Israel has always insisted that it will determine the nature of the solution, and the Palestinians must be resigned to accept it or suffer the consequences of continued oppression. Israel will permit the Palestinians a level of independence that Israel will determine based on its own perception of Palestinian compliance with Israeli interests. The best Palestinians may expect is that Israel will at some point permit a limited autonomy on selected areas of historic Palestine—areas that will be selected by Israel itself. The notion that the two parties need to reach a solution as equal partners is inconceivable to the Zionist state.

The Israeli government always maintained that it has the right to determine who will represent the Palestinians as Israel's negotiating partner, using "security" considerations as the ultimate test. Israel has systematically delegitimized any

Palestinian leader who was unwilling to accept Israel's "right" to total domination of the land and the discourse. This is the primary reason why so many Palestinian leaders have been imprisoned, exiled, or assassinated, and it is the reason Yasser Arafat spent his final days surrounded by Israeli tanks: refusal to accept Israeli superiority and the exclusivity of the Israeli narrative.

"The settlements will be removed one day and peace will be achieved through partition," Rami insisted.

"Rami, this is like Jews waiting for the Messiah and knowing full well that he will never actually come. Every so-called 'peace plan' has only made things worse for Palestinians, and now we have the two people living in one state but governed by very different laws." It was like what the police chief at the Kiryat Arba police station said to me the first time I was arrested in Beit Ummar: "He is an Israeli citizen and he has rights, he is not a Palestinian that I can just throw in jail." No argument I could possibly make demonstrates better than the words of this police station chief that indeed there exist different laws for different people.

Israel created an entire bureaucracy with the sole purpose of making the lives of Palestinians unlivable, so that they will ultimately have no choice but to leave. Israeli human rights attorney Michael Sfard describes it as, "Mountains of movement prohibitions and preventions, and an ocean of walls."[3]

But as Einstein said, the answers have changed. The answer known as the two-state solution belongs to a reality that no longer exists. The West Bank is riddled with cities and shopping malls, industry and highways designated for Jews only and Palestinians in the West Bank and Gaza are prohibited from enjoying any of the development that took place on their land. There is no political will within Israel to give Palestinians their freedom—all of which means that clearly the answers have changed.

The answer to the difficult question of the Israeli-Palestinian conflict could be drawn from the reality that Israel created. By ruling over two nations, Israel has chosen to be a bi-national state. All that remains now is to replace the current system whereby only Israeli Jews enjoy the freedoms and rights of full citizenship, with one that will allow Palestinians to enjoy those rights as well.

Rami was not the only one hurt by my views and my actions. As more and more Israeli friends and acquaintances realized that I supported the call for sanctions and boycotts against Israel, I could see the sadness and pain in their faces. Israelis who live in the United States love finding coffee or pickles or olive oil made in Israel, and they relish the taste of home, as every immigrant does. I remember that feeling myself, finding a piece of home in a supermarket. Young Israelis who are liberal leaning and abhor the treatment of Palestinians by Israel also argue with me,

---

3 Michael Sfard, "Devil's Island: The Transfer of Palestinian Detainees into Prisons within Israel" in *Threat: Palestinian Political Prisoners in Israel*, ed. Abeer Baker and Anat Matar (London: Pluto Press, 2011), 188.

particularly when I tell them they should refuse to serve in the IDF—an organization I began referring to as a terrorist organization. "Are you suggesting that we refuse to serve in the same army that your father helped to build? The first Jewish armed force to protect Jews in over two thousand years?"

"This is very hard for me," Gila would tell me repeatedly. When other Israelis and Jewish friends would ask her what I speak and write about, she'd cringe right along with them as she told them about my views and measures I have taken.

My response is: "If you knew what I know, if you saw what I saw, you would do the same. The pain of knowing what I know is a pain so sharp that sitting around and doing nothing stopped being an option for me a long time ago." Still, Israeli and most Jewish friends look at me with a combination of sadness and uneasiness that is hard to mask.

Rami and I continued talking for hours and we did not notice the time until my mother called, wondering where we were. "The utopian dream," I said to Rami in the end, "is not the one secular democracy in which we all live as equals. What is naïve is the belief, the insistent belief, that Israel can change, that we can have a Jewish democracy in a country that is inhabited by another nation. That is utopian. Struggling to end the segregation and create a secular democracy where two nations live as equals, while difficult, is not naïve, nor is it utopian. Demanding freedom and equality for our friends in Anata, and Bil'in and for the children in Deheishe, and indeed expecting it, is tough but realistic."

One question that hangs in the air and can never be answered is: What would my father have said? My best guess is that since he was always ahead of his time, and he never hesitated to slaughter sacred cows, he would call for a single democracy with equal rights. He would have preferred that, I think, to the Israel that exists today, where racism and violence against Palestinians prevail. I know my mother has said on several occasions that Zionism failed, and there is no reason why we can't all live as equals in one democratic state.

In any case, I don't think Rami was convinced. I think he and I will always find something about which we will argue and raise our voices.

It's what happens when you care so much that it hurts.

Acknowledgments

I learned a great deal from writing this book and I am thankful for all that I learned and to all those who helped me along the way. Iris Keltz who planted the seed, Heidi Schulmann who lovingly helped me to get the writing off the ground. Landrum Bolling for his tireless work for peace and for introducing me to Helena Cobban of Just World Books; and to Helena Cobban for taking on this project with me. I want to thank Pamela Olson for her excellent, tireless work with me on the manuscript. I also want to thank Mike Sirota for helping me with the manuscript, which could not have been easy for him. And I must thank Samar Fitzgerald for her excellent editing and for getting more out of me than I thought I had.

I thank the Foundation for Middle East Peace for their generous grant, without which this book would not have been possible.

Finally, I must thank my family and friends for their inspiration and patience.

—M.P.

A Note on Maps
from Just World Books

The United Nations' Office for the Coordination of Humanitarian Affairs for the occupied Palestinian territory has an excellent collection of regularly updated maps on their website. The portal to their 'Reference Maps' is at <http://bit.ly/P86uUD>. Two Israeli organizations have mapping centers that track Israel's building of settlements and other rights abuses in the occupied territories: Peace Now maps the situation in the West Bank: <http://bit.ly/MV3w9z>; and Btselem has an interactive map with a lot of good information about the West Bank and Gaza: <http://bit.ly/NPArLC>. The Palestinian organization Applied Research Institute, Jerusalem (ARIJ) has many maps describing the situation of Palestinians over time, including in the occupied territories, inside Israel, and in the broad Palestinian diaspora. They can be accessed here: <http://bit.ly/Q2kXpx>.

One informative depiction of the transfer of control over land and resources since 1946 is this one, distributed by <mapcards123@gmail.com>:

Palestinian Loss of Land 1947 to 2012

e obtained at www.ICGtesting.com

2B/15/P

9 781935 982159

CPSIA information can
Printed in the USA
LVOW050658140812

294080LV000